THE POLITICS
OF INDUSTRIAL RECRUITMENT

Recent Titles in
Contributions in Economics and Economic History

THE POLITICS OF INDUSTRIAL RECRUITMENT

Japanese Automobile Investment and Economic Development in the American States

EDITED BY

Ernest J. Yanarella and William C. Green

Contributions in Economics and Economic History, Number 104

Greenwood Press

NEW YORK • WESTPORT, CONNECTICUT • LONDON

Library of Congress Cataloging-in-Publication Data

The Politics of industrial recruitment : Japanese automobile
   investment and economic development in the American states / edited
   by Ernest J. Yanarella and William C. Green.
        p.   cm. — (Contributions in economics and economic history,
   ISSN 0084-9235 ; no. 104)
      Includes bibliographical references.
      ISBN 0-313-26359-0 (lib. bdg. : alk. paper)
      1. Automobile industry and trade—United States—Foreign
   ownership—Case studies.   2. Investments, Japanese—Government
   policy—United States—States—Case studies.   I. Yanarella, Ernest
   J.   II. Green, William C., 1941–   III. Series.
   HD9710.U52P58   1990
   338.8′87292′0973—dc20   89–25997

British Library Cataloguing in Publication Data is available.

Library of Congress Catalog Card Number: 89–25997
ISBN: 0-313-26359-0
ISSN: 0084-9235

First published in 1990

Greenwood Press, Inc.
88 Post Road West, Westport, Connecticut   06881

Printed in the United States of America

The paper used in this book complies with the
Permanent Paper Standard issued by the National
Information Standards Organization (Z39.48–1984).

10   9   8   7   6   5   4   3   2   1

TO
ELIZABETH AND ROWENA

Contents

Figures and Tables

Preface

State governments in the 1980s have pursued an aggressive strategy of public entrepreneurship focused on the recruitment of foreign capital and industry. These state economic development actions have been rooted in state fiscal health interests which have been made more pressing and perhaps more protracted by the momentous structural changes taking place in the international economic system and by the absence of a national economic program to meet the realities of the new international order.

The essays in this volume will explore this phenomenon of foreign industrial recruitment in terms of the experiences of six mid-American states—Michigan, Ohio, Indiana, Illinois, Kentucky, and Tennessee—in attracting Japanese automobile assembly facilities. This experience and the choice of plant site in these states by Mazda, Honda, Fuji-Isuzu, Mitsubishi, Toyota, and Nissan was invariably determined by multistate negotiations and escalating state government incentive packages. To understand this phenomenon and its consequences, the essays in this volume will sketch its comparative historical, economic, and legal dimensions; examine the dynamics of Japanese automobile investment in terms of six site-specific studies; and then place these industrial recruitment experiences within a wider framework of federal-state relations and the prospects for a national industrial policy.

Part I illuminates the background to and comparative setting for the mid-

American competition for Japanese automobile plants in the era of international corporate flight. Susan B. Hansen sets the stage with her essay, "Industrial Policies in the American States: Historical and Comparative Perspectives," in which she explores the legacy of past state economic activity and reviews the changing policies of the American states toward business. Noting the significant alternations in state economic development policy that have taken place, she then offers a broad comparative analysis of the efforts by various states and regions to recruit business, to promote foreign trade, and to design well-articulated industrial policies to foster economic growth. Her brief, but pointed, case study of Pennsylvania's recruitment of Volkswagen serves both as a paradigm of vigorous competition among the midwestern states for Japanese automobile transplants and, given the New Stanton plant's recent closing, as a warning to other states that today's winners in the new "war between the states" may be tomorrow's losers.

In "State Incentive Packages and the Industrial Location Decision," H. Brinton Milward and Heidi Hosbach Newman examine the contours of the industrial location process. First, they investigate the growing literature on the business and nonbusiness factors influencing these corporate decisions and then focus on the character and impact of state inducement packages in this process. Here they offer a comparative study of the six Japanese auto alley cases in order to discern the trends in this increasingly popular state economic policy and to weigh the impacts of such packages on the corporate decision-making process. In conclusion, they acknowledge the ambiguity of their findings and make several recommendations to state and local governments interested in designing an industrial recruitment policy and in honing their business negotiation skills.

William C. Green's "Constitutional Dimensions of State Industrial Recruitment" brings together, often for the first time, a wealth of information from extensive interviews of state policy makers and from scattered incentive package documents in order to assay the constitutional issues involved in the use of sometimes conventional, sometimes creative and dubious state financial incentives. His assessment of the six state experience in America's heartland leads him to question the constitutionality of only two elements in the Illinois and Kentucky financial incentive agreements. He then presents a careful, detailed case study of the Kentucky case, *Hayes v. State Property and Buildings Commissions* (1987), the only incentive package subjected to a state constitutional challenge. His juxtaposition of the majority and dissenting opinions, along with the comparative analysis offered earlier in the chapter, leaves little doubt that the Kentucky Supreme Court bowed to the pressure of a gubernatorial fait accompli and extended the parameters of the state constitution.

Within these historical, economic, and legal contexts, Part II carefully probes the dynamics of Japanese automobile investment and state economic development in terms of six site-specific studies. First, Lynn W. Bachelor examines the decision by Mazda to build an American auto assembly plant. In her chapter "Flat Rock, Michigan, Trades a Ford for a Mazda," she reconstructs the industrial location process showing the lengthy behind-the-scenes interactions between Michigan state officials and Mazda executives as well as consultations between the Mazda and UAW leaders that laid the basis for the negotiations of a Mazda-UAW contract. She then explores the impact of Mazda's location decision on Flat Rock and on Michigan's economic health. While cautious about the short-term results to date, Bachelor clearly indicates that the Michigan case was a storybook model of how state economic development programs should be conducted.

The second study, by Nancy S. Lind, "Economic Development and Diamond-Star Motors," draws upon the spirit of game theory to examine the cooperative and competitive dimensions of Illinois' successful recruitment effort. First she examines the economic development strategy and legislative enactments used by Illinois in its competition to wrest the joint Chrysler-Mitsubishi automobile plant from its chief rivals, Michigan and Indiana. Then her analysis turns to the "cooperation" of Illinois state economic development officials with local public officials in Bloomington and Normal which apparently netted the state and local community this economic plum. Chief among the cooperative mechanisms were the state's enterprise zone and metro zone programs and Build Illinois, the state's economic development fund. In closing, she itemizes the costs and benefits of cooperation and competition, and she suggests that until an active federal presence emerges, interstate competition will be the prevailing ethic in the politics of industrial recruitment.

In the third site-specific study, "Japanese Automobile Investment in West Central Ohio," John P. Blair, Carole Endres, and Rudy Fichtenbaum apply their economic expertise to the problems of economic development and labor-management issues associated with Honda's location of automobile facilities near Marysville, Ohio. The authors probe the decisions over the past decade by Honda and by the State of Ohio to create an automobile complex of assembly plants and their supplier industries in West Central Ohio. After citing a number of locational factors, also highlighted by Milward and Newman in their chapter, Blair and his associates proceed to explore the diverse reasons for the failure of the UAW to unionize the Marysville plant but then suggest that the changing demographics of the workplace, i.e., the aging of the Honda work force, may over time pose new challenges to Japanese management practices. In conclusion, they discuss the policy implications of their study for economic policy entrepreneurs, corporate managers, union leaders, and Japanese executives.

The fourth and fifth studies train their sights on the Indiana and Kentucky experiences. In "Local Images of Japanese Automobile Investment in Indiana and Kentucky," Robert Perrucci and Madhavi Patel examine the role of local newspapers in state economic promotion activities. Working from three potential images of community growth—growth elitist, political-pluralist, and ecological images—generated from different social science research traditions and bodies of theory, the coauthors extrapolate the differing functions for local newspapers. Then they conduct a content analysis of newspaper clippings on the Lafayette, Indiana Subaru-Isuzu plant and on the Georgetown, Kentucky Toyota plant from three local newspapers—the *Lafayette Journal and Courier*, the *Louisville Courier-Journal*, and the *Lexington Herald-Leader*—to test hypotheses about the functions of newspaper reportage drawn from the competing images of community growth. Among their major findings is evidence of strong support for the growth elitist image which holds that the newspapers tend to be a part of the growth coalition and perceive their profit-oriented interests as closely allied to the growth-promoting interests of local public officials and economic elites. As a consequence, the coauthors find that the role of newspapers in educating the public about key issues in the debate over mid-American state industrial recruitment is woefully neglected.

In "Problems of Coalition Building in Japanese Auto Alley: Public Opposition to the Georgetown/Toyota Plant," Ernest J. Yanarella and Herbert G. Reid investigate the efforts of labor leaders, local environmentalists, and small businessmen to take up the challenge of public education in the politics of industrial recruitment. Yanarella and Reid review the rise of opposition to the Georgetown plant's construction in the context of clarifying the critical stakes involved in building coalitions around union representation and environmental issues as a counterpoise to the considerable power and influence of growth coalitions which employ standard appeals to unlimited growth and economic boosterism. Criticizing, but not dismissing, the free market nostalgia and flight from global economic realities evidenced by the protest of a small businessmen's group against the Collins administration's economic incentive package, the coauthors analyze the more weighty challenge presented by the union labor and, to a lesser extent, the environmentalist forces. By comparing this case with an earlier, more successful environmentalist and citizen action group struggle in Georgetown, they show how neglected opportunities from the first battle against the growth coalition hampered efforts in the more recent controversy to forge a winning labor and environmentalist alliance. In their conclusion, they speculate about the incipient issues which might yet ignite significant political protests and coalition building against unlimited growth, heavy state subsidies, union busting practices, and environmental degradation.

In the sixth and last study in Part II, "Japanese Investment in Tennessee," William F. Fox examines the local political and economic impacts of Nissan on Smyrna, Tennessee, the oldest among the transplants in the Japanese automobile alley and the one to which public entrepreneurs and scholars turn first to gather lessons. Fox begins his study by assessing the magnitude of Japanese investment in Tennessee and the policies that state economic development officials have devised to foster this investment. Then he presents the five factors adduced as being important in the choice of Smyrna. From there, Fox delineates the state's role in Nissan's decision and the effects of the plant on the city of Smyrna and on Rutherford County. His conclusion about the experience in Smyrna is mixed, because the verdict seems to be out on the overall economic effects of the plant on the community, although no discernible negative noneconomic consequences appear to have been triggered by the facility.

Finally, Part III places these six state industrial recruitment experiences within the wider framework of federal-state relations. David Lowery's concluding chapter, "The National Level Roots of the Failure of State Industrial Policy," reviews the preceding chapters and finds that the mid-American states' experience with Japanese automobile plants has been a policy failure, because of missed opportunities. Lowery then outlines the requirements and consequences of the return of the activist federal state in generating national and state reindustrialization in the decade of the nineties, as well as implementing a coordinated federalist policy and planning program to overcome the negative consequences of state bidding wars. By asserting a new role and direction for federal macroeconomic policy, Lowery points the way to a federal presence in programs for foreign industrial location and state economic development which might restore a balance between the American states and multinational capital.

Acknowledgments

The editors and contributors to this volume owe a great debt of gratitude to the government officials in the six mid-American states and, in particular, to those men and women in economic development offices and departments, upon whom many of us relied for public information and personal knowledge and insights on their recruitment of the Japanese automobile manufacturers. Their willingness to take time from their demanding schedules to talk with us at length by phone and in person and to supply us with documents has permitted us to capture a significant phenomenon in the history of state economic development.

The editors wish to acknowledge the efforts of the contributors to this volume. Their willingness to accept our suggestions and revisions of their draft chapters has substantially increased the quality of the final product. On behalf of the contributors, we extend our and their thanks to the staff people at their institutions who have also assisted in the production of this volume. We are indebted to three people at the University of Kentucky. Kim Hayden in the Department of Political Science has done her customary stellar typing job. Rob Aken in the Reference Department of M. I. King Library has a marvelous command of bibliographic resources and has tirelessly tracked down obscure citations. Lyle Sendlein, Director of the Institute of Mining and Mineral Research, has once again encouraged a project of ours and has underwritten the production costs for the tables and figures. William Green thanks Morehead State University for the support of his research provided by a Faculty Research Grant. We also appreciate the patience Cynthia Harris, Greenwood Press's history and economics editor, has for the editors of a volume of original essays. In closing, we acknowledge Elizabeth and Rowena's understanding of the time we needed to invest in this volume, and we believe that we have now answered their question: When do we get a book dedicated to us?

Abbreviations

AFL–CIO	American Federation of Labor–Congress of Industrial Organizations
AMC	American Motors Corporation
CETA	Comprehensive Employment Training Act
DCC	Downriver Community Conference (Michigan)
DCCA	Department of Commerce and Community Affairs (Illinois)
EDA	Economic Development Act
EDF	Economic Development Fund (Kentucky)
EPA	Environmental Protection Agency
GM	General Motors Corporation
IDB	Industrial development bond
IEDC	Indiana Employment Development Commission
ILIR	Institute of Labor and Industrial Relations (Michigan)
JTPA	Job Training Partnership Act
MEDA	Michigan Economic Development Administration
mgd	Million gallons per day
MITI	Ministry of International Trade and Industry (Japan)

MOB	Moral obligation bond
MSA	Metropolitan Statistical Area
MSF	Michigan Strategic Fund
NASDA	National Association of State Development Agencies
NEPA	National Environmental Policy Act
NUMMI	New United Motor Manufacturing Incorporated
OITP	Ohio Industrial Training Program
PATCO	Professional Air Traffic Controllers Organization
SEV	State equalized value
SIC	Standard industry classification
SMSA	Standard Metropolitan Statistical Area
UAW	United Auto Workers
UDAG	Urban Development Action Grant
VAT	Value-added tax

PART I

STATE INDUSTRIAL RECRUITMENT AND JAPANESE AUTOMOBILE INVESTMENT

1

Industrial Policies in the American States: Historical and Comparative Perspectives

Susan B. Hansen

The American states' concerted efforts to attract Japanese and other foreign investment is a relatively new development. But even before the American Revolution, the colonies (later states) were heavily involved in efforts to encourage investment and to promote business. The purpose of this chapter is to place current state activities in historical and comparative perspective. What is novel, and what is traditional, about state industrial policy? Which states are most active, and why? And what difference does it make?

STATE ECONOMIC POLICY: THE LEGACY OF THE PAST

State involvement in the economy is not new. In fact, one can find many parallels to current industrial policies in earlier times. Despite the wide acceptance of laissez-faire, another tradition—that of mercantilism—has long characterized relationships between business and government. Alexander Hamilton's youthful ''Report on Manufactures'' recommended an active role for government in financing new enterprises and in sheltering them from foreign competition by means of tariff barriers. Hamilton also advocated the politically unpopular course of paying off the accumulated Revolutionary War debt, because he realized early the importance of foreign capital to the growth of industry and transportation in the thirteen largely agricultural former colonies and in the frontier territories.

Presidents such as Jefferson and Jackson were not convinced by Hamilton's logic, however. Except for an ongoing debate over the tariff, the federal government played little direct role in the development of industry or infrastructure until well after the Civil War.

Mercantilist philosophy found greater acceptance at the state level. Because of its parallels with the pre-laissez-faire era, recent industrial policy has in fact been termed the "new mercantilism" (McGraw, 1986). But current policy efforts cannot be explained in terms of their longevity. Rather, an overview of the history of state involvement in the economy should provide answers to the key questions. First of all, what has been the relative importance of economic development compared to other state policies? And second, what has been the capacity of state governments, either fiscally or politically, to deal with economic issues?

State involvement with economic development has varied over time. In the 1820s and 1830s, large amounts of state monies were spent on canals. Before the Civil War, the total U.S. public investment in internal improvements was $432 million, of which $300 million was provided by the states, $125 million by local governments, and only $7 million by the federal government (Cumberland, 1971: 32). After the Civil War, state government investment declined. Railroad investment became a largely federal activity financed through land grants, but many local governments subsidized railroads as well, and the states contributed 48 million out of the total of 179 million acres allocated to the railroads (North et al., 1983: 93).

After the Morrill Act (1862) many states, particularly in the Midwest, invested heavily in the new land-grant colleges and in agricultural research. Another major role for the states emerged after the mass production of the automobile led to great demand for highways. Federal highway involvement was minimal until the National Defense Highways Act of 1952; thereafter state matching grants contributed 10 percent of the funding of the interstate highway system. As of 1950, 28 percent of state budgets were devoted to highways and 40 percent to education.

Such spending on infrastructure and education varied across states and regions as well. But until after World War II, the bulk of government spending in the United States was state and local rather than federal. Thus the states contributed far more than the federal government to the financing of economic development. The exact proportion depends on how one evaluates federal land grants used to finance railroad construction, as well as on assumptions about the pace of growth in the absence of government activity.

Neoclassical economic history tends to discount the contribution of governments to national and regional economic growth. Government taxing and spending throughout the nineteenth century were modest (less than 5 percent of GNP except during wartime) compared with much larger inputs from capital, the growing labor force, and technological advance. However, the "institutional economics" approach tends to give much greater credence to the role of government in creating the conditions which encourage private entrepreneurial activity. Douglass North et al. (1983: 92ff.) argue that the social rate of return on investment in state-funded education, agricultural research, and public health can be demonstrated to have exceeded their initial direct costs. These are all examples of public goods which would not have been provided without government support. But the benefits varied considerably by sector and also across states.

State taxing, spending, and regulatory activity have all grown tremendously in the twentieth century; the range of state functions has also increased. In earlier years, even if states wished to influence the level or distribution of economic activity, they had few resources with which to do so. Modern broad-based taxes on sales and income were not developed until well into the twentieth century. After numerous scandals and defaults, most state constitutions by 1900 limited the amount of bonded indebtedness which states could incur (Hansen, 1983).

In addition to resource constraints, state capacity to influence economic development positively has been limited by political and institutional factors. In some states, waste, corruption, and lack of planning meant that the public's resources were not efficiently used. Canal construction was a good example. Some canals, such as New York's Erie Canal, were profitable, but Roger Ransom (1964) estimates that only 17 percent of total canal investment produced a profit. In addition, the lack of national planning led to inefficiency, interstate competition, and wasteful duplication of routes. Coordinated national infrastructure efforts, such as those proposed by Jefferson's treasury secretary Albert Gallatin or Henry Clay, never attained much political support in Congress.

The states' capacity for planning and forecasting were likewise limited. Until the development of national income accounts and econometric models in the 1930s, even the federal government had limited capacity to anticipate or influence economic trends. Although the larger industrialized states began to develop professionalized legislatures and large-scale bureaucracies by the 1930s, many smaller states had very limited budgets, part-time legislatures, and minuscule staffs well into the 1960s. Under these circumstances, it is hardly surprising that state economic policy was highly responsive to interest-group pressures, as graphically described by Robert Goodman (1979).

Thus, while state capacity has tended to increase, state involvement in economic development has waxed and waned over the past 200 years. This is reflective of the tension and ambiguity which have long characterized American attitudes toward the proper role of government in the economy. On the one hand, laissez-faire and economic individualism have been consistently held values. On the other hand, there has been strong support for technological progress, for increasing control over the environment, and for the fostering of economic growth. As a consequence, a flexible, pragmatic approach to government's role in the economy has emerged. But direct, large-scale involvement in particular economic enterprises has historically suffered from what Ellis Hawley (1986) termed a crisis of legitimacy. Efforts to create jobs, assist the unemployed, benefit lagging regions, or favor one set of industrial activities over another, have been the focus of considerable political debate over both means and ends.

CHANGING STATE POLICIES TOWARD BUSINESS

While economic development has been on most states' agendas for years, its relative priority and specific policies toward business have varied over time in response to three major factors. The first is the structure and stage of growth of a given industry. The second factor is the political conditions within a state, including the roles of parties, interest groups, the legislature, and the executive branch. The third factor is that of interstate competition: states are well aware of their neighbor's activities and often emulate them.

Stages of Industrial Development

Historically, an active government role has often been important in starting up companies because of the need for credit, for basic infrastructure, for the legal status of corporations, and for tariff protection for "infant industries." As firms mature, however, there is a trend toward monopoly structure, in order to control prices and limit competition. Thus we see a familiar cycle in steel, automobile production, and silicon chips: a very large number of firms is shaken down until only a few survive (Lawrence and Dyer, 1983). Under the ensuing monopoly conditions and controlled prices, little government intervention is necessary to maintain profits and restrict entry. Still, monopolies may be in a better position than individual firms to push for tax subsidies or a favorable regulatory environment. This is more likely to be the case in states dominated by a single industry (coal in West Virginia, copper in Montana) than in states with more diversified economies.

By the mid–twentieth century, however, many large manufacturing industries (including steel and automobiles) faced increasingly serious foreign competition. Monopoly structure was no longer sufficient to guarantee high prices and solid profits. In this environment, many industries have again turned to government for assistance with restructuring and technology development. And state governments, faced with lack of domestic investment, have turned to foreign sources for markets and investment.

Political Conditions within States

These constitute the second set of factors influencing state policies toward business and economic development. The number and strength of interest groups, the regulatory and extractive capacities of state governors and legislators, and the professionalism of state bureaucracies all help determine whether and how a state will act to influence industrial development. For example, the size and strength of organized labor is related to the passage of laws concerning right to work, minimum wages, and workers' compensation. States where a handful of industries are dominant (coal in West Virginia, copper in Montana, gambling in Nevada) are more likely to have laws and tax structures favoring those industries than are more diversified states, where the influence of any particular industry is counterbalanced by others. Thus Sarah Morehouse (1981) ranks states on the basis of interest group influence and finds the least influence in the largest urban states with complex economies.

Mancur Olson (1982), in a widely cited work, sees the increasing strength of state interest groups over time as an impediment to economic innovation and technological change. In his analysis for the period 1965–1980, older states and those with a high proportion of union members do indeed have slower rates of economic growth than newer states in the South and West. But Virginia Gray and David Lowery (1988), in a more recent study using direct measures of interest-group size, failed to duplicate Olson's results; they found little relationship between interest-group structure and state growth. Paul Brace (1988) suggests one reason for this: the development of powers of the state to counteract the influence of private interests. Industrialized states with well-developed parties and professionalized legislatures and bureaucracies, in his analysis, have continued to grow in recent years despite highly developed interest groups.

I have examined the political and economic conditions within states which best predicted state reliance on either tax subsidies or industrial policies (the latter including venture capital programs, enterprise zones, high technology programs, and plant-closing legislation) (Hansen, 1989). Tax subsidies have become widely disseminated over the past few decades, and in more recent years, many states have moved to adopt more innovative and interventionist industrial policies. States with high corporate taxes make more use of tax subsidies, as might be expected. But tax subsidy use is not well predicted by other economic or political conditions, partly because states have emulated each other in offering most tax breaks. However, states which make extensive use of tax subsidies are also the states most active in other industrial policy areas. By contrast, a smaller group of states (mostly rural and with small populations) relies on low overall taxes rather than tax expenditures and prefer to encourage private market initiatives rather than state industrial policy activism.

Overall, my analysis found that industrial policy adoption varied across states based on political rather than economic conditions. Neither unemployment, slow growth in personal income, nor business failure rates are very good predictors of reliance on industrial policy. Instead, the Democratic percentage of the state legislature, legislative professionalism, strong unions, and high representation of blacks in state legislatures are the best predictors. States where governors enjoy broad formal powers tend to be more active than states with many constraints on governors; this relationship holds regardless of party, since many Republican governors of northern industrial states have been proponents of industrial policies.

Actions Taken by Other States

Such actions constitute the third set of factors predicting use of industrial policies. As Jack Walker (1969) noted, states emulate the innovations of regional leaders. Many tax subsidies (for inventories, purchase of equipment, fuels and raw materials) have now been adopted by virtually all states and now confer little comparative advantage on any one state. Several of the more recent industrial policies have also been disseminated quickly. There were only two venture capital programs before 1980, but there are now over 20 (7 adopted in 1986 alone). Enterprise zones, high technology programs, state overseas offices, and foreign trade zones, all innovative policies a decade ago, are now widely employed.

Of course, the mere presence of a program is no guarantee that it will be adequately funded or effectively administered. In fact, my analysis (Hansen, 1989) found that the states with the most programs tended to spend the least per capita on industrial policy (based on budgetary data gathered by the National Association of State Development Agencies). This raises serious questions about the effectiveness of broad-gauge approaches. Rather than emulating their neighbors and trying a little bit of everything, state governments would be well advised to concentrate their efforts on a smaller set of programs and to build on their own strengths or on areas of comparative advantage. Focus on one or two geographic areas can also be recommended, particularly for high technology programs, in order to enhance agglomeration effects (Markusen, 1987). Although North Carolina's Research Triangle Park has been widely admired, it is highly unlikely that all 50 states will be successful in developing a similar high technology focus. Tourism may be a more realistic and more profitable emphasis, especially in poorer and more rural states.

CURRENT STATE INDUSTRIAL POLICY EFFORTS

The focus of state economic policy has changed considerably in recent years. A 1960 report on "the little economies" (Gilmore, 1960) described thousands of small and large state programs to encourage state business growth. The majority of these were tax breaks of various kinds, and advertising constituted the principal function of state departments of economic development. Such policies provided generalized benefits to many types of businesses, but a few policies were more focused. In order to reduce regulatory burdens, small businesses were often exempt from corporate income taxes, antipollution laws, minimum wage requirements, and provisions for occupational health and safety. In states where one or two businesses dominated (copper in Montana, automobiles in Michigan, tobacco in North Carolina, dairy farming in Wisconsin), those businesses were often able to persuade the state legislature to enact provisions (usually tax breaks) benefitting their particular industry. But in states with more diversified economies, interest groups tended to counterbalance one another, and industrial policies spread benefits more widely. Neither sectional nor sectorial policies have been the norm in most major industrial states.

Southern states have been the real pioneers in promotion of business, particularly manufacturing, beginning with Mississippi in the 1930s. Philip Wood (1986) describes state and local government efforts to diversify agricultural economies. Their inducements included advertising, tax subsidies, free land, factories built to suit, and customized worker training programs. Beginning in the 1950s, many northern states emulated the Southern tactics in their efforts to keep their factories from relocating in the Sunbelt. At least in the short term, however, the lure of low wages and union-free environments proved compelling. New England lost most of its textile and shoe industries, and Birmingham became a leading steel producer as Pittsburgh lost its price advantage.

After about 1960, however, major industries (agriculture, forestry, and primary metals, as well as manufacturing) in many states faced growing foreign competition and the necessity to reduce production. State policies of tax breaks and advertising campaigns were of little help as potential markets were lost. Nor, in an interdependent national economy, could states adopt production controls or marketing agreements to limit surplus capacity, although pressure for import quotas was brought to bear on the federal government. Instead, the recessions of 1979–1980 and 1981–1982 led many states to make economic development a priority and to attempt much more activist policies than had hitherto been the practice.

Industrial policies differ in three main ways from tax subsidies. First, they involve a degree of economic forecasting and planning to select the businesses or activities which are to be encouraged. Second, they often involve direct expenditure of state funds, rather than tax exemptions. And third, they are often focused on specific businesses or industries, rather than being available to all. Table 1.1 shows the current mix of traditional and innovative state policies toward industry. Under "tax exemptions" are listed those in effect as of 1986, according to NASDA's (1986) compilation. Several (such as goods in transit, machinery and equipment, fuels and raw materials) are nearly universal. But others are more unusual. Only 20 states, for example, have an investment tax credit; only 17 offer a tax credit for job creation.

The listing in Table 1.1 includes a few policies which have been widely disseminated (customized job training, local IDBs) as well as policies limited to a subset of states. Such a summary listing cannot capture the actions of individual states, several of which offer unique programs. (Michigan's business tax, for example, resembles a VAT [value-added tax] rather than a corporate income tax; California gives tax breaks for businesses which hire disabled or disadvantaged workers.) It should be noted that states vary widely in the particular features of these programs, as well as in the availability of funding. (See Clarke, 1986; NASDA, 1986; Fosler, 1988; and Hansen, 1989, for further discussion of state differences in focus and emphasis.)

The shift from general promotion to industry-specific incentives has not been

Table 1.1
Number of American States Employing Current Business Tax Exemptions,
Industrial Policies, and Foreign Trade Promotion Activities

Tax Exemptions

Fuels, raw materials	43
Goods in transit	42
Machinery and equipment	42
Pollution control equipment	40
Energy, fuel consumption	37
Business inventory	35
Property tax abatement	31
Investment tax credit	20
Job creation tax credit	17
Research and development	14
No unitary tax	41
No income tax	7
No sales tax	5

Industrial Policies

Local industrial development bonds	45
Customized industrial training	42
High technology programs	37
Direct state loans	27
State industrial development bonds	25
Enterprise zones	22
Venture capital programs	20
Right-to-work laws	20
Loan guarantees	15
Umbrella bonds	15
Plant closing legislation	4

Foreign Trade Promotion

Export development programs	50
Free trade zones	43
Overseas offices	32

Sources: NASDA, 1986; Clarke, 1986; Hansen, 1989; U.S. Department of Commerce, 1988

easy. Most states still attempt to avoid identifying "winners" and "losers," and economic planning remains a hard sell. As of 1985, according to a survey by the National Governors Association, over 20 states were identified as targeting specific industries or regions within the state. In addition, many other states were encouraging specific activities (high technology, research and development, job creation) in both old and new industries. But traditional, nontargeted policies (advertising, aid to small business, tax breaks) continue to dominate the industrial policy mix. As Margery Ambrosius (1986) noted, the value of tax expenditures in many states is substantial and far exceeds direct expenditure on industrial policy programs.

Table 1.1 also indicates the degree to which states have become involved in the international economy. Export promotion programs, free trade zones, and overseas trade offices are all widely disseminated, and most of these are new to the 1980s. As of 1977, for example, only 13 states had free trade zones. The controversial unitary tax (listed among tax exemptions) should also be mentioned in the international context. The nine states which currently have this levy (Florida and Massachusetts recently repealed theirs) tax the overseas and out-of-state activities of businesses headquartered within the state, and the tax is generally unpopular with business for that reason. Despite its unitary tax, however, California has greatly expanded its trade with Pacific Rim countries, and has made such trade the centerpiece of its industrial policy efforts.

The states have also been increasingly active in efforts to encourage direct foreign investment. As of 1983, net foreign investment totaled $47 billion and was estimated to produce over 2,500,000 jobs (Clarke, 1986: 81); by 1988, foreign investment had grown to over $150 billion (Council on Competitiveness, 1988). State leaders in this area included Texas, Alaska, and Louisiana (oil-related investment), California, New Jersey, Pennsylvania, Kentucky, and New York.

Foreign investment has in many ways substituted for lack of domestic capital and the low U.S. savings rate. According to many analysts (notably Zysman, 1983), capital is the key element in economic growth. Financial resources are necessary to develop innovations through research, to turn innovations into prototypes, and to mass-produce and market them. Capital is likewise necessary for the upgrading of production processes, managerial practices, and workers' skills. Lack of investment in basic industries is often cited as a reason for declines in U.S. productivity and rates of innovation.

But access to capital is by no means equal across states. Commercial bank deposits per capita in 1983 ranged from over $12,000 in Delaware to less than $3000 in South Carolina. Venture capital was even more highly concentrated; in 1985, over 48 percent of all U.S. venture capital was invested in California (Brody, 1985). Furthermore, California's share of venture capital resources had increased over the past decade, and only six states (California, New York, Massachusetts, Illinois, Texas, and Connecticut) accounted for over 80 percent of all venture capital raised in the U.S. as of 1983 (cited in Brody, 1985).

The attraction of foreign investment, regardless of its importance to states lacking in ready access to capital, is not always welcomed by state residents, particularly unions and companies fearful of losing business to foreign competitors. A 1987 national survey (NASDA, 1987) found the public supportive of a long list of state economic development policies, but not of overseas offices or trips abroad by state officials (often described as junkets in the media). Former Kentucky Governor Martha Layne Collins was widely criticized for spending more time in Tokyo than in Frankfort as she negotiated for the Toyota plant which eventually settled near Lexington.

From the perspective of most states, foreign investment is a goal worthy of increased state effort and financial support. Not all state interests may agree, however, since export and investment potential are usually concentrated in a few high tech or service industries. As Murray Weidenbaum (1987: 9) notes, 17 states had by 1987 imposed some sort of "Buy America" requirements for state procurement. Thus Michigan insists that all motor vehicles purchased by the state be of American manufacture—even if Mazda now has a factory in Flat Rock, Michigan. State and local building codes and other regulations may also be used to discriminate against foreign products. These protectionist tendencies are likely to invite retaliation by foreign businesses and thus will not assist state efforts to internationalize their markets.

THE EFFECTIVENESS OF STATE INDUSTRIAL POLICIES

Let us now consider the evidence for the impact of state economic development policies. The most extensive research, over the longest time period, has been devoted to the impact of taxes on industrial location. But it is difficult to reach an overall assessment: one can cite studies showing no effects (the preponderance), positive effects (tax breaks encourage industry), or negative effects (low taxes are detrimental, largely because of the resulting underfunding of services such as education.) Many of these studies are limited as to time period, and several have serious methodological flaws.

The most useful approaches for state policy makers interested in industrial recruitment would be those which show how tax effects differ across industrial sectors. Michael Wasylenko and Theresa McGuire (1985) thus compare the impact of state taxes on six different industrial sectors, including manufacturing and services (finance, insurance, real estate). They find that overall, nominal and effective personal and corporate income tax rates have an insignificant impact, but there are considerable differences across sectors. High personal income taxes and high overall taxes discourage economic growth in several sectors (particularly manufacturing). But higher state and local spending on education favorably affects job growth for the period they consider (1973 to 1980). They then calculate, for several individual states, the percentage change in total employment growth attributable to their taxing and spending variables.

Wilbur Thompson (1986) reviews research which shows that industries based on routine operations (most mature manufacturing) prefer low tax locations and are willing to tolerate the inconvenience of poor quality public services. But industries with a larger proportion of employees in research would be willing to pay higher taxes for better schools and universities. He concludes:

The near-zero correlation between local taxes and employment change is really a blurring of a negative correlation between local taxes and routine operations in almost all industries and a positive correlation in their sophisticated work. The question "Do taxes hurt or help in local economic development?" begs the prior question, "What does the community aspire to be?" (1986: 21)

Thompson advises state and local governments to target not specific industries but specific types of operations within industries. Michigan, for example, has focused economic development incentives on high tech operations in automobile production and supply. The Ben Franklin Partnership in Pennsylvania uses a similar strategy, emphasizing advanced technology regardless of the industry involved.

Thomas Plaut and Joseph Pluta (1983) also find, contrary to their expectations, positive relationships between tax rates and business location decisions. A definitive recent study of this topic is that of L. Jay Helms (1985). He argues that tax rates matter less than how tax monies are used. Using a general equilibrium model and allowing for a budgetary constraint, he finds that transfer payments (welfare) discourage growth in personal income, while expenditures serving some broader public purpose (education) exert a positive influence.

Tax expenditures have several limitations as a tool for economic development. Since so many states offer them, they may confer little comparative advantage, despite the often substantial revenue losses involved. In most cases, tax subsidies are used to reduce taxes on a firm's profits and thus are of little use to firms just starting up, which seldom have profits to offset. Further, as David Rasmussen et al. (1984) argue, many state tax breaks end up enriching federal coffers by reducing state or local tax or interest deductibility against federal income taxes. Nevertheless, state business associations continue to plead for tax reductions, and states are likely to continue to grant them—if only because their neighbors are doing so.

Let us now turn to evidence as to the effects of other state industrial policies. Here the research record is much leaner. Many of these policies are quite recent; relatively few have been subject to systematic evaluation. Ideally one would wish to have budgetary data available in order to weigh the costs and benefits of different incentives, but such data is nearly impossible to obtain in a comparable form across states.

When other measures were used, the most common result is that state policies have little if any impact. Michael Luger (1986) devised a series of "effort" measures (mostly ordinal) of state policy initiatives in order to predict wage and unemployment rates in 1981 and 1982. He found very little relationship between his measures and these economic outcomes, but noted that his highly aggregated measures may not predict the impact of explicit policies targeted to particular industries. Ambrosius (1986) compared rates of unemployment and personal income growth before and after the adoption of industrial policies by particular states. She also found little impact on the basis of comparison of the slopes of the regression lines before and after policy adoption (allowing for a three-year lag). But her choice of time-series methodology sacrificed numerous degrees of freedom and resulted in conclusions based on a subset of states for the mid-1970s. As does Luger's, her analysis does not consider the impact of more recent policy efforts.

I have examined a variety of recent industrial policy efforts in the states over the period 1970–1986 (Hansen, 1989). The purpose of this research was twofold: (1) to consider a range of economic outcomes, not just unemployment; and (2) to compare aggregate economic effects in states with and without particular policies, as well as within individual states over time. The overall conclusion reached was that a few state policies (particularly venture capital and high technology programs) did show a positive relationship to indicators of business activity such as productivity growth, increase in exports, or rates of new business formation. However, I was unable to establish positive causal relationships between unemployment rates and state policy efforts. Instead, states with high unemployment rates were those most willing to experiment with industrial policy initiatives. The indicators of business activity produced only marginal rates of growth in employment over a considerable lag time. It was apparent that there were no easy, cheap, short-term solutions to problems of unemployment and that assistance to business did not produce much payoff in terms of jobs.

Some additional results from this research deserve mention here. First, neither plant-closing laws nor absence of right-to-work laws have a deleterious impact on economic growth, as their business opponents have often predicted. This conclusion is based on analysis over time of the few states which have changed their status on these issues during the 1970–1986 time period: little change in either direction is apparent. Second, state programs continued to have high variations in unemployment rates across SMSAs both before and after adoption of enterprise-zone programs. The unemployment problems of the inner cities thus remain a troubling issue for state and local decision makers. On a more positive note, however, states that have had free trade zones in place since before 1980 have experienced considerably faster growth in exports than states which have only recently acquired free trade zones, and this relationship holds for both coastal and interior states.

This sort of aggregate-level analysis cannot isolate the success or failure of particular state programs or incentive packages. Nor can a broad-gauged investigation of state industrial policy predict effects on specific industries. As Wasylenko (1981: 160) noted, tax cuts designed to attract heavy manufacturing may be inappropriate, even detrimental, for the investments in infrastructure, education, and services necessary to attract and retain high technology industries.

Thus, as the automobile industry becomes increasingly high tech in production techniques and organization, state and local governments must reexamine their industrial policy priorities. It is a long road from Volkswagen in Pennsylvania to Saturn in Tennessee and from Saturn to the automobile factories in the future. Yet, however successful a particular package or program may be, if there is no ascertainable impact on state economic aggregates (particularly employment), scholars as well as citizens may question the relative costs and benefits of costly incentives to individual firms.

State policy effectiveness must also be compared to that of federal government initiatives. Ambrosius (1986) noted that federal macroeconomic policies tend to dominate state policy efforts. She found that the best single predictor of state-level unemployment was the national unemployment rate and that state productivity trends also tracked national trends (see also Brace and Bauman, 1988, and Rasmussen et al., 1984). An ongoing task for state government officials as well as for policy analysts is to sort out the appropriate industrial policy roles for different levels of government. (See John, 1987, for a thoughtful attempt to do so.) Certainly one focus of state efforts has been to lobby Washington for import restrictions, EDA monies, Defense Department procurement, and other policies to the advantage of particular states. Import restrictions, interest rates, and the value of the dollar may have far more to do with foreign investment than the efforts of individual states.

VOLKSWAGEN IN PENNSYLVANIA: A CAUTIONARY TALE?

In the 1980s, as we have seen, the states engaged in increasingly sophisticated and expensive industrial policy efforts. It is too soon to test for the economic effects of many of these. But it has been over ten years since one noteworthy instance of foreign automobile investment occurred in Pennsylvania. The economic development prize of the 1970s was the Volkswagen automobile plant. The German manufacturer decided to reduce production costs (due in part to Germany's overvalued mark) and import fees by locating a VW Rabbit production facility somewhere in the United States. When this plan was announced, a bidding war ensued among the states, with Pennsylvania the ultimate victor over Ohio and West Virginia. But it was a costly victory. The Commonwealth agreed to an incentive package worth between $70 and $80 million. (For 3000 jobs, this works out to between $23,000 and $26,000 per job.) As David Osborne (1987) notes, however, this package of concessions depleted Pennsylvania's principal loan fund, the Industrial Development Authority, for several years. Ron Chernow (1979) describes the whole bidding war in a critical article entitled "The Rabbit That Ate Pennsylvania," and he alleges that Pennsylvania was induced to make additional concessions even after Volkswagen had decided on its preferred location.

Subsequent events have tended to prove the skeptics right. The VW plant was a modern production facility, with considerable quality control equipment. But the Rabbit did not do as well as expected in the American market after gasoline prices dropped in the 1980s. The plant in New Stanton, Pennsylvania switched over to Golf and Jetta models, but was never able to find another profitable niche in the small-car market and was forced to reduce operations considerably. The New Stanton plant was plagued by labor unrest (perhaps because the initial contract paid VW workers about 20 percent less than their counterparts at Ford or GM) and by 1983 was operating only one shift. Finally, in July 1988, it closed its doors completely, idling nearly 3000 workers and greatly reducing tax revenues in New Stanton and Westmoreland County. As of this writing the state has not been able to locate another buyer for the facility, although negotiations have been undertaken with several auto makers (Oravecz and Citron, 1988). The number of employees never reached expectations, and the plant operated on reduced shifts during the last years of its existence.

The major negative consequence of the Rabbit facility was the amount of state investment foregone. The highway link was expensive, and tax concessions to the surrounding communities were only partially offset by sales tax revenues and increased real estate values. In a year in which it produced over 80,000 Rabbits, VW's total property taxes were less than the value of one vehicle (Allan, 1986). With its depleted loan fund, the Commonwealth could not pursue other potential manufacturers in later years even if it had wanted to do so. Republican Governor Richard Thornburgh, elected in 1978, did not want to, and his own economic development program emphasized homegrown entrepreneurship and small business development rather than smokestack chasing. Pennsylvania's pursuit of the Saturn facility was noticeably restrained. Thornburgh (along with three dozen other governors) did make the requisite pilgrimage to GM headquarters in Warren, Michigan, to pitch the state to General Motors. But he made a point of flying there in a propeller plane rather than a jet and insisted he would discuss concessions only after Saturn agreed to locate in Pennsylvania.

The state's Democrats were highly critical of Thornburgh's restrained approach, since unemployment in the state was over fourteen percent at the time. But Thornburgh insisted that Pennsylvania had learned from the VW Rabbit experience and would no longer engage in costly bidding wars for major manufacturing facilities. Instead, his administration (with Democratic support) developed and implemented a strategy centered on the Ben Franklin Partnership. This program uses state funds to leverage private investment and to encourage joint efforts of businesses and universities to develop advanced technology. Four regional centers have been established, and proposals are reviewed and funded on a competitive basis, with job creation potential a major criterion.

Whatever its economic logic, Thornburgh's restraint had its political costs. The Ben Franklin approach failed to create as many new jobs or businesses as expected and did not address problem areas such as the Monongahela Valley, the former steel-producing region near Pittsburgh. Democrats in the state legislature introduced legislation to set up a Sunny Day Fund specifically to attract out-of-state firms. Thornburgh was constitutionally prohibited from running for a third term. His lieutenant governor, William Scranton, lost to Democrat Robert Casey in a race in which economic development policy was one of the major issues. Casey pledged a more activist stance regarding unemployment and has pursued out-of-state plants more vigorously than Thornburgh did, but nevertheless continues to emphasize the retention of existing business and the support of entrepreneurship rather than costly bids for outside investment. (See Hansen, 1989, for further discussion of Pennsylvania's industrial policy.)

Although Pennsylvania continues to lag behind other Middle Atlantic states with respect to increases in new business and labor force participation, its unemployment rate is now lower than the national trend for the first time since the 1970s. Its Ben Franklin partnership program has been widely emulated. In short, deemphasizing the pursuit of out-of-state and foreign manufacturing has not seemed to hurt, although pockets of high unemployment still linger in the former steel- and coal-producing regions.

AN UNRESOLVED DEBATE: ATTRACT JOBS OR PEOPLE?

An ongoing debate in the scholarly literature concerns the relationship between population and employment growth. Do jobs follow people, with growth in the labor force a consequence of general population growth? Or do people follow jobs, migrating to areas of higher wages or lower unemployment? This is an important issue of budgetary priorities for state governments, particularly in states with stable or declining populations. Should they invest public resources in industry or job-related activities? Or should they pay attention to more general components of the quality of life, such as education and environmental protection, in order to retain population? In short, is industrial policy a waste of money?

Richard Muth (1968) used simultaneous equation models to estimate population and employment trends in cities. For two-thirds of the urban areas in his study, people followed job opportunities, but for the remainder, one additional employed immigrant led to more than one additional job. Donald Steinnes (1977) found, based on state-level data, that jobs followed people.

A recent comprehensive analysis of the determinants of growth in total employment, manufacturing employment, and population is offered by Gerald Carlino and Edwin Mills (1987). They use 1970s data (mostly from *County Business Patterns* and the *City-County Data Book*) on 3000 U.S. counties to analyze the determinants of growth between 1970 and 1980. Their purpose was to investigate three separate, concurrent movements of jobs and people: from metropolitan central cities to the suburbs, from metropolitan to nonmetropolitan areas, and from the Frostbelt to the Sunbelt. They found that family income has a powerful effect in stimulating both population growth rates and employment density: a 10 percent increase in family income leads to a 7.9 percent increase in total employment and a 9.2 percent increase in manufacturing employment.

High family income, in their view, stands for high demand and therefore draws both firms and households. Thus, based on their structural equations and estimates of elasticities, jobs follow people—especially high-income house-holds—rather than people following jobs. Carlino and Mills are thus skeptical of state and local efforts to attract jobs and industry:

Since population and employment growth are interrelated, one policy prescription for local economic development officials is to formulate strategies to retain or attract population and employment will follow. To the extent that income serves as a proxy for good neighborhoods and good schools, the population equation suggests that public funds may be better spent on educating the resident population than used to lure employment. (1987: 52)

Despite the breadth of scope of their article and its careful methodology, several criticisms can be made. One is that, although the article is recent, the data are from the 1970s, and there is no evidence that the same trends have continued unchanged. Second, no direct measures of amenities (climate, quality of schools, quality of life) are used, and the authors make inferences about these factors from other variables such as family income. Finally, taxes and industrial development bonds are the only policies they consider, even though dozens of others have been adopted by local governments. Because of such issues, state officials might be best advised to hedge their bets—to continue efforts to attract industry, but to also maintain high qualities of public services in order to maintain or increase population. In an era of constrained budgets, however, it may be impossible to do both well, and hefty incentive packages for industrial recruitment may necessitate substantial cuts elsewhere.

CONCLUSION

I have described current state industrial policy in both historical and comparative perspective. What does this tell us about the possible long-term effects of state efforts to attract large-scale foreign investment?

Both positive and negative outcomes must be considered. First, on the positive side, foreign investment has emerged as a major source of capital. The U.S. savings rate is low and has been declining, while the soaring federal deficit has crowded out domestic sources of capital. Foreign investment is therefore a welcome substitute, especially for the many states that have little access to private venture capital. Also on the positive side, states that have actively pursued foreign investment have become more aware of the increasing internationalization of the American economy. Their efforts to transcend cultural barriers, retrain workers, and promote education and high technology should auger well for the ability of other corporations in such states to tap into overseas markets. Governors have been subject to popular criticism for their foreign ''junkets,'' but many governors whose previous experience has been entirely in subnational domestic politics have presumably learned something of value in the process.

On the negative side, however, foreign investment strategies are in many ways hazardous for states. Considerable loss of tax revenue has occurred, and the cost of tax breaks and other subsidies has been increasing over time. State and local governments have many other demands for services and can ill afford additional erosion of their tax base. Jobs forecasts have in several instances been over-optimistic. As state economies move into international markets, they also become more vulnerable to outside forces. As Pennsylvania discovered, its investment in Volkswagen produced payoffs over a much shorter period than originally forecast, and the New Stanton plant ended up with a very different cost-benefit ratio than had been anticipated. Any long-term predictions of jobs and payrolls, whether calculated by the state or by a prospective foreign investor, should therefore be taken with a large grain of salt.

Further, based on previous industrial policy efforts, the geographic distribution of benefits from foreign investment is likely to be somewhat limited within a state. While Pennsylvania was successful in bringing Volkswagen into an area of high unemployment, this is often not the case; Governor Casey was recently criticized for costly state efforts to attract an Eastman Kodak plant, which ultimately located in one of the state's wealthiest counties. North Carolina has found it difficult to spin off positive effects of the Research Triangle into other regions of the state, despite its efforts at "balanced growth" (Johnson, 1983). States have been more successful in targeting by sector than in targeting industrial policy efforts on poor regions. Some form of sharing of the tax benefits of growth could overcome such problems, but the political difficulties involved should not be underestimated.

The states thus face a difficult dilemma. It may make economic sense to concentrate economic development efforts on a few programs, a few industries, or a limited geographic area. But it will not be easy to justify such a strategy to state residents or regions which do not directly benefit.

This discussion has raised serious questions concerning the ability of either the states or the federal government to deal with statewide unemployment by means of industrial incentives. Although considerable public money has been spent, this has not been sufficient to have much impact on a large and dynamic economy. While creative financing has been a hallmark of state industrial policy efforts to date, popular opposition to tax increases and the demands of other state spending programs limit the monies available for investment in industrial development. Competitiveness in the international marketplace may well require state investment in education, infrastructure, and the environment, rather than in efforts to attract foreign firms by means of expensive incentive packages. State experiences may therefore inform the current national debate over a competitiveness strategy.

REFERENCES

Allan, William. 1986. "Disassembled Dreams: Market Realities Cast Pall over VW Car Plant." *Pittsburgh Press*, 16 February, D15–16.

Ambrosius, Margery M. 1986. "Effects of State Economic Development Policies on the Health of State Economies." Paper presented at the annual meeting of the Midwest Political Science Association, Chicago.

Bartik, Timothy. 1984. "Business Location Decisions in the United States: Estimates of the Effects of Unionization, Taxes, and Other Characteristics of States." *Journal of Business and Economic Statistics* 3: 14–22.

Bendik, Marc, Jr., and David W. Rasmussen. 1986. "Enterprise Zones and Inner-City Economic Revitalization." In George E. Peterson and Carol W. Lewis, eds., *Reagan and the Cities*. Washington, D.C.: Urban Institute Press, 186–203.

Brace, Paul. 1988. "Legislatures and Economic Performance." Paper presented at the American Political Science Association annual meeting, Washington, D.C., September.

Brace, Paul, and Philip Bauman. 1988. "Isolating the Political Economic Nexus in the American of States." Paper presented at the annual meeting of the Midwest Political Science Association, Chicago.

Brody, Herbert. 1985. "The High-Tech Sweepstakes." *High Technology* 4 (January): 16–46.

Carlino, Gerald A., and Edwin S. Mills. 1987. "The Determinants of County Growth." *Journal of Regional Science* 27: 39–54.

Carlton, Dennis W. 1983. "The Location and Employment Choices of New Firms." *Review of Economics and Statistics* 65: 440–449.

Chernow, Ron. 1979. "The Rabbit That Ate Pennsylvania." *Mother Jones*, October, 254–258.

Clarke, Marianne. 1986. *Revitalizing State Economies*. Report prepared for the National Governors Association. Washington, D.C.

Council on Competitiveness. 1988. "Reclaiming the American Dream: Fiscal Policies for a Competitive Nation." *Challenges* 2 (December): 5–8.

Cumberland, John H. 1971. *Regional Development Experiences and Prospects in the United States of America*. The Hague: Mouton.

Fosler, M. Scott. 1988. *The New Economic Role of the American States*. New York: Oxford University Press.

Gilmore, Donald R. 1960. *Developing the Little Economies*. New York: Committee for Economic Development.

Goodman, Robert. 1979. *The Last Entrepreneurs*. New York: Free Press.

Gray, Virginia, and David Lowery. 1988. "Interest Group Politics and Economic Growth in the American States." *American Political Science Review* 82: 109–132.

Hansen, Susan B. 1983. *The Politics of Taxation: Revenue Without Representation*. New York: Praeger.

———. 1987. "State Governments and Industrial Policy in the United States." In J. J. Hesse, ed., *Regions, Structural Change and Industrial Policies in International Perspective*. Frankfurt: Nomos Verlag.

———. 1989. *The Political Economy of State Industrial Policy*. Pittsburgh: University of Pittsburgh Press.

Hawley, Ellis W. 1986. "Industrial Policy in the 1920s and 1930s." In Claude Barfield and William A. Schambra, eds., *The Politics of Industrial Policy*. Washington, D.C.: American Enterprise Institute, 63–86.

Helms, L. Jay. 1985. "The Effect of State and Local Taxes on Economic Growth: A

Time Series-Cross Section Approach." *Review of Economics and Statistics* 67: 574–582.

Hughes, Jonathan R. T. 1977. *The Governmental Habit*. New York: Basic Books.

John, Dewitt. 1987. *Shifting Responsibilities: Federalism in Economic Development*. Washington, D.C.: National Governors Association.

Johnson, W. Lee. 1983. "Balanced Growth Policy in North Carolina: A Case Study in Realities." *State Government* 56: 112–119.

Lawrence, Paul R., and Davis Dyer. 1983. *Renewing American Industry: Organizing for Efficiency and Innovation*. New York: Free Press.

Luger, Michael I. 1986. "The States and Industrial Development: Program Mix and Policy Effectiveness." In John Quigley, ed., *Perspectives on State and Local Finance and Public Policy*. Greenwich, Conn.: JAI Press.

Markusen, Ann. 1987. *Regions: The Economics and Politics of Territory*. Totowa, N.J.: Rowman & Littlefield.

McGraw, Thomas K. 1986. "Mercantilism and the Market." In Claude Barfield and William A. Schambra, eds., *The Politics of Industrial Policy*. Washington, D.C.: American Enterprise Institute, 33–62.

Morehouse, Sarah McCalley. 1981. *State Politics, Parties, and Policy*. New York: Holt, Rinehart, and Winston.

Muth, Richard F. 1968. "Differential Growth among Large U.S. Cities." In J. P. Quirk and A. M. Zarley, eds., *Papers in Quantitative Economics*. Lawrence: University of Kansas Press.

National Association of State Development Agencies. 1986. *Directory of Incentives for Business Investment and Development in the United States: A State-by-State Guide*, 2nd ed. Washington, D.C.: Urban Institute Press.

Newman, Robert J., and Dennis H. Sullivan. 1988. "Econometric Analysis of Business Tax Impacts on Industrial Location: What We Do Know, and How Do We Know It?" *Journal of Urban Economics* 23: 215–234.

North, Douglass C., et al. 1983. *Growth and Welfare in the American Past*. Englewood Cliffs, N.J.: Prentice-Hall.

Olson, Mancur. 1982. *The Rise and Decline of Nations: Economic Growth, Stagflation, and Social Rigidities*. New Haven: Yale University Press.

Oravecz, John D., and Rodger Citron. 1988. "VW's Westmoreland Plant Story Coming to Sad End." *Pittsburgh Press*, 10 July, B8.

Osborne, David. 1987. *Economic Competitiveness: The States Take the Lead*. New York: Economic Policy Institute.

Plaut, Thomas R., and Joseph E. Pluta. 1983. "Business Climate, Taxes and Expenditures, and State Industrial Growth in the United States." *Southern Economic Journal* 50: 99–119.

Ransom, Roger. 1964. "Canals and Development: Discussion of the Issues." *American Economic Review* 44: 360–380.

Rasmussen, David W., et al. 1984. "A Methodology for Selecting Economic Development Incentives." *Growth and Change* 15: 18–25.

Steinnes, Donald N. 1977. "Causality and Intraurban Location." *Journal of Urban Economics* 4: 69–79.

Thompson, Wilbur R. 1986. "Cities in Transition." *Annals of the American Academy of Political and Social Sciences* 488 (November): 18–34.

U.S. Department of Commerce. 1988. "Free Trade Zones in the U.S." Washington, D.C. Mimeo.

Walker, Jack L. 1969. "The Diffusion of Innovation among the American States." *American Political Science Review* 63: 880–889.

Wasylenko, Michael. 1981. "The Role of Taxes and Fiscal Incentives in the Location of Firms." In Roy Bahl, ed., *Urban Government Finance: Emerging Issues.* Beverly Hills, Calif.: Sage, 155–190.

Wasylenko, Michael, and Theresa McGuire. 1985. "Jobs and Taxes: The Effect of Business Climate on States' Employment Growth Rates." *National Tax Journal* 38: 497–510.

Weidenbaum, Murray L. 1987. "International Trade and Economic Development." *Economic Development Quarterly* 1: 4–12.

Wood, Philip. 1986. *Southern Capitalism: The Political Economy of North Carolina.* Durham, N.C.: Duke University Press.

Zysman, John. 1983. *Governments, Markets, and Growth.* Ithaca, N.Y.: Cornell University Press.

2

State Incentive Packages and the Industrial Location Decision

H. Brinton Milward and
Heidi Hosbach Newman

The 1980s has become the decade of industrial recruitment and the state incentive package. Recent media exposure has heightened public awareness of and controversy over the extent to which state governments are willing to give incentives to large corporations to locate in their state. Although state and local governments have long offered companies inducements to retain, expand, or create facilities within their borders, recent negotiations have led to a war between the states characterized by ever increasing bids.

This chapter provides an analysis of the industrial location process. Various studies will be reviewed in an effort to determine the relevant business and nonbusiness factors involved in industrial location decisions and to note any shifts in their relative importance. In addition, six case studies are presented to provide an overview of the state incentive packages which have recently led to the development of the Japanese Auto Alley in the American Midwest (see Figure 2.1).

THE LOCATIONAL DECISION

The industrial location decision is a complex, multistep process which occurs

Milward, H. B. and Newman, H. H. *Economic Development Quarterly*, vol. 3, no. 3, pp. 203–222. Copyright 1989 by Sage Publications, Inc. Reprinted with Permission of Sage Publications.

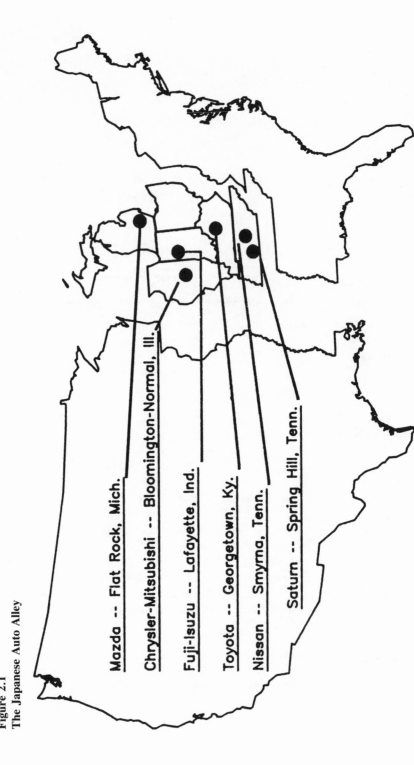

Figure 2.1
The Japanese Auto Alley

Mazda -- Flat Rock, Mich.

Chrysler-Mitsubishi -- Bloomington-Normal, Ill.

Fuji-Isuzu -- Lafayette, Ind.

Toyota -- Georgetown, Ky.

Nissan -- Smyrna, Tenn.

Saturn -- Spring Hill, Tenn.

only after the relevant corporation has formulated a strategic plan, devised a forecast of future capacity requirements, and determined the necessity of additional and/or improved facilities.

A major problem with the popular view of locational decision-making is the importance attached to the role of the city or the state in influencing a firm to locate one place rather than another. In Kentucky a major issue in the 1987 gubernatorial campaign revolved around why the governor gave Toyota such a large incentive package (a fair question) and why she did not tell Toyota to locate in a part of the state where there is high unemployment. Yet, although governors can locate universities, prisons, and national guard armories wherever they want, it is firms, not states or cities, that decide where they will locate (Milward, 1986).

In "Major Factors in Industrial Location: A Review," John Blair and Robert Premus (1987) outline the findings of the industrial location literature and stress the necessity of understanding that the location decision is merely a subset of the larger process of corporate planning. Once a corporate plan has been devised, future capacity requirements determined, and the decision to expand or create an existing or new facility made, Blair and Premus list eight additional steps in the site selection process:

1. Determine the structure and composition of the site selection committee/team;

2. Develop a list of characteristics that are pertinent to the location of the new facility;

3. Develop a "must and want" list of site selection criteria based upon the economic and noneconomic aspects of locational choice;

4. Gather information on possible sites and compare each against the "must and want" list of step 3;

5. Conduct elimination rounds (a) by region/multistate level, (b) by state, (c) by specific community, and (d) by specific site;

6. Narrow the locational choices and begin discussion with local/state public officials regarding potential problems and incentives;

7. Prepare preliminary estimates of construction costs for inclusion in the corporation's capital budget;

8. Conduct a feasibility study.

However, once step 5 is reached, the factors deemed important to the site selection shift as one moves from multistate to the specific site levels. According to a Fortune, Inc. publication (1977), *Facility Location Decisions*, over 50 percent of all location decisions make the first elimination at a regional or multistate level. At the macro level, the selection committee will focus on labor factors, state tax variables, climate, market proximity, and transportation access. However, as the elimination rounds continue, the importance of microgeographic features (i.e. education, land cost, and public attitudes) gain importance. Therefore, it is imperative that state and local government officials understand the site selection process and the relevant location determinants if they hope to intervene in and influence the final site selection decision.

Historical Overview

Although a myriad of articles have been published on industrial location, the results vary with each study. The differences appear to reside in the specific industry chosen, the age of the sample firms, the production technology changes which have occurred over the years, and the array of methodological approaches employed. Therefore, a review of the industrial location literature can be a journey into both the contradictory and the ambiguous. The impact of state taxes on a region's economic development has long been a concern for economists, and the findings have been less than conclusive. A review of studies by Due, Bloom, Campbell, Floyd, Larson, and Garwood suggests that state taxes have had no significant effect on the trend or magnitude of industrial movement (cited in Newman, 1983: 76–78). Further, Dennis Carlton's 1977 examination of three four-digit SIC industries revealed that corporate tax differentials between states did not explain the observed variation in "new births" of companies. However, in a subsequent study by Hodge, taxes significantly affected regional investment patterns in an industry not studied by Carlton. Also in 1983, Robert Newman (1983) published the results of a study which gave considerable support to the belief that tax rate differentials between states is a major factor influencing industry's movement southward.

Further, complications arise when assessing the industrial location decision. Recent studies in economics have used computerized models, and, like the studies of past decades, these statistical models are predominantly based upon quantifiable data. Although such studies have expanded an earlier focus on both transportation and production costs to include quantifiable variables associated with plant location, a significant problem still exists when one attempts to incorporate nonquantitative variables. G. Michael Epping (1982) claims that, in fact, qualitative and subjective factors can be just as important as the quantitative when determining industrial location.

The following is an overview of the current literature and includes the results of both econometric and survey techniques. Although a brief analysis of the 1982 Heckman study, John Steinnes's 1984 model of economic development, Schmenners's 1987 analysis of geographic differences and the location decision, *Industry Week*'s 1984 survey, Carlton's 1982 econometric model, Newman's 1982 study on industry migration and the growth of the South, and Mamoru Yoshida and Edwin Coleman's studies on Japanese and foreign direct investment, cannot provide confirmation of specific findings, it can offer a basis upon which to derive important generalizations and trace subtle shifts in factor significance.

From 1977 to 1981, John Heckman conducted mail/telephone interviews with the business executives of 204 firms in North Carolina, South Carolina, and Virginia (Heckman, 1982). The executives were asked to rate 19 business location factors and 12 quality-of-life factors. Heckman found that the most important location factors were state and local industrial climate, labor productivity, transportation, land availability (including room for plant expansion), and cost of land and construction. Of particular note is the lack of significance attributed to market proximity. However, this could be a direct function of the type of firms used in Heckman's study, which were predominantly branch operations of multiplant firms. Heckman found that a good business climate/attitude and labor productivity were of primary importance to firms when making site selection decisions.

Further, Heckman determined from his sample that quality-of-life factors were indeed important in the location decision. Of primary importance were the educational system, the cost of living, housing, quality of the environment, and the amount of personal taxes. However, although quality-of-life factors were significant, Heckman found that their overall rating was less than that of the traditional business location factors.

In the following year, Dennis W. Carlton (1983) published the results of a study of the location and employment choices of new firms, using an econometric model with discrete and continuous endogenous variables. Although Carlton's research dealt only with the location and employment choices of new branch plants across SMSAs, many of his findings are particularly significant. Carlton concluded that: (1) taxes and state incentive programs do not seem to have major effects, and (2) available technical expertise is likely to be important for highly sophisticated industries. In addition, Carlton found that when using the model, the tax variables are frequently of the wrong sign, usually very small, and always statistically insignificant. Carlton does concede, however, that taxes may have a statistically significant indirect impact. He speculates that if taxes are levied to finance highly valued public goods, workers will be attracted to the area, wages will fall, and new industrial "births" will be stimulated by the drop in wages. Finally, Carlton found no justification for claims that a favorable business climate could alone substantially stimulate new plant location.

Later that year, Robert J. Newman (1983) published the results of a 1981 study of the Sunbelt phenomenon. The focus of the research was to understand the effect of interstate differentials in corporate tax rates, unionization, and "business climate." Newman concludes that interstate corporate tax rate differentials, the prevalence of unionization, and a favorable business climate (here defined as the legislative enactment of right-to-work laws) are, in fact, major factors in industry's southern drift. Newman attributes the seemingly contrary results to the flawed design of previous studies. Newman provides evidence that a significant variation in the coefficient estimates across industries exists, and thus past research based upon limited industry samples cannot be generalized. For example, Newman found that the durable goods sector was more sensitive to alterations in the corporate tax differentials than the nondurable sector.

In 1984 Mark L. Goldstein published the results of a survey of 1000 executives (Goldstein, 1984). Goldstein found that transportation (land, air, train, and sea) was the most statistically significant locational factor, and that higher worker productivity was ranked by 59 percent of the respondents as "vitally important." The survey also pointed to both unionization and tax credits/exemptions as important locational factors. However, no attempt was made in the survey to distinguish between the importance of local tax incentives and the level of state taxes. Further, like Heckman, Goldstein emphasized the importance of the industrial climate and the growing significance of quality-of-life factors, particularly education.

Also in 1984, Steinnes developed a dynamic model of economic development which utilized a pooled time series–cross sectional set of data in conjunction with a lagged dependent variable (Steinnes, 1984). Steinnes insists that there is little statistical evidence to substantiate the claim that tax incentives or business climate variables effectively stimulate economic growth. In fact, his study suggests that higher taxes are positively related to economic growth. The author speculates that economic growth may be a function of the mix rather than the level of taxes. Steinnes found that the majority of positive (wrong) signs were associated with sales tax and the fewest, for property tax. Therefore, the author suggests that state legislators may stimulate growth by shifting the tax burden from the property tax to other methods of taxation (i.e., sales tax). Further, Steinnes proposes that the higher taxes of a state may indicate a corresponding level of public services or a higher quality of life. Therefore, industries dependent upon state-of-the-art technology may settle in high tax states if the taxation level reflects a well trained work force and a higher level of public amenities.

Finally, Mamoru Yoshida published *Japanese Direct Manufacturing Investment in the United States* in which he dedicates one chapter to the investment decision-making process (Yoshida, 1987). Yoshida's findings are based upon extensive personal interviews conducted in the summer of 1984 with executives and managers of 15 Japanese companies and officials from both the Ministry of International Trade and Industry (MITI) and the Federation of Economic Organizations (Keidanren). When studying the relative significance of various factors effecting the location decision, Yoshida only considered those companies which were selecting a U.S. plant site for a start-up venture rather than a plant expansion.

All interviewees were asked to rank the importance of 12 locational factors, using a four-point scale ranging from "very important" to "not important." Table 2.1 summarizes Yoshida's results.

The three most significant location factors were quality of labor (here synonymous with Heckman's labor productivity and Goldstein's worker productivity), proximity to markets, and lack of labor unionization. An analysis of the table reveals marked differences between the concerns of large Japanese companies and those of the small firms. The majority of the large firms ranked proximity to suppliers as an "important" factor; the small firms, on the other hand, did not. Also noteworthy is that quality-of-life was rated more important than special tax incentives by both the large and small firms.

Table 2.1
Relative Importance of Factors Influencing Location Decision

| | | Average Rating | |
	Total	Large Firms	Small Firms
Number of cases	20.00	14.00	6.00
Quality of labor	3.40	3.64	2.83
Proximity to markets	3.10	3.14	3.00
Labor unionization (lack of)	3.10	3.43	2.33
Cost of land	2.70	2.71	2.67
Cost of labor	2.60	2.57	2.67
Quality of life	2.50	2.64	2.17
Special tax incentives	2.40	2.57	2.00
Proximity to suppliers	2.35	2.64	1.67
Proximity to educational and research institutions	2.30	2.14	2.67
Other state and local government incentives	1.95	2.07	1.67
Proximity to a Japanese community	1.65	1.71	1.50
Proximity to competitors	1.55	1.57	1.50
Total average rating	2.47	2.57	2.22

Note: The average ratings are based on a four-point scale: 4 = very important,
        3 = important, 2 = less important, and 1 = not important.

Source: Yoshida, 1987: 7.

Yoshida further elaborates on the concerns of the Japanese companies directly investing in the United States. Yoshida found that the primary concern of the firms interviewed was with labor, including the quality and availability of engineers, the level of union activity, and the history of management-employee relationships in a particular region. Also, during site investigations, the Japanese firms were interested in the local community's attitude toward their direct investments.

The industrial location literature has thus provided a myriad of contradictory results. The majority of published studies have minimized or dismissed the significance of tax differentials or tax incentives while others claim that taxes do have an important effect on industrial development. Similarly, some researchers have heralded the importance of wage and unionization differentials while others claim their effect is statistically insignificant. However, a recent publication by Roger W. Schmenner and associates (Schmenner, Huber, and Cook, 1987) provides an overview of the location decision, and he, like Blair and Premus, views the decision as a sequential process. Their study complicates the econometric model by inserting two additional factors: (1) the decision is made in stages and the factor weights differ from stage to stage; and (2) the weights prescribed to the various factors depend not only on the stage of the decision but also on the characteristics indigenous to the new plant being considered and the company making the decision. The model designed by the authors accommodates state-specific characteristics which affect expected profitability, plant characteristics which affect expected profitability, plant characteristics which alter the importance of state characteristics, and independent variables which either operate to advance or retard the anticipated profitability of building a plant within a particular state, or plant-specific characteristics that magnify or reduce the state effects.

In *Making Business Location Decisions*, Schmenner (1982) provides the results of research spanning a five or six year period during which he garnered and analyzed information from 410 of the Fortune 500 companies and from industrial concerns within the Cincinnati metropolitan area and New England. According to the study, an analysis of data from the 1970s indicates a trend toward the Sunbelt's superior performance relative to the Frostbelt in attracting new plants. Therefore, the author suggests the promotion of internal industrial growth in the North and the advertisement of attractions for new plants in the South. In addition, he argues, governmental taxation and financing have only a minimal effect on the selection of new plant locations. In fact, relatively high taxes are more likely to "push" businesses away than low taxes "pull" corporations in from other states. Further, it is the particularly visible taxes (i.e., high income tax or workers' compensation) which seem most detrimental to a state's recruitment strategies. However, Schmenner's research indicated that long-distance movers and new plant openings are the most likely to move to an area of lower tax rates, although this is not a major consideration for the companies in the Fortune 500. Schmenner asserts that tax and financial incentives appear to be significant only when companies are evaluating otherwise equivalent locations. The author also states that state right-to-work laws appear a successful inducement to industrial economic development and that right-to-work states are frequently preferred for new plant locations.

Schmenner provides a summary of those economic development programs used by the plants in his various surveys (see Tables 2.2 and 2.3). Clearly, comparatively few programs are employed by even the large corporations. However, certain programs are used more frequently in specific geographical areas. For example, labor training programs are widely used in the South Atlantic states and moderately in the East and West South Central areas. From a state policy perspective, Schmenner's research indicates that states and localities should focus their resources on the physical assistance associated with plant selection, construction, and start-up.

Conclusions from the Literature

Traditionally, the overriding concerns in an industrial location decision have been access to labor, transportation, markets, and raw materials. Although these business factors are still of paramount importance, research has recently highlighted the salience of state economic development programs and the fact that the location decision is a multistage process. Consideration is now given to local and state tax systems, education, the industrial climate, and labor skills. Further, as Blair and Premus (1987) assert, the nation's continued shift to more advanced technologies will lead to an increase in the importance of nontraditional locational

Table 2.2

The Use of Government Aid by New Plants: Frequencies by Which Different Kinds of Plants Used Specific Government Assistance

| Item | Cincinnati Data Mover Plants | | New England Mover Plants | | Fortune 500 Data Nationally | | |
| | Single Plant Companies | Plants of Multiplant Companies | Single Plant Companies | Plants of Multiplant Companies | Newly Opened Plants | Mover Plants | Newly Opened Plants |
Number of Plants	53	11	74	38	82	36	161
Financial Help							
Industrial revenue bonds	4%	18%	7%	8%	29%	14%	21%
Industrial revenue bonds for pollution control	NA	NA	NA	NA	NA	3%	5%
Tax concessions of any sort	NA	NA	14%	16%	11%	28%	14%
Physical Help							
Roads, sewers, water	NA	NA	NA	NA	NA	3%	38%
Labor training	NA	NA	NA	NA	NA	6%	30%
Help with environmental permits	NA	NA	NA	NA	NA	6%	22%
Zoning changes	2%	0	3%	2%	3%	8%	12%
Expansion of sewage treatment	NA	NA	NA	NA	NA	0	10%
Traffic, parking adjustment	NA	NA	NA	NA	NA	3%	6%
Character of Dealings							
Highly attentive and helpful	NA	NA	31%	42%	46%	NA	NA
Only modestly helpful	NA	NA	29%	19%	12%	NA	NA
No dealings	NA	NA	38%	40%	40%	56%	29%

Source: Schmenner, 1982: 55.

Table 2.3
Percentage of Plant Openings by Major Manufacturers Using Various Public Policies, by Region

Public Policy	New England	Mid-Atlantic	South Atlantic	East North Central	East South Central	West North Central	West South Central	Mountain	Pacific
						Regions			
Physical Help									
Roads, sewerage lines, water mains, etc.	56	29	56	20	18	21	44	80	22
Labor training	0	21	61	13	36	21	35	0	0
Environmental permits	22	29	31	20	5	7	17	40	26
Zoning changes	0	7	11	13	14	0	9	60	17
Expansion of sewage treatment	22	14	11	7	5	7	9	20	9
Traffic, parking adjustments	22	0	8	13	0	0	0	20	4
Financial Help									
Industrial revenue bonds	0	21	14	13	50	21	13	20	13
Industrial revenues bonds for pollution control	0	0	8	7	0	0	13	0	0
Tax abatements holidays, or other tax concessions	0	14	8	7	32	14	22	0	4
Number of plant openings from region	9	14	36	15	22	14	23	5	23

Source: Schmenner, 1982: 56.

factors (i.e., education, quality of life) and a relative decrease in the significance of the traditional determinants.

The next section offers a discussion of six cases where states actively recruited large automobile concerns and offered the firms substantial "state incentive packages" in an effort to influence the corporations' site selections.[1] The cases provide verification of that part of the location literature which stresses the importance of market access, transportation, a state's perceived business climate, and the state's ability to provide both worker training and the improvement of the physical infrastructure.

STATE INCENTIVES AND INDUSTRIAL RECRUITING

Although nonbusiness and business factors were discussed in the prior section, further explanation must be provided to explain the recent rash of Japanese direct manufacturing investment and the mounting recruitment packages that states are willing to offer. Although Japanese and American automobile concerns are committed to short run and/or long run cost minimization and profit maximization, the Japanese were faced with the decision to establish facilities in the United States or risk losing the competitive advantages they had achieved over the decades. As previously cited, Yoshida (1987) found that a significant factor for Japanese locational decisions was proximity to market. However, for firms operating in mature industries dominated by a few conglomerates and largely dependent upon economies of scale rather than product differentiation, the size of the market is critical. The United States offers that market. Further, and perhaps of more immediate concern to the Japanese, is the growing protectionist sentiment. Congress has repeatedly threatened to enact strict quotas and tariffs in an effort to curb foreign imports, strengthen the domestic industrial sector, and restore a balance of trade. Therefore, the most effective offensive measure may be to establish a supply source in the United States and at least partially employ American materials and labor. Finally, given the desire to gain direct access to a large market and to decrease the risk of protectionist legislation, the dramatic rise in the yen has reportedly made investments in the United States fifty percent cheaper than in 1986 (*Chicago Tribune*, 5 April 1987).

Acting in conjunction with the rapid increase in direct Japanese manufacturing investment are the state governments which are attempting to lure these investors with rapidly increasing incentive packages. Toyota was offered a package estimated at a value of $158.7 million (not including the cost of debt) in 1986, an incentive worth approximately 395 percent more than the package provided to Nissan in 1980. The company investment and employment projections are relatively equivalent in both instances (see Table 2.4).

Public officials are actively recruiting both foreign and domestic firms in an attempt to create jobs, to improve both the local and state tax bases, and to address public concerns regarding unemployment. All five of the states discussed in the case studies exceeded national unemployment levels during the period

Table 2.4
Recent Industrial Recruiting: An Overview

Plant	Location	Companies Involved	Ownership
Nissan Motor Manufacturing Company	Smyrna, Tennessee	Nissan	Wholly Owned
Mazda Motor Manufacturing (USA) Corporation	Flat Rock, Michigan	Mazda *Ford will buy about 50% of the cars but will not invest in the plant *Ford acquired a 24.4% Stake in Mazda in 1979	Wholly Owned
Saturn Corporation	Spring Hill, Tennessee	General Motors	Wholly Owned
Diamond-Star Motors Corporation	Bloomington-Normal, Illinois	Chrysler Mitsubishi *Chrysler owns 24% of Mitsubishi Motors	Joint Venture 50% Chrysler 50% Mitsubishi
Toyota Motor Manufacturing USA Incorporated	Georgetown, Kentucky	Toyota	Wholly Owned
Fuji-Isuzu	Lafayette, Indiana	Fuji Heavy Industries *Nissan Motor Corp. owns 6.1% of Fuji stock Isuzu Motors Limited *General Motors Corp. owns 38.6% of Isuzu Stock	Joint Venture 51% Fuji 49% Isuzu

Company Investment	State Investment
Reportedly between $745 to 848 million (includes a 1984/85 expansion)	22 million - Road Access 11 million - Worker Training $33 million - Total
$745-750 million	19 million - Worker Training 5 million - Road Improvement 3 million - On-Site RR Improvement 21 million - Economic Development Grant Loan (to be recaptured) .5 million - Water System Improvement $48.5 million - Total *Michigan also posted a $32 million pollution control bond
Reportedly $3.5 to 4.79 billion (split into two phases)	30 million - Worker Training 50 million - Road Improvement $80 million - Total
Reportedly between $500-700 million	17.8 million - Road Improvement 11.0 million - Site Acquisition 14.5 million - Water System Improvement 40.0 million - Worker Training $83.3 million - Total
$823.9 million (a $23.9 million overun in site preparation is expected to be paid by Toyota)	12.5 million - Land Purchase 20.0 million - Site Preparation 47.0 million - Road Improvements 65.0 million - Worker Training 5.2 million - Toyota Families' Education $149.7 million - Total Miscellaneous Fees are estimated at an additional 9 million (ie. legal fees, an impact survey) and bond interest payments are estimated at between 166.7 to 224 million.
$480 to 500 million	55 million - State Funds 26 million - Federal Subsidies 3 million - Water System Improvement 2 million - Road Improvement $86 million - Total Phase II: An Estimated $25 million in Additional Support

Table 2.4 (continued)

Employees	Estimated Production	Announcement Year	Estimated or Actual Start Up
3,000 (1900 for Phase I and 1100 for 1984/85 expansion)	120,000 light trucks 240,000 light trucks and Sentras (after expansion)	October 1980 May 1984	Phase I: 1983 Expansion: 1985
3,500 by 1988	240,000 mid-sized Mazdas and Fords	November/December 1984	September 1987
Phase I: 3,000 by 1990 Phase II: 6,000	250,000 Sports Compacts	July 1985	Phase I: June 1990 Phase II: Indefinite, based on market demand
2500 - 2,900 in 1989	180,000-240,000 (2 door hatch-back Sports Model & 4 Door Sedan split evenly between firms)	October 1985	Spring 1988
3,000 by 1988	200,000 Camry's	December 1985	1988
Phase I: 1700 Phase II: 3200	240,000 Subarus and Isuzus	December 1986	1989

Other States Seriously Considered	Financial Incentive Cost Plant Employee
Phase I: Georgia & Tennessee were bidding	$11,000.00
Alabama Iowa Kansas Michigan Missouri Nebraska North Carolina Oklahoma South Carolina Tennessee	$13,857.14 (however, modified given $21 million grant to be recaptured)
Illinois, Indiana, Kentucky, Michigan, Montana Minnesota, New York, Ohio (38 states total)	$26,666.67 (based on only Phase I) $13,333.33 (based on Phase II)
Indiana Michigan Ohio	$33,320 (based on 2500 workers) $28,724.14 (based on 2900 workers)
Georgia Indiana Kansas Missouri Tennessee (by the final decision 31-34 states had entered the competition)	$49,900.00 (even based upon the State's claim of $125 million, the incentive/worker = $41,666.67)
Illinois Kentucky (12 states from the South and Southeast were asked to submit bids)	$50,588.23 (based on Phase I) $34,687.5 (based on Phase II)

from 1980 to 1986 (Indiana, however, fell below the national average in 1986), and most surpassed the national figures by more than 15 percent (see Table 2.5). However, it must be noted that the actual plant locations, although in states suffering from high unemployment, are frequently in geographical areas where a number of the surrounding counties have relatively low unemployment rates (see Table 2.6).

Business relocations and plant creations are frequently viewed as direct and effective methods to ensure economic development. In fact, the form that a foreign direct investment takes can have a significant effect on the expected economic impact. If a merger or acquisition simply constitutes the transfer of ownership and the purchase of the existing assets, very few, if any, new jobs are created. On the other hand, if new plants are built and equipped, the economy is stimulated immediately (Coleman, 1986).

What follows is a review of six automotive plant creations, each of which represents a substantial company investment and dramatic financial commitments by the host state and community. The information provided was compiled from interviews with state representatives and various periodical sources. No judgment as to the success or failure of any given incentive package is offered since economic development policies are long-term considerations. However, final remarks on this survey of the six location cases and the literature review are provided in the conclusion and offer a basis upon which to begin an analysis of the effectiveness of given incentive packages.

Nissan Motor Manufacturing Company and Smyrna, Tennessee

In late October 1980, Nissan announced its intention to build a wholly owned automobile plant in Smyrna, Tennessee which would produce 120,000 light trucks. Both Georgia and Tennessee actively sought the Nissan facility; however, Tennessee's offer of extensive worker training, road access and improvements, tax inducements, the state's commitment to establish an open dialogue with the investing company, and a positive business climate helped to convince Nissan to locate there. The reported $11 million committed by the state to job training supplemented a $64 million expenditure by Nissan. Although 90 percent of the hourly workers were hired from Tennessee, all assembly line workers were required to be present for 48 to 60 hours of uncompensated training before even being considered as job applicants.

In May 1984, Nissan announced its decision to expand its Smyrna facility in an effort to combat a lower demand for Nissan trucks than forecast and to recover its investment in the Smyrna facility. Further, it was believed that U.S. production of the Sentra would ease the auto-trade tension which was mounting domestically and which limited Nissan to an annual shipment of 480,000 automobiles since those cars produced within the United States were exempt from the trade restrictions. Therefore, through an additional direct investment, Nissan could pro-

Table 2.5
Total Unemployed and Percentage over the National Average, 1980–1986

STATE	1980	1981	1982	1983	1984	1985	1986
U.S.							
Number (1000's)	7637	8273	10678	10717	8539	8312	8237
% Unemployed	7.1	7.6	9.7	9.6	7.5	7.2	7.0
% over National	0.00%	0.00%	0.00%	0.00%	0.00%	0.00%	0.00%
ILLINOIS							
Number (1000's)	458	474	632	640	512	513	461
% Unemployed	8.3	8.5	11.3	11.4	9.1	9.0	8.1
% over National	16.90%	11.84%	16.49%	18.75%	21.33%	25.00%	15.71%
INDIANA							
Number (1000's)	252	264	310	286	226	215	185
% Unemployed	9.6	10.1	11.9	11.1	8.6	7.9	6.7
% over National	35.21%	32.89%	22.68%	15.63%	14.67%	9.72%	15.71%
KENTUCKY							
Number (1000's)	133	140	178	198	160	161	156
% Unemployed	8.0	8.4	10.6	11.7	9.3	9.5	9.3
% over National	12.68%	10.53%	9.28%	21.88%	24.00%	31.94%	32.86%
MICHIGAN							
Number (1000's)	534	529	661	610	487	433	385
% Unemployed	12.4	12.3	15.5	14.2	11.2	9.9	8.8
% over National	74.65%	61.84%	59.79%	47.92%	49.33%	37.50%	25.71%
OHIO							
Number (1000's)	426	492	640	622	480	455	426
% Unemployed	8.4	9.6	12.5	12.2	9.4	8.9	8.1
% over National	18.31%	26.32%	28.87%	27.08%	25.33%	23.61%	15.71%
TENNESSEE							
Number (1000's)	152	193	252	251	190	180	185
% Unemployed	7.3	9.1	11.8	11.5	8.6	8.0	8.0
% over National	2.82%	19.74%	21.65%	19.79%	14.67%	11.11%	14.29%

Source: Bureau of Labor Statistics, *Unemployment in States and Local Areas, 1980–1986.* Microfiche.

Table 2.6
The Unemployment Rates of Counties Surrounding the Case Locations (for the Year of Announcement and the Prior Year)

Company	Site Location	Counties	Unemployment Rates (in %)							
			1979	1980	1981	1982	1983	1984	1985	1986
Nissan	Smyrna, Tennessee	Davidson	4.0	5.2						
		Rutherford	4.5	6.1						
		Williamson	2.8	4.2						
		Wilson	5.1	6.4						
Mazda	Flat Rock, Michigan	Monroe					15.1	12.7		
		Washtenaw					9.5	7.2		
		Wayne					14.5	11.1		
Saturn	Spring Hill, Tennessee	Marshall						6.6	10.2	
		Maury						8.2	8.3	
		Williamson						3.4	2.8	
Diamond-Star	Bloomington-Normal, Illinois	Dewitt						9.4	11.2	
		McClean						6.6	6.3	
		Tarewell						11.8	11.8	
		Woodford						8.8	9.1	
Toyota	Georgetown, Kentucky	Bourbon						4.3	6.0	
		Fayette						4.5	4.9	
		Harrison						7.2	7.4	
		Scott						4.3	4.8	
		Woodford						4.0	3.8	
Fuji-Isuzu	Lafayette, Indiana	Benton							7.9	8.2
		Carroll							7.1	5.8
		Clinton							9.4	7.3
		Tippecanoe							4.6	3.9
		Woodford							4.0	3.8

Source: Bureau of Labor Statistics, *Unemployment in States and Local Areas, 1980–1986.* Microfiche.

tect itself from protectionist legislation and actively seek an increased U.S. market. The expansion provided an additional 1100 jobs and improved the incentive/worker ratio from $17,368.42 to $11,000 per worker.

Mazda Motor Manufacturing (USA) Corp. and Flat Rock, Michigan

In making its locational decision, Mazda considered 10 states as sites for a U.S. facility modeled after its Hofu plant in southwestern Japan, a state-of-the-art production facility requiring increased automation. In determining the site, Toyo Kogyo Ltd. said that three criteria were of paramount importance: (1) local sourcing of components, material handling, and distribution; (2) labor relations and conditions of employment and work; and (3) government grants and incentives (*Wall Street Journal*, 10 July 1986).

In November and December of 1984, facing an annual unemployment rate of 11.20 percent or 49.33 percent over the national unemployment level, the state of Michigan was "awarded" the new Mazda facility. In its first major attempt to lure Japanese direct investment, Michigan offered Mazda an incentive package including bonds, grants, training funds, and infrastructure improvements totalling $53 million in recaptured investments and $27.5 million in direct expenditures. Michigan is committed to $19 million in training funds, $5 million ($4 million in federal grant funds and $1 million in a community development grant) for road improvements, $3 million in on-site railroad improvements (the Grand Trunk Western Railroad has also pledged an additional $5 million to off-site improvements), and $500,000 to expand water and sewage systems. The state also posted a $32 million pollution bond which, although committed, is not an out-of-pocket expense, and loaned Mazda $21 million in the form of an Economic Development Grant. Both will eventually be recaptured by the state. If one considers only direct and unrecaptured expenditures, the incentive/worker ratio is $7,857.14 to each employee; however, given the "out-of-pocket" nature of the development grant, $13,857.14 per worker seems more appropriate.

In response to Michigan's cooperation, Mazda has sought the development of good community relations. According to Read Ross of the Michigan Department of Commerce, Mazda gave an unconditional gift of $100,000 to the city of Flat Rock and developed educational scholarships for employees' children to study in Japan for a year.

The Saturn Corporation and Spring Hill, Tennessee

In 1984, General Motors Corporation committed itself to "Project Saturn," the auto maker's attempt to build a competitive small car and establish its position in a Japanese dominated segment. Through Saturn, GM hopes to render the assembly line obsolete, to dramatically reduce the number of parts and labor hours needed to manufacture an automobile, and to pioneer in the use of state-of-the-art robots (Nal, 1984).

On January 8, 1985, GM formed the Saturn Corporation and officially sought a U.S. location for a new production facility. In response, 38 states made direct appeals to GM, making Saturn one of the most sought-after investments in industrial history. The demand greatly outweighed the supply, and the competition among the states mounted. Governors traveled to Detroit, and, in fact, the first state presentation was given January 10, 1985, two days after the official Saturn announcement. The projected enormity of GM's investment made Saturn's appeal undeniable. At full production, the plan was to provide 6000 jobs, and the company was reported to be investing $5 billion into the project with $3.5 billion in land, site preparation, buildings, and equipment. In July 1985, GM announced that the Saturn Corporation would build an assembly plant in Spring Hill, Tennessee, a community approximately 30 miles south of Nashville.

GM's decision to locate its "factory of the future" in Spring Hill was affected by factors related to both business and quality-of-life. Transportation appears to have been a primary factor in the location decision; GM wanted to establish its plant close to its potential market and to its suppliers. Further, Tennessee's relatively low cost of electricity lured GM since the plant would make extensive use of electric power. Also, the state of Tennessee offered GM an incentive package with an estimated value of $80 million, by far the highest state incentive accepted to that date.

Some $20–30 million was committed to worker training and $50 million to improvements in the road infrastructure. However, state representatives claim that a portion of the road improvements would have been done regardless of GM's decision. In accordance with state policy, Tennessee's package did not include state tax concessions. Yet, local property tax reductions are provided at an estimated savings of $70 million. It should be stressed though that a fully taxed Saturn plant (an investment four times larger than the current value of all taxable property in Maury County) would cause the local property tax rate to plummet since revenues at the existing rate would significantly exceed the need for expenditures (Fox and Neel, 1987).

Tennessee's incentive package to the Saturn Corporation represents a 92.4 percent increase over the incentive cost per worker offered by Michigan to Mazda. The dramatically increasing incentives may be a function of the number of states bidding on projects (even if not seriously considered) and the number of states maintaining unemployment rates substantially above the national average. It may also be based on the certain knowledge that there were only a few investments of this magnitude that would ever be "put up for bid." In a market of many buyers and only one seller, the only thing that can go up is the price.

Yet, Spring Hill and the state of Tennessee were not the only sites and states to offer access to markets, relatively cheap electricity, and an attractive inducement package. In fact, other states reportedly offered more attractive incentives. What specifically then lured GM to Tennessee and Spring Hill?

In "Saturn: The Tennessee Lessons," William Fox and Warren Neel point to the following critical factors. First, although labor costs for the Saturn plant are set in the national market via a GM-UAW labor agreement, GM officials believed Tennessee's labor force to be more productive because of the perceived strength of the traditional "work ethic." Secondly, they note, although no effort by state and local governments could compensate for the basic business requirements (i.e., location, transportation, weather, labor productivity, and topography), Tennessee's probusiness attitude is an important factor in attracting industry. A probusiness attitude includes a willingness to aid a firm in transition, to reduce burdensome taxes, and to foster a regulatory environment which will not inhibit corporate activity. In addition, Fox and Neel (1987) suggest that Saturn officials sought a sight where employees could choose from a variety of housing, recreational, cultural, and educational opportunities. Although Spring Hill has a population of 1100 people, it is located only 30 miles from Nashville. Recent improvements in Tennessee's educational system are indicative of the policies which foster a positive business environment. Given the type of employee Saturn desires to run its factory of the future, a solid educational system is vital.

The sophistication Tennessee officials have acquired since their first major industrial recruitment in 1980 is a testament to the state's commitment to the business community and its development of a recruitment policy. Although the plant has recently announced a 50 percent reduction in employment, the relationship between the state and Saturn has remained cooperative. State officials are renegotiating their job training commitment, given the anticipated decrease in available jobs and the likelihood that recently laid off GM workers will be given preferential treatment at the new Saturn Plant.

Diamond-Star Motors Corp. and Bloomington-Normal, Illinois

On April 6, 1985, the Chrysler Corporation and Mitsubishi Motors Corp. of Japan announced a tentative agreement to jointly build Mitsubishi-designed subcompact cars in the United States. By announcing the joint venture, Chrysler emphasized its decision to abandon plans to build small cars domestically on its own and to rely on its past affiliate, Mitsubishi, to service the small-car segment of the total U.S. auto market. At the time of the announcement, Chrysler owned 15 percent of Mitsubishi Motors. By October 8, 1985, the two auto makers announced the formation of a $500 million plant (recent estimates place that closer to $700 million) near the adjacent central Illinois towns of Bloomington and Normal. The 1.7 million square foot plant would be able to produce 180,000 cars, employ 2500 workers, and create an estimated 9000 supplier jobs.

Although on October 7, 1985, Iacocca and Tate (the presidents of Chrysler and Mitsubishi, respectively) defended their site selection on the basis of a modern transportation system, a superior education system, cultural advantages, a good labor climate, and a favorable tax base (*PR Newswire*, 7 October 1985), a statement published the following day cited Illinois' financial incentives as the deciding factor (*Wall Street Journal*, 8 October 1985). To lure Chrysler and Mitsubishi, Illinois provided a package valued at $83.3 million. Although Governor Thompson was quoted as saying, "We didn't buy this car plant. We invested in our future" (*Wall Street Journal*, 1985), the state committed $17.8 million to road improvements, $11 million to site acquisition, $14.5 million to the water/sewage system, and $40 million to worker training. The package represents an incentive cost of $28,724.14 per worker if calculations are based upon 2900 employees, an estimate often cited by state representatives, or $33,320, using 2500, the number given by company representatives in 1985. Therefore, at its most optimistic, the incentive represents an 107.3 percent increase in the incentive cost per worker committed by Michigan in 1984. Both the Saturn and the Diamond-Star inducement packages altered the course of future industrial recruiting, as an upward trend was firmly established (see Figure 2.2).

Toyota Motor Manufacturing USA Inc. and Georgetown, Kentucky

On December 11, 1985, before more than 200 people, Toyota's President, Shoichiro Toyoda, announced that Scott County, Kentucky had been selected as the site for Toyota's new U.S. facility. With this announcement the cost of industrial recruitment reached new levels. After nearly 17 months of both passive and active recruiting, Kentucky had succeeded in luring Toyota and its estimated $800 million plant at a reported cost of $125 million.

Part of Kentucky's "success" is attributed to Jiro Hashimoto, the Far Eastern representative of Kentucky's state government. It was Hashimoto who initially provided Toyota with information on Kentucky in July 1984; who arranged for Kentucky to be the first state to provide information concerning suitable sites, climate, living conditions, site acquisition, local auto parts makers, tax regulations, and labor costs; and who performed the roles of liaison, expediter, and coordinator (Miyauchi, 1987).

The Georgetown Toyota plant, by recent estimations, will be a $823.9 million investment. The plant, scheduled to produce 200,000 Camrys at full production, presently employs 3000 workers.[2] However, Kentucky officials' claim that only $125 million of state funds would be committed to the project was misleading, at best. A more realistic estimate, albeit not totally inclusive, is $149.7 million, for $12.5 million was spent on land purchases, and $43.9 million is currently estimated for site preparation, although Toyota is expected to assume $23.9 million of that figure. The expenditures on road improvements are expected to total $47 million. Federal funds will cover $22 million in highway improvement, but the money spent in relation to the Georgetown plant will not be used on other needed highway projects. Further, Kentucky committed itself to an unprecedented $65 million in job training, including the construction of a $10 million training facility. State officials had originally claimed that only $43

Figure 2.2
Incentive Cost per Plant Employee

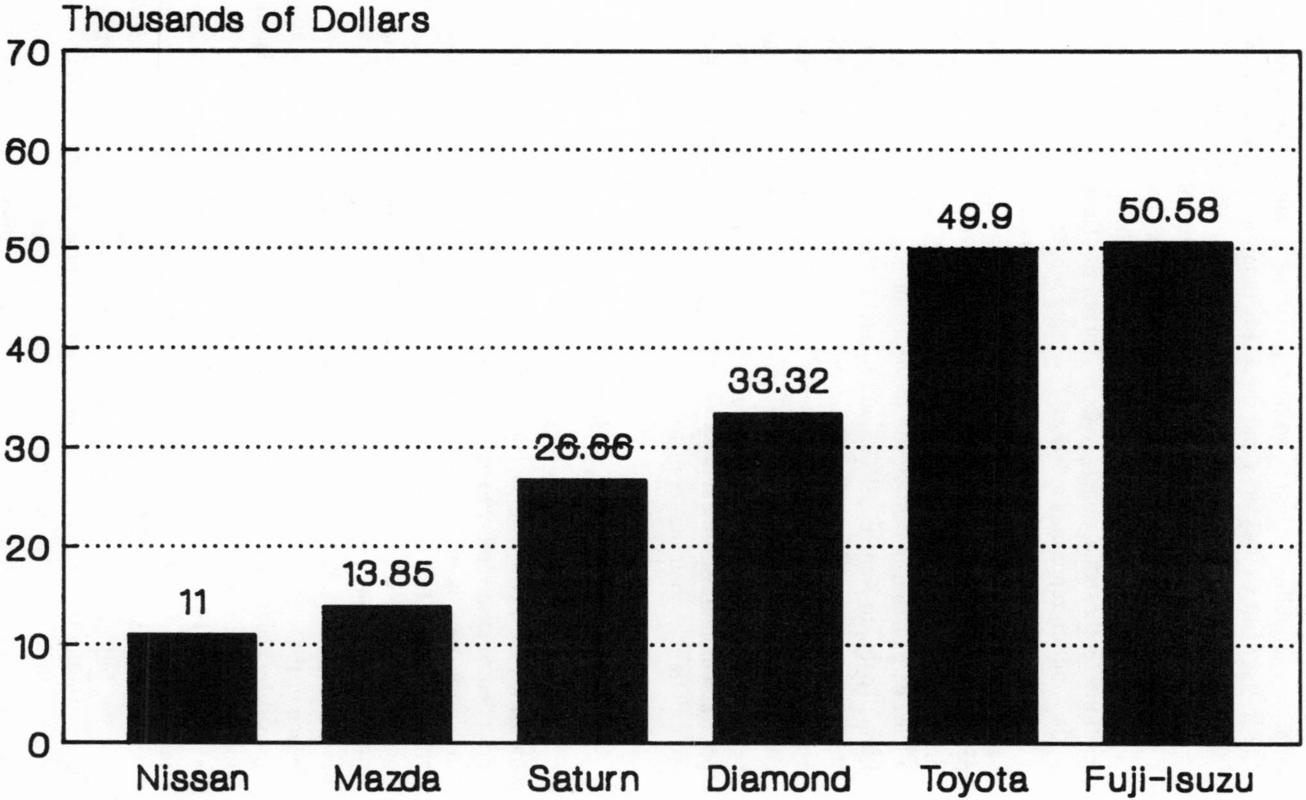

Thousands of Dollars

Source: Table 2.4

million would be spent from the state budget on training and the remainder would be covered by federal funds through the Job Training Partnership Act. However, employee eligibility is highly suspect given the relatively low unemployment rate in the Scott County area and the JTPA requirement that only workers not fully employed are covered. Finally, the state has made a 20-year commitment to provide a Saturday school program for the children of Toyota employees and a 10-year commitment to provide Toyota employees and families with English language classes. An estimated $5.2 million will be needed to cover these alterations to the educational system. Therefore, Kentucky's commitment of $149.7 million represents a $49,900 cost per worker.[3]

Why did Kentucky offer Toyota considerably more than any other state that had been successful in attracting a major auto manufacturer? The intense competition between the states definitely contributed to the escalated cost; by the final decision, 31 to 34 states had joined the competition. Further, Toyota drives a hard bargain and is well-versed in the art of negotiation. In "The Man Who Lured Toyota to Kentucky," Takeo Miyauchi (1987) claims that Toyota played state against state. The company made it apparent that unless Kentucky offered a satisfactory incentive, Toyota would settle in "a neighboring state," an apparently thinly veiled reference to Tennessee. It must be noted that just months before, Kentucky had lost the Saturn Project to that same state. Kentucky's state pride and mounting political pressure on the governor for an industrial "success" were definitely contributing factors.

Fuji-Isuzu and Lafayette, Indiana

On December 2, 1986, representatives of Isuzu Motors Ltd. and Fuji Heavy Industries Inc., two rival Japanese car and truck producers, announced an unprecedented joint venture to be located in Lafayette, Indiana. Isuzu, 38.6 percent of whose stock is owned by General Motors, and Fuji, a company in which Nissan owns a 6.1 percent interest, have joined forces to minimize the risk associated with being among the last major Japanese auto makers to directly invest in the United States. Fuji and Isuzu are seeking to expand their position in the U.S. market, a position seriously limited by the auto export quotas that began in 1981. The joint venture will be 51 percent owned by Fuji and 49 percent owned by Isuzu. The total direct investment is estimated at a value of $480 million, and the plant is expected to create 1700 jobs.

In May of 1985, after Fuji and Isuzu agreed jointly to produce cars and trucks in the United States, the companies invited incentive plans from a dozen states in the South and the Southeast, including Kentucky, Illinois, and Indiana. Lafayette, Indiana, heralded by managing directors Soejima and Yamamoto as an area offering the best combination of manufacturing benefits, business climate, and quality-of-life, attracted the Fuji-Isuzu plant at a cost to the state of $86 million. Included in the package was $55 million directly from the state's 1987 to 1988 and 1989 to 1990 budgets, $26 million from the federal government

($18 million from funds generated by the settlement of the oil-overcharge lawsuits and $8 million expected through the Job Training Partnership Act), $3 million from the city of Lafayette for the water/sewage system, and $2 million from Tippecanoe County for road construction. However, the anticipated $8 million through the JTPA is questionable. According to August 1986 figures, the Lafayette area's unemployment level was 3.8 percent (*Louisville Courier-Journal*, 2 December 1986). The JTPA only covers those workers who are not fully employed. Indiana's inducement package represents a cost of $50,588.23 per worker employed by the Fuji-Isuzu plant. However, Lieutenant Governor John M. Mutz claims that the potential for a second phase at the Fuji-Isuzu plant is enormous and would double production, creating 1500 more jobs while requiring only $25 million in additional state support. If this proposed expansion were to occur, the cost/worker ratio would decrease to $34,687.50 per employee.

Conclusions

A general review of Table 2.4 and the six case histories reveals the importance of transportation, a rapid escalation in the costs associated with industrial recruitment, and a dramatic increase in the number of states vying for new auto assembly facilities. Goldstein's claim (1985) that transportation is paramount in any industrial location decision appears relevant in an analysis of the plant locations presented here. All of the plants are located in a relatively central area within the United States and are located on or near major interstate highways. Further, the plants are or will be close to the largest part of the U.S. market. Of particular note are the three plants located in Kentucky and Tennessee, states which Schmenner et al. (1987) categorizes as East South Central. These states are centrally located and can expect to continue attracting plants for which transportation costs to predominantly national markets are critical concerns. Without question, transportation is a priority for automotive manufacturers who require easy access to the nation as a whole. Further, Figure 2.2 graphically depicts the surge in the incentive cost per worker ratio introduced in Table 2.4. The limited supply of major industrial plants and the seemingly increasing demand for them by states is forcing the market price to skyrocket, giving the auto makers increased power. States, particularly those whose unemployment rates have significantly exceeded national levels for years and who have not benefitted from the effects of a "bicoastal economy," are actively seeking to attract large manufacturing concerns.[4]

In response to political pressure to improve their economies and in accordance with much of the literature, the five states discussed are seeking methods which present an image of positive business climate. However, it must be recognized that the term "business climate" defies precise definition and is a multifaceted concept. According to Schmenner (1982: 53), the term

remains a rough metric of a location's expected ability to maintain a productive environment over the foreseeable future. Attitudes are important to the business climate: the attitude of working people to hard work, to quality work, to unionization; the attitude of government to business, as reflected in government aid in solving joint problems, and in regulations, tax rates, and financing; the attitude of government in managing itself, its services, its schools.

Therefore, states have sought methods to improve their business image and to eliminate the traditional perception of having slow moving and red-tape-laden state bureaucracies. In the case studies examined here, one sees a commitment to work with the facility on a direct and continuous basis and to deal with problems that arise during the development of the plant. Tennessee worked with GM to scale down the state's commitment to job training in response to GM's decision to hire fewer workers for the Saturn plant than originally planned. Further, the degree to which the governor becomes involved in the recruitment process surfaces as a factor in the creation of a positive business climate. It is symbolic and yet reflective of the importance a state attaches to new investment. In recruiting Toyota to Kentucky, Governor Martha Layne Collins frequently traveled to Japan to meet personally with business people and to assure them of Kentucky's commitment to foreign investment.

Also, the six cases studied support Schmenner's claim (1987) that the Southern states most successful in attracting new plant openings advertise their company-specific, preemployment training programs and concentrate their limited resources on the provision of physical aid. In all but one of the incentive packages discussed, significant funds were committed to worker training. In fact, 33 percent, 39 percent, 38 percent, 48 percent, and 43 percent of the packages offered to Nissan, Mazda, General Motors, Chrysler, and Toyota, respectively, were dedicated to worker training. Finally, all of the six cases chosen demonstrate the relevant state's commitment to the improvement of the site's physical infrastructure (i.e., roads, sewage, water, and/or waste treatment). In all six of the cases, road improvement/access was contained within the incentive package. In three of the six, funds were set aside for water improvement, and in three cases, monies for site improvement and/or acquisition were specifically allocated.

Although the cases have supported a number of the research findings previously presented, they do not substantiate either Newman (1983) or Schmenner's claims (1982) regarding the importance of right-to-work legislation. In fact, right-to-work laws appear to have a minimal effect on the recruitment of automobile manufacturers. Of the six cases presented, four of the companies located in states not having right-to-work laws; and in the one state, Tennessee, where the law does exist, the Saturn Corporation supposedly had no intention of opening a nonunion plant. The observed contradiction of the literature may rest in the size of the new plants considered. A facility employing an estimated 3000 workers at full production is without question a primary union target.

Research on the development and benefits of state incentive packages is undeniably in its infancy stages. Of particular interest is the importance of tax structures in the state's ability to successfully recruit large corporate concerns such as automotive manufacturers. Have the five states considered here stimulated industrial growth by shifting the tax burden from property taxes to other, perhaps less obvious, methods of taxation (i.e., sales tax) as suggested by Steinnes (1984)? Are there particular state tax structures more favorable to the automotive industry than to other manufacturers of durable products?

Further research is also needed on the economic impact over time of the various state incentives offered to large corporations. Any in-depth analysis of state industrial recruitment is significantly limited, however, by the apparent lack of data and information made available to the public. Most government agencies are reluctant to discuss the details of an industrial recruitment for fear of negative political ramifications or providing too much information to competing states. The garnering of information can also be complicated by personnel and organizational changes in state government which typically occur every four years. Further, few states appear to have conducted an in-depth economic study of an automotive plant's impact after the inducement package was offered and the locational decision announced. Kentucky, the host of the new Toyota plant, however, has sought to establish an understanding of the impact of the plant. The governor's office funded the University of Louisville, to conduct an impact study on Scott County, Kentucky (Koebel et al., 1987), and the Center for Business and Economic Research at the University of Kentucky, to study the trends and the economic value of the automotive supplier industry (Center for Business and Economic Research, 1988). Also, in 1986, the Center for Business and Economic Research prepared a report entitled "The Estimated Impact of Toyota on the State's Economy."

However, of particular importance to both an analysis of a given automaker's impact on the state's economy and a determination of the effectiveness of a state's industrial recruitment policies is the creation of relevant and easily accessed data bases. Initially, a central agency should be awarded the responsibility of designing, implementing, and maintaining a data base which would track the automotive supplier industry (on a state, multistate, or national level depending on the available resources and funding) by compiling information on employment, location, ownership, automaker affiliation, product, and sales. Only through an analysis of the secondary industries (i.e., the automotive supplier industry) can a state determine the benefits and disadvantages of its industrial recruitment of automotive manufacturers and the recently escalating incentive packages.

NOTES

1. Information regarding the state incentive packages and the relevant plants were predominantly obtained from articles published in the *Wall Street Journal*, the *Louisville Courier-Journal*, and the *Lexington Herald-Leader*. Particularly informative articles were: Swasy (June 28, 1987) and Loftus (December 4, 1986).

2. Recently, the Toyota Motor Corporation announced its plans to build a new engine

plant in Scott County. The proposed engine plant would reportedly employ up to 1,000 workers.

3. It must be stressed, however, that the figure $149.7 million does not include the $9 million estimated in miscellaneous costs by the Center for Business and Economic Research (i.e., legal fees and an economic impact study by the University of Louisville) nor the $166.7 million to $224 million interest payments on the tax-exempt Economic Development Bonds. (See: CBER, 1986).

4. "Bi-coastal economy" is a term coined by the Joint Economic Committee to explain why both California and the Atlantic Coast with 42 percent of the U.S. population account for 58 percent of the national job growth since 1981 (U.S. Congress, July 9, 1986).

REFERENCES

Blair, John P., and Robert Premus. 1987. "Major Factors in Industrial Location: A Review." *Economic Development Quarterly* 1: 72–85.

Carlton, Dennis W. 1983. "The Location and Employment of New Firms: An Econometric Model with Discrete and Continuous Endogenous Variables." *Review of Economics and Statistics* 65: 440–449.

Center for Business and Economic Research. 1986. *The Estimated Economic Impact of Toyota on the State's Economy.* Lexington: University of Kentucky, CBER.

———. 1988. *Kentucky's Automotive Supplier Industry: Trends and Implications.* Lexington: University of Kentucky, CBER.

Coleman, Edwin J. 1986. "Regional Aspects of Foreign Direct Investment." Presented at the 20th annual meeting of the Pacific Northwest Regional Conference, 6 May.

Epping, G. Michael. 1982. "Important Factors in Plant Location in 1980." *Growth and Change*, April.

Fortune, Inc. 1977. *Facility Location Decisions.* New York: Fortune, Inc.

Fox, William F., and Warren G. Neel. 1987. "Saturn: The Tennessee Lessons." *Forum for Applied Research and Public Policy*, Spring, 7–16.

Goldstein, Mark L. 1985. "Choosing the Right Site." *Industry Week*, 15 April, 57–60.

Heckman, John S. 1982. "Survey of Location Decisions in the South." *Economic Review*, June, 6–19.

Koebel, C. Theodore, and Associates. 1987. *Impacts of the Toyota Plant on Scott County, Kentucky.* Louisville, Ky.: University of Louisville.

Loftus, Tom. 1986. "Indiana Auto-Plant Incentives to Go Beyond $55 Million from Tax Funds." *Louisville Courier-Journal*, 4 December, B2.

Milward, H. Brinton. 1986. "Can a Governor Determine the Location of Private Industry?" *Kentucky Economy: Review and Perspective* 10 (Summer): 3–4.

Miyauchi, Takeo. 1987. "The Man Who Lured Toyota to Kentucky." *Economic Eye*, March, 23–27.

Nal, Amal. 1984. "Gearing Down: To Build a Small Car, GM Tries to Redesign its Production System." *Wall Street Journal*, 14 May, 1.

Newman, Robert J. 1983. "Industry Migration and Growth in the South." *Review of Economics and Statistics.* 65: 76–86.

Schmenner, Roger W. 1982. *Making Business Location Decisions.* Englewood Cliffs, N.J.: Prentice-Hall.

Schmenner, Roger W., Joel Huber, and Randall Cook. 1987. "Geographic Differences and the Location of New Manufacturing Facilities." *Journal of Urban Economics* 21: 83–104.

Steinnes, John. 1984. "Dynamic Model of Economic Development Using a Pooled Time Series-Cross Sectional Set Along with a Lagged Dependent Variable." *Growth and Change*, April, 38–47.

Swasy, Alicia. 1987. "Dollars, Doubts Line Japan's 'Auto Alley.' " *Lexington Herald-Leader*, 28 June, A1.

U.S. Congress, Joint Economic Committee. 1986. *Bi-Coastal Economy, Regional Patterns of Economic Growth During the Reagan Administration.* 99th Cong., 2nd Sess., 9 July. Washington, D.C.: U.S.G.P.O.

Yoshida, Mamoru. 1987. "The Investment Decision-Making Process." *Japanese Direct Manufacturing Investment in the United States.* New York: Praeger Publishers, 41–74.

3

Constitutional Dimensions of State Industrial Recruitment

William C. Green

State governments have become increasingly involved in the new international economic order. One aspect of this participation has been the intense competition between states to recruit foreign industry, including the major Japanese automobile manufacturing corporations. Six mid-American states—Michigan, Ohio, Indiana, Illinois, Kentucky, and Tennessee—have been winners in this industrial recruitment competition. A major feature of this competition has been the financial incentives these states have offered and the Japanese automobile firms have accepted including land purchases and improvements, highway and railroad extensions, employee recruitment and training, and tax exemptions and abatements.

This state government industrial recruitment activity has occurred within the context of six different constitutional environments (Ledebur, Hamilton, and Rabinowitz, 1986). At the same time, the six state constitutions commonly contain fiscal provisions which limit and structure the freedom of their state officials to use public monies or to extend public credit for the benefit of private industry. This chapter will explore the constitutional fiscal dimensions of the financial incentives the six mid-American states have used to attract Japanese automobile manufacturers.

The first section will examine the state constitutional fiscal landscape in the six states. The next will examine the constitutional consequences of using general tax revenues and revenue bonds to provide interest and production subsidies.

This chapter originally appeared in *The Urban Lawyer*, 22:2 (1990) under the title, "State Constitutions, Industrial Recruitment Incentives, and Japanese Investment in Mid-America" and is republished with the permission of *The Urban Lawyer* and the section of urban, state, and local government law of the American Bar Association.

The third section will examine the one case, *Hayes* v. *State Property and Buildings Commission* (1987), which arose as a consequence of Kentucky's purchase and improvement of the Toyota plant site and its conveyance to the automaker. Finally, section four will then draw some conclusions about the meaning of the six state mid-American experience for understanding the political role of state constitutions and courts in state industrial recruitment activities.

STATE CONSTITUTIONAL FISCAL LANDSCAPE

State government recruitment of Japanese automobile manufacturers has occurred within a long tradition of state and local government commitment to economic development (Kline, 1985). This state industrial investment has relied on the use of financial incentives to influence corporate location decisions (Gray and Spina, 1980). A state's collective offer to private industry, its incentive package, typically contains three types of inducements (Rasmussen, Bendick, and Ledebur, 1984: 19). First, interest subsidies in the form of subsidized direct loans, loan guarantees, or industrial development bonds permit the firm to acquire capital below the commercial market rates. Second, production input subsidies relying upon the use of public funds for land acquisition, plant site preparation and construction, equipment purchases, and worker training are especially attractive to industries because they "lower the total initial investment required by a firm" (Rasmussen, Bendick, and Ledebur, 1984: 22). States frequently provide a variety of associated production incentives including highway, railroad, and utility improvements. Third, tax subsidies in the form of state sales tax exemptions, state income tax deductions, state investment tax credits, local property tax exemptions, and local utility tax rebates for a period of years provide a long term benefit to industry. Of all these incentive package components, interest and production subsidies are the most constitutionally significant, because their use encounters constitutional fiscal provisions which are intended to limit state government financing of private enterprise. They, rather than tax subsidies, will be the principal focus of this analysis.

State constitutions formally limit the authority of state governments to offer interest and production subsidies with three types of fiscal provisions originally incorporated into nineteenth century state constitutions (Pinsky, 1963: 277–282).[1] First, taxation clauses require uniform taxation; limit taxing power to public purposes; and prohibit gifts, loans, and donations to private persons and corporations from current tax receipts. Second, current expenditure clauses prohibit appropriating money, extending public credit, and stockholding in any private corporate venture. Some constitutions also include internal improvements clauses which forbid the state from being "a party to or interested in any work of internal improvement, nor engage in carrying out such work" (Pinsky, 1963: 281). Third, borrowing and debt provisions limit state and local debt to a specific dollar amount without electoral approval in order "to protect taxpayers by preventing legislatures from mortgaging the future with expenditures in excess of current revenues'' (Graves, 1960: 232).

These state constitutional provisions advanced sound fiscal policy objectives. ''They constituted an 'effort to prevent corruption, curb extravagance, and maintain [state and] municipal finance on a sound basis' '' (Bowmar, 1967: 867). In fact, they frequently have an overlapping and interlocking character, well designed to frustrate evasion. As Justice Liebson of the Kentucky Supreme Court observed about his state constitution's fiscal provisions, any attempt ''to escape one or the other of the various constitutional provisions . . . [will] serve only to trigger another'' (*Hayes* v. *State*, 1987: 807). At the same time, these fiscal limitations which virtually limited government spending to current revenues meant that states and municipalities, confronted with the need to increase public services and to promote economic development, were ''precluded from realizing their development potential'' (Bowmar, 1967: 867–868).

Constitutional provisions governing state debt have been the most troublesome. Three mid-American states have constitutions which severely limit general obligation debt. The 1870 Tennessee Constitution prohibits all state debt while the 1851 Indiana Constitution prohibits all debt except to meet the ''casual deficits in revenue.'' The 1891 Kentucky Constitution, somewhat less harsh, limits the Commonwealth's debt to $500,000 except to meet ''casual deficits,'' unless the debt is authorized by the General Assembly and approved by a popular majority.

Three other states have replaced or amended their nineteenth century constitutional debt provisions to increase the opportunities for their governments to use general tax revenues and general obligation bonds. The 1851 Ohio Constitution imposes a $750,000 debt limit, although ten constitutional amendments from 1947 to 1987 permit a total debt of $4 billion for specific purposes including veterans compensation, education, highways, and public buildings and infrastructure. The 1963 Michigan Constitution is more flexible. It permits short-term debt up to 15 percent of undedicated revenues and unspecified long-term debt subject to a statute passed by a two-thirds legislative majority and approved by a simple popular majority. The 1970 Illinois Constitution, even more generous, permits state debt up to 20 percent of appropriations.

These state governments have continued to finance public services and economic development within their constitutional parameters by using general tax revenues and by selling general obligation bonds: full faith and credit obligations ''secured by the promise that both the principal and interest will be paid through the exercise of the . . . taxing power'' (Gelfand and Salsich, 1985: 143). The need to make a more substantial financial commitment has led state governments to create nonconstitutional debt financing devices, the most popular of which is the revenue bond. Michigan, Illinois, and Ohio have rewritten or amended their constitutions explicitly to authorize the use of revenue bonds (Gold, 1985). In other states, legislatures have created public commissions, corporations, and authorities legally independent of state government which issue the bonds, build and operate the facilities to which they hold title, and retire the bonded indebtedness by collecting tolls, rents, or user fees from the operation of the public projects including public highways, buildings, and recreational facilities.

Supreme courts in these states have generally deferred to their legislature's judgment and upheld the use of revenue bonds by broadly interpreting their constitution's public purpose clause and by narrowly construing their credit and debt limitation provisions. These courts have, in particular, relied upon the special funds doctrine which holds that "obligations payable solely from funds separate from general taxes are not considered debt . . . and, therefore, are exempt from debt ceilings and related limitations on debt financing" (Gelfand and Salsich, 1985: 161). These state courts have also upheld the use of three variations on the traditional revenue bond which are used by state governments to finance economic development: the industrial development bond (IDB), the moral obligation bond (MOB), and the serial lease.

Industrial development bonds are used by municipal, county, and state governments to finance the construction of industrial facilities which are then leased to a private enterprise (Marlin, 1987). The rental payments made by the company are used to retire the bonds after which the ownership of the facility passes to the private enterprise. IDBs have posed more of a constitutional problem than traditional revenue bonds, but, once again, state courts have upheld IDB use "under an expansive view of public purpose and restrictive view of lending of credit . . . provided there is a clear state legislative authorization for the particular project" (Gelfand and Salsich, 1985: 172).

A moral obligation bond is a revenue bond which contains a promise that if the revenues to be derived from the project are not sufficient to pay the principal and interest on the bonds, then tax revenues will be used. If the pledge of tax revenues is an express legal promise, it may raise a major constitutional problem, because the use of tax receipts may convert an MOB into a general obligation bond. If it does, then the statute providing for its use may violate the state constitution's debt limitation provision. Most state courts have, however, found that the pledges are not legally binding. Despite the mandatory language for repayment from general tax revenues, these courts have held that the legislature did not intend to create a binding obligation, because "one legislative body may not commit a successor legislative body to [appropriate] . . . tax revenues" (Gelfand and Salsich, 1985: 166).

A serial lease allows a public authority which has issued revenue bonds to lease a project to a state executive department which uses or operates the project by paying rent, in part or full, from its annual or biennial appropriations to the authority. Serial leases have also encountered constitutional challenges, but state courts have generally exempted them from constitutional debt limitation provisions on the basis of the contingent obligation doctrine: "That the payments are not due until a particular condition has occurred . . . [e.g. the availability of the rental property] and that the contract may be terminated before this condition is satisfied" (Gelfand and Salsich, 1985: 237).

In sum, the six mid-American state constitutions in the 1980s still contain many of their nineteenth century taxation, current expenditure, and debt limitation clauses. But the revision and amendment of their constitutions and the creation and legitimation of constitutional and nonconstitutional debt financing mechanisms by their state legislatures and courts have expanded the constitutional legal parameters for state industrial recruitment. As a consequence, the six states have greater legal freedom to use interest and production subsidies as components in their industrial recruitment packages. How have these states used this freedom to recruit Japanese automobile manufacturers?

MID-AMERICAN STATE CONSTITUTIONAL FISCAL EXPERIENCE

State governments have negotiated multi–hundred million dollar agreements with Japanese automobile manufacturers which have contained interest, production, and tax subsidies.[2] The interest and production subsidies in these agreements have included site acquisition and improvement, plant construction, employee training, and infrastructure improvements. These incentive package components have been financed with general tax revenues and nonconstitutional debt monies which have been supplemented by local and federal funds.[3] What have been the constitutional consequences of using these funds to finance economic development? The following analysis will frame an answer in terms of two major features of the government financing provided by the six mid-American states: first, worker training and infrastructure improvements; and, second, site acquisition and improvement and automobile facility construction.

Worker Training and Infrastructure Financing

The mid-American states have all used general tax revenues as the principal, but not exclusive, source of worker training and infrastructure improvements: Tennessee has provided $7.35 million; Ohio, $8.4 million; Michigan, $19 million; Kentucky, $33 million; Indiana, $35 million; and Illinois, $38.6 million. Four states have provided subsidies which have been funded, in part or whole, from a single annual or biennial general fund appropriation.[4] Tennessee limited itself to a single budgetary appropriation of $7.35 million to its Industrial Training Service program for Nissan worker training (Parsons, 1989). Kentucky also agreed to make a one-time $33 million general fund appropriation to its Human Resources Cabinet to be spent for Toyota worker training over a five-year period (Furr, 1989).[5] Ohio provided $741,000 in four separate legislative appropriations to its Industrial Training Program for Honda worker training assistance and $7,669,000 in four separate legislative appropriations to its Industrial Inducement Fund for on-site road, utility, and rail spur improvements (Ohio Department of Development, 1988).[6]

The appropriation of these funds from one legislative budget raises no genuine constitutional issue. That issue was settled long ago in the leading case of

Albritton v. *City of Winona* (1938) where the Mississippi Supreme Court said that "the care of the poor, the relief of unemployment, and the promotion of agriculture [and industry] are undoubtedly proper governmental purposes, [which] are recognized everywhere and by all" (*Albritton* v. *City of Winona*, 1938: 804).

Since then, state courts have generally deferred to legislative determinations of what constitutes a public purpose and upheld statutes which authorize spending for housing, education, and economic development against public purpose challenges. In *State Property and Buildings Commission* v. *Hayes* (1986), the Kentucky Court of Appeals rejected, without comment, the claim that House Bill no. 398 which appropriated funds for Toyota worker training did not serve a public purpose in violation of Section 3 of the Kentucky Constitution (*Maddox* v. *Mills*, 1986). *Bazell* v. *City of Cincinnati* (1968) and *McConnell* v. *City of Lebanon* (1958) suggest that Ohio and Tennessee courts would also be inclined to reject any similar claims and to hold that statutes which authorized spending for worker training fulfilled the public purposes, broadly defined, of alleviating and preventing unemployment, even if those funds also benefited private individuals and corporations.

The state incentive agreements have also called for a series of annual or biennial general fund appropriations. Michigan's $19 million commitment to Mazda worker training was fulfilled by means of three successive legislative appropriations to the state's Business and Industrial Training Program (Fraser, 1989). In Illinois, the $40 million for Diamond-Star worker training funds came from a general revenue program, the Illinois Industrial Training Program, which will provide $38.6 million over five years (Dennis, 1989). Indiana has financed its $55 million in Fuji-Isuzu interest and production subsidies from its general treasury over three bienniums of which $21 million for Fuji-Isuzu worker training was appropriated to the state Industrial Training Program (Preston, 1989) and $14 million to the state's Industrial Development Fund in grants and loans for highway and utility improvements.

These appropriations by successive sessions of the Michigan, Indiana, and Illinois legislatures will not likely raise any meaningful constitutional questions, because the incentive agreements and understandings provide that the executive branch of the state government will make a "best faith effort" to acquire future monies from future legislatures. The Indiana Memorandum of Understanding with Fuji and Isuzu, for example, clearly states: "It is expressly understood . . . that the execution of this Understanding . . . merely expresses the commitment of the executive branch of the State to use its best efforts to seek to cause compliance with the proposals made to the Joint Venture . . . [and] that the . . . proposals . . . are subject to governmental funding [and] . . . legislative authorization" (Memorandum of Understanding, 1986). The Indiana agreement has not been challenged nor have those made by Michigan and Illinois. If they were, it is unclear how the Illinois Supreme Court would rule. However, *In Re Request for Advisory Opinion enrolled Senate Bill 558* (1977) and *Steup* v. *Indiana*

Housing Finance Authority (1980) suggest that the Michigan and Indiana Supreme Courts would likely reject those challenges by holding that the agreements may create a moral obligation, but their constitution's state debt provisions have not been violated, since the agreements do not impose a legal obligation on future legislatures.

Four mid-American states have also used dedicated revenue sources, highway revenue bonds, and limited obligation bonds to finance infrastructure improvements. Michigan's $3.1 million cost for on-site railroad improvements came from the state Department of Transportation's Comprehensive Urban Transportation Fund which is supported by 10 percent of gasoline tax revenues (Bachelor, 1989). Tennessee's $9,383,000 for Nissan-related highway improvements came from its Industrial Access Road Program funded by state gasoline tax receipts (Wallace, 1989). Kentucky financed the $30,788,000 in Toyota access road improvements with road revenue bonds which will be retired from highway user tax proceeds (Cole, 1989; Transportation Cabinet, 1989). Ohio spent $35,128,000 for improvements to state Route 33 from its highway trust fund which is supported by gasoline tax receipts (Wise, 1989). Illinois has, however, relied upon the proceeds from two limited obligation bond-driven economic development programs, authorized by its Build Illinois Act, to finance $35.5 million in Diamond-Star infrastructure improvements (Giscala, 1989). The water and sewer improvements, $11.4 million, were funded by the Public Infrastructure Program grant. The highway improvements, $24.1 million, came from successive annual appropriations to the Highway Access and Interchange Program (Dees, 1989).

Michigan, Ohio, and Kentucky's use of state gasoline tax receipts and/or highway revenue bonds are highly unlikely to encounter any constitutional objections. Their courts in *Eaves* v. *State Bridge Commission* (Michigan, 1936), *State* v. *Griffiths* (Ohio, 1940), and *Turnpike Authority* v. *Wall* (Kentucky, 1960) had, long ago, approved these two means of financing highway improvements. The Build Illinois Act and its companion statute, the Build Illinois Bond Act, are, however, constitutionally untested. The Build Illinois Bond Act, passed by the General Assembly in 1985, authorizes the state to issue $998 million in limited obligation bonds. The proceeds from these bond sales are deposited in a separate fund, the Build Illinois Bond Fund, and are appropriated by the legislature to agency programs devoted to public infrastructure improvements and economic development activities. The bonds are retired on the basis of mandated legislative fund appropriations from dedicated sales tax revenues to the Build Illinois Bond Retirement and Interest Fund. If the legislature fails to act, the statute will serve as "an irrevocable and continuing appropriation" to pay the principal and interest (Illinois Annotated Statutes, Chapter 127, Section 2811). The bonds are not, however, general obligations of the state, but limited to a "first priority pledge of and lien on monies on deposit in the Build Illinois Bond Retirement and Interest Fund" (Illinois Annotated Statutes, Chapter 127, Section 2812).

Illinois Supreme Court's review of the Build Illinois statutes would, most likely, focus on the constitution's debt provision: Article 9, Section 9(a) defines state debt as "bonds or other evidences of indebtedness which are secured by the full faith and credit of the state or are required to be paid, directly or indirectly, from tax revenues" (Illinois Constitution, Section 9[a]). Are the Build Illinois Bonds state debt? Section 9(f) of the Illinois Constitution permits state government agencies to "issue bonds which are not secured by the full faith and credit or tax revenues of the State nor required to be repaid directly or indirectly from tax revenues" (Illinois Constitution, Section 9[f]). The Court will be hesitant to accept the Build Illinois Bond Act's declaration that the bonds are not a pledge of the state's full faith and credit, because of the statute's requirement that the bonds be repaid from successive annual legislative appropriations. The Court may, however, be tempted to rely, inter alia, upon *People* v. *Illinois State Toll Highway Commission* (1954) and *Rosemont Building Supply* v. *Illinois Highway Trust Authority* (1970) and to uphold the statute by finding that Section 9(a) is not offended, since the appropriations come not from general tax revenues but from dedicated revenue sources including state use taxes, service occupation taxes, and retailers occupation taxes.

In sum, worker training monies have not encountered constitutional problems because, long ago, state courts had accepted the expenditure of general tax revenues to alleviate unemployment as a valid public purpose. Multilegislative session appropriations are unlikely to encounter any constitutional challenge because their legislatures are only morally obligated to make the appropriations. Infrastructure improvements, particularly highway construction, based on the use of public authorities, revenue bonds, and dedicated revenue sources have also been judicially approved as not creating state debt. The Build Illinois' limited obligation bond program, the source of the Diamond-Star worker training and infrastructure improvements, is, however, constitutionally suspicious because it requires the legislature to provide continuing appropriations to pay the principal and interest on the bonds.

Financing Site Acquisition and Improvement and Facility Construction

Japanese automobile manufacturers have privately financed, in whole or part, the purchase and improvement of the plant sites and the construction of the automobile facilities in Michigan, Ohio, Indiana, and Illinois. At the same time, these states, along with Tennessee and Kentucky, have employed four interest and production subsidy approaches which have relied upon general tax revenues and revenue bonds to finance the purchase and improvement of the site and the construction of the automobile facility. Figure 3.1 distinguishes these four approaches on the basis of their financing and ownership status: who has financed and owns the site and the facility. What are the state constitutional implications of each of these approaches to industrial financing?

Figure 3.1
Financing and Ownership of Industrial Sites and Facilities

Facility

	Automaker	Government
Automaker	I. Industry Owner- ship & Financing Ohio Illinois Michigan	II. Mixed Ownership & Financing II Kentucky
Government	III. Mixed Ownership & Financing I Indiana	IV. Government Owner- ship & Financing Tennessee

Site

Industrial Ownership and Financing

One approach to industrial development is private financing of both the purchase and improvement of the site and the construction of the automobile facility. In Ohio, Honda purchased the sites and constructed its Marysville and Anna facilities solely with financing from the Mitsubishi Bank (Wise, 1989).[7] Honda's purely private approach to industrial financing has also been followed with minor but constitutionally significant variations in Michigan and Illinois.

In Michigan, Mazda purchased the Flat Rock site, and the Michigan Strategic Fund (MSF) supported the automaker's private financing of the plant's construction with a $21,138,000, 20 year, 8 percent loan (Benkelman, 1985: 1A, 12A). Mazda will repay a private lender to which the MSF sold its loan obligation in order to recoup the funds for loans to other companies (Pentilla, 1989). The Mazda loan had its origins in Public Act no. 70 (1982) which created the Michigan Economic Development Authority (MEDA), the predecessor to MSF, and gave to MEDA general powers to issue notes and bonds and to make grants and loans. In 1982, MEDA sold $45 million in economic development revenue bonds, and from the proceeds of that sale, it used $21,138,000 to make the Mazda loan (Pentilla, 1989).

MEDA and MSF are both "public bodies corporate" authorized by Article 9, Section 13 of the Michigan Constitution to borrow money and to issue their securities evidencing debt, as limited by Sections 12, 14, and 15 governing general obligation debt and by Section 18 prohibiting the state's credit from being granted to or in aid of a public or private person, association, or corporation.

The MEDA statute makes it clear that its bonds and loans are "not a general or moral obligation of the state," that no state funds will be used to repay the bonds, and that the state "has not in any way pledged its credit to repay" (Public Act no. 70, 1982, Title 3, Section 541[6][f]). Moreover, MEDA bonds and loans are secured solely by a dedicated revenue source: state oil and gas receipts (Lontz, 1989).

MSF's loan to Mazda raises no constitutional issue. As the Michigan Supreme Court observed in *Schureman* v. *State Highway Commission* (1966), neither is state debt created nor is the state's credit pledged for the payment of revenue bonds which are retired from special tax revenues earmarked for that purpose (*Schureman* v. *State*, 1966: 62). Moreover, no loan offends the constitution, as the Court said in *Request for Advisory Opinion In Re Enrolled Bills 1385 and 1387* (1977), as long as no pledge of the state's full faith and credit is made and the provisions for repayment are strictly limited to dedicated revenues (*Advisory Opinion*, 1977: 129).

In Illinois, Diamond-Star financed the construction of its automobile facility through the Mellon and Mitsubishi Banks. The 625-acre plant site was a gift from the state which used $11.2 million from its Large Business Attraction Program, a Build Illinois Act program, to purchase an 820-acre tract (Pitcher, 1989). The state will eventually recover $5 million: approximately $3 million from the sale of the remaining 195 acres to automobile supplier industries and a $2 million Bloomington-Normal contribution from the proceeds of a $5 million local revenue bond sale (Giscala, 1989). Does the Diamond-Star real estate donation offend the Illinois Constitution?

The 1970 Illinois Constitution contains no donation provision. State real property donations are limited only by the constitution's public purpose clause, Article 8, Section 1(a), which provides: "Public funds, property or credit shall be used only for public purposes" (Illinois Constitution, Article 8, Section 1[a]). The Illinois courts in such cases as *People* v. *McMakin* (1972) and *O'Fallon Development Company* v. *City of O'Fallon* (1976) have held that Section 1(a) does not prohibit appropriations of public funds to private corporations. Yet none of this state case law directly addresses the question of whether a state agency's use of the proceeds from the sale of limited obligation bonds to purchase private property and then to convey a major portion of it to a private corporation violates the Illinois Constitution, Article 8, Section 1(a).

If this use of Build Illinois Act funds were challenged, its constitutionality would initially depend upon how the Supreme Court of Illinois interpreted Section 1(a)'s public funds and property language. The monies for the plant site purchase did not come directly from general tax revenues; they came instead from the sale of limited obligation bonds which had been deposited in a separate account, the Build Illinois Bond Fund. Still public funds were involved, because the bonds were retired with statutorily mandated appropriations even though they were deposited in a separate account: the Build Illinois Bond Retirement and Interest Fund. As a consequence, it is necessary, as the Supreme Court of Illinois said in *People* v. *McMakin* (1972), that public purpose test had to be examined, since "public funds or property in some manner may be involved" (*People* v. *McMakin*, 1972: 812).

The Supreme Court of Illinois, like other state courts, would take a broad view of "the scope of activities which may be classified as serving a public purpose especially in the area of economic welfare" (*Marshall Field* v. *Village of South Barrington*, 1981: 1282). The Court would not, however, be unwilling to review the expenditure of Build Illinois monies by the state Department of Commerce and Community Affairs. As the Illinois Court of Appeal observed in *Marshall Field & Company* v. *Village of South Barrington* (1981):

The determination of whether a proposed public expenditure serves the public purposes is initially to be made by the legislative body . . . [and] is not to be lightly set aside upon judicial review. However, a self-serving recitation that public purposes are served is not conclusive of that question. (*Marshall Field* v. *Village of South Barrington*, 1981: 1282)

To determine whether the Diamond-Star property donation served a public purpose, the Court would likely employ the principal purpose and effect test which the Illinois courts have used on numerous occasions and which requires them to examine "the goals sought by and the actual effects of the public funds" (1282). That a private interest is incidentally benefited does not matter; "the crucial test," as the state Court of Appeals said in *O'Fallon Development Co.* v. *City of O'Fallon* (1976), "is whether the attempted use . . . subserves the public interest and benefits a private interest or individual only incidentally. If the private benefits are purely incidental to the public purposes of the act then art 8, section 1(a) . . . is not violated" (*O'Fallon Development Co.* v. *City of O'Fallon*, 1976: 1229).

The Build Illinois Act clearly declares a public purpose: to issue bonds in order to finance programs which will attract new businesses and, thereby, assure that the growth of the state's economy will benefit its citizens and business community (Illinois Annotated Statutes, Chapter 127, Section 127–2[a-e & k]). The Build Illinois Bond Act specifically authorizes $50 million in bonds to be issued for the purpose of economic development activities including "acquiring real properties for commercial or industrial developments" (Illinois Annotated Statutes, Chapter 127, Section 2804[b]). The Supreme Court of Illinois would undoubtedly accept the statute's broadly defined economic objectives but then critically address the question of whether the statute, as applied, serves a public purpose. Here the Court will find it difficult to avoid the conclusion that this use of Build Illinois Bond monies to purchase private land and then convey it to Diamond-Star Motors does not offend Article 8, Section 1(a). Granted that the expenditure will provide a direct $6.2 million benefit to a private corporation, but this direct private benefit would be seen as clearly incidental to the $700 million investment Diamond-Star has made and to the substantial impact it and its supplier industries will have on the state's economic health.

Government Ownership and Financing

A second approach to industrial development is state and local government financing of both the purchase and improvement of the site and the construction of the automobile facility. State and local governments customarily accomplish this objective by issuing industrial development revenue bonds (Marlin, 1987). In Tennessee, state and local governments are permitted by statute to create industrial development boards which are authorized to own, lease, and dispose of property for industrial development purposes (Tennessee Code Annotated, 1980: Sections 7–53–101 to –311). The Industrial Development Board of Rutherford County financed both the purchase of the site and the construction of the Nissan facility from the private sale of $700 million in industrial development bonds to Nissan Motor Corporation, the parent corporation (Sellers, 1989). The agreement raises no state constitutional issues, because it provides that Nissan will pay rent for the use of the facility sufficient to retire the bonds by the year 2011, at which time it will be able to purchase the facility for a nominal sum (Memorandum of Agreement, Sections 2[d] and 3[d], 1980: 3–4).

Mixed Ownership and Financing I

A third approach to economic development, based on shared private and government ownership and financing, involves government ownership of the improved site and private ownership of the automobile facility. In Indiana, Fuji-Isuzu privately financed the construction of its automobile facility, and the state agreed in its Memorandum of Understanding with the automakers to finance the purchase and improvement of the 869-acre Lafayette plant site. To this end, the Indiana Employment Development Commission (IEDC) entered into a purchase agreement with the Indiana Bond Bank whereby the Bond Bank used the proceeds from an issue of its Special Program Notes to loan IEDC $20.9 million (Purchase Agreement, 1987). IEDC used these funds to acquire and develop the site as an Industrial Development Project and then to lease it to Fuji-Isuzu for $100 a year. IEDC will repay the Bond Bank loan solely from its Industrial Development Fund, the monies for which will come from three biennial general fund appropriations—$5.6, $13.5, and $8 million—totalling $26.1 million. When the loan is repaid, the site will be conveyed to Fuji-Isuzu at a nominal cost (Dorman, 1989).

Any challenge to this public financing arrangement would be based primarily on the state constitution's public purposes, state debt, and public credit provisions. Article 1, Sections 1 and 21, limit the expenditure of state funds to public purposes. In construing these provisions, the Indiana Supreme Court would acknowledge that "[p]ublic purposes are matters of legislative determination" (*Steup* v. *Indiana Housing Finance Authority*, 1980: 1221) and would indulge a presumption of constitutionality in favor of a statute which authorizes the expenditure of public monies, even though it incidentally benefited private individuals.

The Court, employing a deferential due process standard, said in *Edwards* v. *Housing Authority of City of Muncie* (1939): "The amount, and manner, and method of the expenditure, must be left to legislative discretion" (*Edwards* v. *Housing Authority*, 1939: 744). Here, the Court would find that the Indiana Employment Development Law created the IEDC to serve a public purpose: "for promoting opportunities for gainful employment and business opportunities by the promotion of industrial development" (Burns Indiana Statutes Annotated, Section 4–4–11–2[b]). To carry out this purpose, the Commission is authorized to borrow money; enter into loan agreements and development projects; sell obligations of the commission; and purchase, improve, and lease land for industrial development projects (Burns Indiana Statutes Annotated, Sections 4–4–11–15[a], 9, 12, 13, 20, & 24–26). Moreover, the Court would find that the $20.9 million benefit Fuji-Isuzu will receive from the conveyance of the property for a nominal consideration will be clearly incidental to the overwhelming economic benefit the state will receive from the construction and operation of a $700 million automobile assembly plant and its associated supplier industries.

Article 11, Section 12 states: "Nor shall the credit of the state ever be given, or loaned, in aid of any person, association, or corporation" (Indiana Constitution, Article 11, Section 12). In construing this provision in *Ennis* v. *State Highway Commission* (1952) and *Orbison* v. *Welch* (1961), the Indiana Supreme Court held that Section 12 "is applicable only to private corporations and not public bodies" (*Steup* v. *Indiana Housing Finance Authority*, 1980: 1220). The Bond Bank and IEDC are neither. The Bond Bank is a body "corporate and politic . . . not a state agency . . . [but] separate from the state in its corporate and sovereign capacity" (Indiana Revised Code, Section 5–1.5–2–1). The Indiana Employment Development Commission Law employs similar language when it states that the IEDC is "a body politic and corporate, not a state agency, but an independent instrumentality exercising essential public functions" (Indiana Revised Code, 1980, Section 4–4–11–4[a]). In sum, the Indiana Supreme Court would find that neither the Bond Bank notes nor IEDC's loan and subsequent purchase, lease, and conveyance of the Lafayette site would violate Section 12, because that provision only applies to an agency of the state in its sovereign capacity or to a private corporation.

The IEDC loan raises one final constitutional issue, because Article 10, Section 5 prohibits the contracting of any state debt. In construing this provision, the Indiana Supreme Court held in *American National Bank and Trust* v. *Indiana Department of Highways* (1982) that constitutional debt is not created if the project is "paid for by bonds issued by a separate corporate entity or agency that committed payment of the bonds out of a special fund created from the income of the special project" (*American National Bank & Trust* v. *Indiana Department of Highways*, 1982: 1132).

The Indiana Bond Bank and the Indiana Employment Development Commission, as noted above, satisfy the separate entity requirement. The Bond Bank statute specifically provides that "every issue of bonds or notes shall be general obligations of the bank payable out of the revenues or funds of the bank'' (Burns Indiana Statutes Annotated, 1980, Section 5–1.5–4–1) and that a bond or note of the bank ''is not a debt, liability, loan of credit, or a pledge of the full faith and credit of the state'' (Burns Indiana Statutes Annotated, 1980, Section 4–4–11–22). The IEDC loan documents recite similar language adding not only that ''taxing power of the state is [not] pledged to the payment of the principal or interest'' of the loan (Purchase Agreement, 1987: 5 and Promissory Note, 1987: 4), but also providing further that the loan is not a general obligation of the IEDC, but is ''limited exclusively to the assets of the IEDC Industrial Development Fund'' (Promissory Note, 1987: 3). Finally, the IEDC Industrial Development Fund satisfies the special fund requirement even though its assets will not come from the revenues derived from any project but from three successive biennial appropriations.

As the Indiana Supreme Court held in *Steup* (1980), appropriations made by the legislature and deposited in the Indiana Housing Finance Authority's capital reserve fund for the ''direct and unconditional satisfaction of the Authority's obligations'' did not constitute debt, because ''the Act allows but does not require such appropriations'' (*Steup* v. *Indiana Housing Finance Authority*, 1980: 1218–1219). In like fashion, the Indiana legislature may be morally bound to appropriate tax revenues to retire the IEDC loan, but, because it is not legally obligated, no state constitutional debt is created in violation of Section 12. In conclusion, the IEDC purchase, improvement, and conveyance of the Lafayette site to Fuji-Isuzu would be unlikely to offend the state constitution's public purpose, state debt, and public credit provisions.

Mixed Ownership and Financing II

A fourth approach to economic development, also based on shared private and governmental ownership and financing, is private ownership of the improved site and public ownership of the facility. In Kentucky, Toyota is the owner of the improved site which the state purchased and improved with proceeds from the sale of $35 million in bonds and then conveyed to the automaker.[8] The facility was financed jointly by the state and the automaker. Toyota privately financed its equipment purchase while the Kentucky Development Finance Authority (KDFA) owns the buildings, having financed their construction from the sale of $400 million in taxable industrial revenue bonds. Toyota will lease the buildings from KDFA and pay a rent sufficient to retire the bonds by the year 2007 (Bratcher, 1989).

The industrial development revenue bonds were clearly authorized by statute and case law, but the Kentucky-Toyota Agreement's site financing provisions required the enactment of legislation.[9] Senate Bill no. 361, broadly drafted to permit the financing of future Economic Development Projects, contained three major provisions which relied upon the revenue bond financing mechanism and the vehicle of incremental taxes.[10] First, the statute authorized the Commerce Cabinet to initiate industrial development (i.e., site acquisition and preparation) projects and to finance these projects by entering into agreements with the State Property and Buildings Commission (Senate Bill no. 361, 1986. Section 2(4)).[11] Second, the statute authorized the Commission to issue revenue bonds and provided for the Cabinet to make payments to retire the bonds solely from its successive biennial appropriations (Senate Bill no. 361, 1986, Section 3(3) [d]). Third, the statute provided for the immediate conveyance of industrial development projects and then declared that the increased, or incremental, taxes—taxes not received but for the establishment of such facilities—paid by private industrial facilities would constitute "the receipt by the Commonwealth of the fair market value for any industrial development project conveyed" (Senate Bill no. 361, 1986, Section 3[3]).

Almost immediately the Kentucky-Toyota Agreement became politically and legally troublesome. There was a frivolous effort by the president of a citizens organization to impeach the governor and leading state officials (Chellgren, 1986: B–7). The Kentucky State Buildings and Trade Council attempted to convince first state and then federal courts to enjoin the state Natural Resources and Environmental Cabinet's issuance of the Toyota air pollution and sewage treatment permits (Hammond, 1988). A landowner's challenge to the Transportation Cabinet's action to condemn his property, needed to widen the road near the plant site, led to a state court trial which involved two former governors as counsel for the respective parties and the incumbent governor as a witness (Cohen, 1986: B–1). These legal actions, all unsuccessful, were dwarfed by the fundamental political and legal issue: the constitutionality of Senate Bill no. 361.

HAYES V. STATE PROPERTY AND BUILDINGS COMMISSION (1987)

Governor Martha Layne Collins decided to silence critics who claimed that the Kentucky-Toyota Agreement and Senate Bill no. 361 were a giveaway and to assure brokerage firms that the land transfer and incremental tax financing provisions were constitutional.[12] The litigation began in Franklin Circuit Court as a declaratory judgment action brought by the state Budget Director Larry Hayes against the State Property and Buildings Commission (Duke, 1986: B-1). The Kentucky Supreme Court named R. Scott Plain, an attorney, to serve as its special amicus curiae. Two labor union leaders, Jerry Hammond, the Executive Secretary-Treasurer of the Kentucky State Building Trades Council, AFL-CIO, and Charles Hoffmaster, a union pipefitter, were also permitted to intervene.[13] Circuit Court Judge Ray Corns heard one day of oral argument on September 23, 1986 (Brammer, 1986: B1-2). Three and one-half weeks later, October 17, he ruled that the Collins Administration had acted legally in offering Toyota $35 million in land purchase and site improvements and that the legislation approved by the General Assembly was constitutional (Brammer and Swasy, 1986: A–12). All the parties then appealed the decision for a final ruling by the Kentucky Supreme Court.

Constitutional Issues

The Kentucky Supreme Court heard oral argument on January 14, 1987 (Brammer, 1987: B-1). At issue were five provisions in the 1891 Kentucky Constitution which place limitations on the exercise of the legislature's fiscal powers: Sections 3, 49, 50, 171, and 177. These sections address two basic intentions of their framers: to provide in Sections 49 and 50 for a general limitation on any General Assembly's power to amass a large debt whatever the purpose; and, second, to provide in Sections 3, 171, and 177 for specific limitations on the General Assembly's authority to obligate public revenues for private purposes.

Oral argument centered on questions raised by these two basic intentions. Did the statute's provision for the use of biennial appropriations to service the revenue bonds violate Section 3's limitation of public emoluments to public services and Section 171's requirement that taxes be used only for public purposes? Did the statute's provision for Toyota's payment of incremental taxes as consideration for the purchase and improvement of the site, which taxes Toyota would have paid in any instance, violate Section 171's requirement that taxes be uniform? Did these incremental taxes, if sham consideration, also violate Section 177's credit and donation clauses? Did the Agreement's use of the revenue bond mechanism violate Sections 49 and 50's limitations on the power of the General Assembly to contract debt? Legal counsel rooted their answers to these questions in terms of the Court's leading general obligation bond, mortgage bond, and revenue bond cases which had defined the meaning of these constitutional provisions. What did existing case law reveal about the Court's general disposition toward the state's incentive agreement and its likely decision in the *Hayes* case?

First, the Kentucky court, like other state supreme courts, had deferred to its legislature's judgment and upheld the use of current revenues and tax-based plans to finance industrial development by broadly interpreting the meaning of Section 171's public purpose clause and narrowly construing Section 177's public credit clause. In *Dyche* v. *City of London* (1956), the Court approved a municipality's use of general obligation bonds to finance the construction of buildings to be leased to private industry. Section 171's requirement that taxes be levied for a public purpose was not infringed, because the relief of widespread unemployment was a public purpose for which the city's taxing power could be used.

The use of current tax revenues by the state Industrial Development Financing Authority to provide mortgage loans to private non-profit corporations had also met with the Court's approval. In *Industrial Development Authority* v. *Eastern Kentucky Regional Planning Commission* (1960), the Court held that neither Section 3's limitation of public emoluments and privileges to public services, nor Section 171's requirement that taxes be levied for a public purpose were violated. Citing *Dyche*, it found a reasonable basis for the legislature's determination that attracting new industry would further the public purpose of eliminating unemployment. Moreover, the loan of state funds did not violate Section 177's prohibition against the loaning of the state's credit, because "the Authority would not be undertaking to become a surety on, or guarantor of the payment, of any bonds or other obligations in which the state's money was invested" (*Industrial Development Authority* v. *Eastern Kentucky Regional Planning Commission*, 1960: 278).

Second, the Kentucky Supreme Court, like most state supreme courts, had also deferred to its legislature's judgment and upheld the use of revenue bonds by broadly interpreting the state constitution's public purpose clause to include relief of unemployment and by narrowly construing its debt limitation provision by relying upon the special funds doctrine. In *Faulconer* v. *City of Danville* (1950), the Court's principal industrial revenue bond case, the Court upheld a municipality's use of revenue bonds to construct and lease industrial property to a private manufacturer in order to provide adequate opportunities for industrial employment. The Court found a "reasonable relation to the public interest or welfare" (*Faulconer* v. *City of Danville*, 1950: 83).

The Kentucky Supreme Court also relied upon the special funds doctrine in *J.D. van Hooser* v. *University of Kentucky* (1936) and *Preston* v. *Clements* (1950) to find that the use of revenue bonds to finance public buildings did not offend Sections 49 and 50, because the bonds were authorized to be "payable solely from the income to be derived from the operation of the buildings" (*J.D. van Hooser* v. *University of Kentucky*, 1936: 1031). Then in *Turnpike Authority of Kentucky* v. *Wall* (1960), the Court confronted a statute which used two revenue bond variants: a serial lease and a moral obligation bond. The Turnpike Authority Act empowered the state Turnpike Authority to issue bonds to finance toll roads which were to be leased to the state Department of Transportation. The department would pay rental on a biennial basis with an option to renew for the following legislative bienniums until the bonds were retired and would make up any deficiency from the tolls it received, first from motor vehicle taxes and then from the department's general fund appropriation. The Court approved the statute's serial lease provision: a contingent pledge of general revenues to cover rental obligations beyond the current biennium. The constitution's debt limitation was not infringed, because the statute gave the department the option to not renew the rental at the end of each biennium.

The Court also upheld the limited use of motor vehicle taxes as an additional source of rent, arguing that they could be "reasonably identified as derived from vehicular use of particular turnpikes being financed" (*Wall* v. *Turnpike Authority*, 1960: 557), that they were payable into a special fund, and that there was no statutory commitment that they would continue to be levied. But the Court objected to a provision that authorized the department to make up any deficiency in turnpike revenues "from any funds or tax revenues available for general purposes of the department and not required by law to be devoted to some other purpose" (*Turnpike Authority* v. *Wall*, 1960: 553). This created a constitutional debt in violation of Sections 49 and 50, since "a prior contract amounting to a 'pledge' would require satisfaction out of . . . general revenues [appropriated to the department] ahead of all other requirements" (*Turnpike Authority* v. *Wall*,

1960: 558). Any doubt about *Wall* was disposed of in *Blythe* v. *Transportation Cabinet of the Commonwealth of Kentucky* (1983). There the Court further expanded the revenue bond mechanism by upholding the payment of biennial rentals solely from general motor vehicle taxes.

In sum the Kentucky Supreme Court's decisions had redefined the state's constitutional infrastructure. The appropriation of economic development funds from current revenues and the use of mortgage loans and general obligation bonds did not offend Section 171's public purpose provision, nor did they amount to a loaning of the state's credit in violation of Section 177; but their use was limited, however, by means of the dual barrier erected by Section 49 and 50. The state could, however, avoid these constitutional barriers by relying on the nonconstitutional mechanism of state revenue bonds to provide financing for an industrial enterprise the magnitude of an automobile assembly plant.

The Court had upheld revenue bond financing by relying on a series of broad interpretations of the constitution's public purpose, cre   nd debt provisions. Section 171's public purpose requirement was not   d if the industrial facility were constructed and leased in order to reliev mployment. Sections 177 and 179's prohibitions on the giving, pledging,   ning of the state's credit were not violated if the government held title   property until the industry had paid for its cost. Sections 49 and 50's   imitations were not abridged if the bonded indebtedness were payable from rents, placed in a separate fund and derived, not just from the project's revenues and those revenues "reasonably attributable" to it, but also from the executive department's general fund appropriation beyond the current biennium, as long as the department was not required to commit more funds than it could anticipate during the biennium. Sections 49 and 50 were also not offended as long as the department was not bound to renew the lease in future bienniums. Was this judicial craftsmanship sufficient to uphold the constitutionality of the Kentucky-Toyota incentive agreement?

Majority Opinion

Six months, almost to the day, the Court by a one vote margin, 4–3, upheld the constitutionality of Senate Bill 361 (Brammer and Miller, 1987: A-1, 16; Note [Rouse], 1988). Justice Donald Wintersheimer, speaking for himself and Chief Justice Robert Stephens and Justices William Gant and Joseph Lambert, wrote the majority opinion. The Court, he said, would not sit as a "super legislature" and review the economic wisdom of the project, but would merely interpret the statute "in light of the constitution," acknowledging that the statute was "entitled to a presumption of validity" and to be "liberally construed" to carry out the legislature's intent (*Hayes* v. *State*, 1987: 799).

Turning to the constitutional issues, Justice Wintersheimer considered first the specific constitutional limitations on the legislature's authority to obligate public revenues for private purposes set forth in Sections 3, 171, and 177. Sections 3 and 171 only briefly detained the Court. Section 3 prohibits exclusive or public emoluments, except in consideration of public services. Section 171 restricts the use of taxes to public purposes. "Common sense," he boldly declared, "dictates that the words [public purpose and public service] are totally compatible" (*Hayes* v. *State*, 1987: 801). If the purposes served by the statute "constitute public purposes for which revenues may be levied and expended under Section 171, the manner of the use and expenditure is also proper under Section 3" (*Hayes* v. *State*, 1987: 801). Did the statute serve a public purpose? "Relief of unemployment," he concluded, "is a public purpose that would justify the outlay of funds" (*Hayes* v. *State*, 1987: 801).

Did Senate Bill no. 361 nevertheless violate Section 177 which prohibits the state from giving, loaning, or pledging its credit or from making a donation to a private corporation, unless there was a valid public purpose? The prohibition on donations did not apply, he concluded, because the "incremental taxes to be collected [estimated at $13 million annually] . . . constitute sufficient consideration for the conveyance of the property" (*Hayes* v. *State*, 1987: 800). Nor did Section 177's prohibition on the lending of the state's credit apply to the statute's provision allowing the property to be initially conveyed to Toyota as long as the financing agreement assured the receipt of fair market value. The State Property and Buildings Commission, he found, had made the statutorily mandated written determination that the incremental taxes "are reasonably expected to be equal to the principal amount of the proposed revenue bonds" and that the private industry had agreed in the event it conveyed the industrial development project to a third party it would pay the state "the difference between the taxes collected . . . and the amount of the bonds" (*Hayes* v. *State*, 1987: 799). Senate Bill no. 361 did not offend Section 177's credit provision for one additional reason: the two year limitation in the statute and financing agreements "does not commit any future funds to the Toyota project" (*Hayes* v. *State*, 1987: 800). The statute only requires the Commerce Cabinet to include a request for appropriations in its biennial budget to pay for the bond service, but "there is no guarantee that the General Assembly will affirmatively act on [that] request. Toyota is clearly at the mercy of the Kentucky legislature" (*Hayes* v. *State*, 1987: 801).

Second, Justice Wintersheimer examined Sections 49 and 50's limitations on the General Assembly's power to amass large debts and to financially obligate future legislatures without a direct popular vote. The Court, he said, had held that no debt was created within the meaning of these provisions if the state issued revenue bonds. Here the revenue bonds were, in a sense, retired by the payment of incremental taxes, but, in fact, depended upon successive biennial general fund appropriations. However, Sections 49 and 50 were still not offended, because the debt service for the bonds was based on the serial lease upheld in *Wall* (1960) and *Blythe* (1983):

The reason no debt has been created is because the financial obligations of the Commonwealth are confined to a particular two-year period and the General Assembly appropriates general fund revenues for debt service accruing during that two year period only. (*Hayes* v. *State*, 1987: 803)

At the same time, Senate bill no. 361's serial lease, unlike those in previous bond issues, limited the security of bond holders to the Commonwealth's promise to seek general fund appropriations to retire the bonds. Still the Court was unwilling to find this innovative legislative approach constitutionally infirm (*Hayes* v. *State*, 1987: 804).

Dissenting Opinions

Three strongly worded dissents written by Justices Charles Liebson, James Stephenson, and Roy Vance argued that the Court had succumbed to powerful nonjudicial arguments. Justice Liebson spoke for his dissenting colleagues when he declared that the Toyota proponents had put overwhelming pressure on the Court to "judicially amend" the Constitution: "Pressure on the judiciary to find some way around the constitution in the name of political expediency has proved to be overwhelming" (*Hayes* v. *State*, 1987: 806). As a consequence, he argued, the majority had approved "a transparent evasion of the plain meeting of constitutional provisions . . . as a matter of judicial expediency" (*Hayes* v. *State*, 1987: 806–807). Two features of Senate Bill 361, the dissenters claimed, could only have been approved by judicially amending the Kentucky Constitution: its use of the revenue bond concept and the incremental tax mechanism.

The state's revenue bonds, the dissenters found, had previously been based on legislation which had authorized a public agency to issue the bonds which would be retired from the income realized from the project they were issued to finance. In *Hayes*, Justice Liebson argued, the Court had made two substantial alterations in the meaning of the revenue bond as an instrument "payable solely from a revenue producing public project" (*Hayes* v. *State*, 1987: 809). First, it upheld the use of bonds which were not revenue producing. Senate Bill no. 361 provided for revenue to cover the project cost through the mechanism of "incremental taxes" which were "deemed sufficient to satisfy the requirement of rent," but, as Justice Liebson observed, it was the Commerce Cabinet which would make the rent payments (*Hayes* v. *State*, 1987: 809). Second, the revenue bonds did not involve a public project. Senate Bill no. 361 authorized the use of the revenue bonds for the establishment of an economic development project, a mechanism which provided that a private corporation, not a state agency or department, would own and occupy the project from the outset and that the Commerce Cabinet, not the private corporation, would pay the rent from its biennial appropriation from the general treasury.

Previous public projects had provided some security, because they involved state-held assets capable of producing revenues. However, the dissenters argued that since the industrial development project is immediately conveyed to a private corporation, the only security the bond holders had, if any, was the promise that the Commerce Cabinet would seek future appropriations to pay the debt service as a current operating expense. "As a practical matter," Justice Vance observed, "a future General Assembly will find it powerless to refuse to appropriate funds. . . . To default upon the [Toyota] 'revenue bonds' would instantly destroy the credit of the Commonwealth" (*Hayes* v. *State*, 1987: 819–820). Therefore, he concluded, debt service on the bonds was a continuing state government obligation at odds with purpose of Sections 49 and 50.

The incremental tax mechanism, the dissenters claimed, constituted a double counting of future taxes not enjoyed by other taxpayers. Toyota's incremental tax payments, Justice Liebson argued, would give it a double tax credit "first satisfying current tax obligations and next applying the same taxes towards the 'rent' required for the issuance of revenue bonds" (*Hayes* v. *State*, 1987: 809). This would violate Section 3 of the Kentucky Constitution which prohibits "exclusive, separate public emoluments" and Section 171 which requires that taxes be "uniform upon all property of the same class" (Kentucky Constitution, Section 3 and 171). The Court's conclusion that reduction of unemployment and the generation of future tax revenues satisfies Section 171's requirement that "taxes . . . be levied and collected for 'public purposes,' " was also incorrect, according to Justice Liebson, because "the public purpose in Section 171 requires that . . . public means, not private means be used" (*Hayes* v. *State*, 1987: 814). Senate Bill no. 361 also failed to satisfy Section 3's public service provision which does not permit the state to "pay a private corporation for conducting its business in Kentucky unless it is performing a service directly for the government. [But] the economic activities of the Toyota Corporation . . . are conducted for a private purpose" (*Hayes* v. *State*, 1987: 813).

The Court's decision that the statute's incremental tax mechanism did not violate Section 177's prohibitions on lending the state's credit and governmental donations to private corporations was also flawed. In Justice Liebson's view, incremental taxes were a temporary lending of credit, because "Toyota is going to pay for the property through future taxes" (*Hayes* v. *State*, 1987: 811). The incremental tax mechanism also violated Section 177's prohibition that the "credit of the Commonwealth shall not be given, pledged, or loaned to any individual, company, corporation, or association" (*Hayes* v. *State*, 1987: 811). As Justice Liebson observed: the state had certainly lent the money in the meantime, because "there is no security for the bonds, except the state's promise to pay the debt service from the biennial appropriations from the general fund" (*Hayes* v. *State*, 1987: 811). As a consequence, it was "irrelevant whether incremental taxes are ever collected . . . [because they] are not even credited against the 'rent'. . . . The Commonwealth's credit is all that stands behind the bonds" (*Hayes* v. *State*, 1987: 811).

The incremental tax mechanism also violated Section 177's donation provision. In Justice Stephenson's view, incremental taxes were not a payment for the property conveyed by the state but a double counting of the obligation of every taxpayer and, as a consequence, "the transaction with Toyota is a gift. The state will purchase and deliver a deed to Toyota with no lien or other reservation" (*Hayes* v. *State*, 1987: 816). The incremental taxes were not consideration for the conveyance, because they were the "taxes paid by any other business for the benefit of government, including . . . payment of principal and interest on the revenue bonds" (*Hayes* v. *State*, 1987: 816). It was also incorrect to argue that Section 177 was "not offended even in situations where the conveyance occurs without consideration" as long as it served a public purpose, because Section 177 does not mention public purpose. As a consequence, Justice Stephenson concluded that the Court had "judicially amended Section 177 by adding 'except for a valid public purpose' " (*Hayes* v. *State*, 1987: 815). In the process, the Court had overruled its decision in *McGuffey* v. *Hall* (1977) where it had said: "Clearly . . . whether the objects of an expenditure are 'public' or otherwise is irrelevant to Constitution Section 177" (*Hayes* v. *State*, 1987: 816).

In sum, the dissenters argued that the Court succumbed to powerful nonjudicial arguments and in the name of political expediency "eviscerated the Kentucky Constitution" (*Hayes* v. *State*, 1987: 816) by destroying the "overlapping and interlocking" character of the fiscal restraints in the 1891 Constitution in order to allow the state government to use Senate Bill no. 361's revenue bond concept and incremental tax mechanisms to finance economic development. Justice Vance concluded that the Court was willing to "wink at apparent evasions of the Constitution when they are considered to be imperative for the process of the state and the benefit of the public" (*Hayes* v. *State*, 1987: 821). As a consequence, he and Justice Stephenson agreed with Justice Liebson that the *Hayes* decision was "a watershed opinion in constitutional law, confirmation that so long as the Governor and General Assembly perceive the need, there are no constitutional restraints on the power of state government to raise and spend money for the benefit of a private business" (*Hayes* v. *State*, 1987: 805).

Summary

The Kentucky Supreme Court's decision in *Hayes* v. *State Property and Buildings Commission* (1987) was a great decision. As Justice Holmes observed: "Great cases . . . make bad law . . . because of some accident of immediate overwhelming interest which appeals to the feelings and distorts the judgment. These immediate interests exercise a kind of hydraulic pressure . . . before which even well settled principles of law will bend" (*Northern Securities Co.* v. *U.S.*, 1904: 400–401). In *Hayes*, the Court could have turned to its revenue bond cases from *J.D. van Hooser* to *Blythe* which, as the dissenters correctly argued, would have provided more than sufficient authority to strike down Senate Bill no. 361. If the Court had declared the statute unconstitutional, the Collins Administration would still have had three constitutional financing options.

First, the revenue bond would have authorized the State Property and Buildings Commission to sell bonds, to purchase and improve the property, and, while holding title to the property, to retire the bonds from the rents received from Toyota. The Court's revenue bond cases clearly indicate that this approach would have offended none of the state constitution's public purpose, credit, and debt provisions. Second, a general obligation bond could have been used to finance the land purchase and improvements. The Court's precedents would also have upheld the constitutionality of this industrial financing mechanisms, as long as the general obligation bond, per Sections 49 and 50, had received electoral approval. Third, a constitutional amendment could have legitimized the Kentucky-Toyota Agreement by specifically authorizing the state to use the Economic Development Project mechanism.

The Collins administration must have rejected all these options as threats to the agreement it had negotiated with Toyota. A general obligation bond and revenue bond would not have permitted the immediate conveyance of the property to Toyota as the Kentucky-Toyota Agreement provided. The use of a general obligation bond and constitutional amendment would have imposed a considerable time delay, because both would have required voter approval. As a consequence, all three options would have required a differently written agreement and consumed more time, either of which might have led Toyota to choose another location in a competitor state.

The Kentucky Supreme Court succumbed to the "hydraulic pressure" of the Collins administration's arguments about the compelling need for economic growth by choosing none of these options. Instead, the Court chose the politically more deferential path and upheld the statute's Economic Development Project mechanism by creating two new constitutional legal fictions.

First, the *Hayes* decision legitimized a public financing creature which may be called an Economic Development Project (EDP) revenue bond. The EDP revenue bond is not a revenue bond; it is instead a moral obligation bond which dispenses with the reality of a biennial serial lease and the rent payment mechanism while continuing to use their language. The Commerce Cabinet does not really use its biennial general fund appropriation to pay rent to the Commission, because it has no project to lease. The Cabinet merely transfers its general fund appropriation to the Commission which uses it to repay the bonds as long as the General Assembly meets its moral obligation to appropriate the funds.

The second legal fiction is the incremental tax mechanism. The terminology appears to have been borrowed from one form of industrial financing bond: the tax increment bond. Here incremental taxes refer to "[t]he difference between the frozen property taxes at the beginning of development and the increased value of property due to the improvements" (Hamilton, 1986: 11). These tax receipts are placed in a special fund and are to be used solely to retire the bonded indebtedness. However, the tax receipts used to pay off the Toyota Industrial Development Project are assigned from the state's general fund. As a consequence, these incremental taxes "will be used . . . merely as a bookkeeping device which the legislature proposes to use as one measure of the consideration provided by Toyota to the state in exchange for the conveyance of the property at no cost to Toyota'' (Hamilton, 1986: 11).

In sum, the Court's use of these two legal fictions has permitted it to judicially amend the state constitution's fiscal barriers contained in Sections 3, 49, 50, 171, and 177. In the future, these judicial changes will permit the state to issue economic development project revenue bonds to purchase and improve large tracts of land which it will convey in fee simple to a private corporation in consideration of that corporation paying the taxes that any other corporation doing business in Kentucky is obligated to pay. The state will then pay the debt service on the bonds from successive biennial appropriations from the state's general fund.

CONCLUSION

What conclusions can be drawn regarding the competitive advantages states may derive from their constitutions and the comparative status of the funding sources and mechanisms states have used to provide interest and production subsidies?

Constitutions may confer advantages upon or place impediments in the way of state economic development programs. Were Michigan and Illinois with their twentieth century constitutions necessarily advantaged? Their constitution's taxation and current expenditure clauses resemble those of the other four mid-American states. Their state courts have not interpreted those clauses in a manner sufficiently different to provide their governments with a constitutional advantage. The Michigan and Illinois Constitutions do, however, have more liberal debt provisions. Yet these clauses have not provided any meaningful advantage. One state, Ohio, has liberally amended its debt provision. What about the other states? Two significant constitutional mechanisms have equalized state industrial recruitment activities: the public authority and the revenue bond. In Illinois and Ohio both state government agencies and public authorities may issue revenue bonds. Michigan and the other three states require revenue bonds to be issued by public authorities, but this formality has imposed no meaningful impediment to state industrial recruitment. Public authorities, revenue bonds, and revenue bond variants—the industrial development bond, and moral obligation bond, and the serial lease—have almost always been upheld against challenges that they violate the state's constitutional debt provision.

State courts have played a significant role in expanding the constitutional parameters for industrial recruitment. This judicial edifice, most of which was constructed before the recruitment of Japanese automobile manufacturers, focused on the means states may employ and the ends they may serve.

State constitutions uniformly limit state action to public purposes. The six state courts have commonly deferred to legislative declarations of public purpose. These courts have also upheld worker training, infrastructure improvements, and industrial development projects as serving public purposes: increasing employment opportunities, the business climate, and the state's economic health. As a consequence, no one had any constitutional doubts about these elements of incentive agreements. The plant site financing, in part, is more constitutionally troublesome in Illinois, because the site was donated to Diamond-Star and in Indiana, because it was conveyed for a nominal sum. Yet, as I have argued, if these issues were to come before their respective state courts, those courts would likely decide in the legislatively deferential manner their courts have previously decided similar cases by finding that the donations and conveyances serve a primary public purpose while providing only an incidental benefit to the private corporation. Clearly these courts would reach to find a public purpose much as the Kentucky Supreme Court did in *Hayes* (1987) by not only equating Section 3's public service with Section 171's public purpose clause, but also by reading a public purpose requirement into Section 177's credit and donation clauses.

If the economic development ends, which state legislatures have sought to promote, have not long delayed state courts, the means employed—the appropriation of money, the extension of credit, and the making of gifts and donations—along with the public consequences, principally the creation of public debt, have invited substantially greater judicial scrutiny. The principal object of judicial attention has been the bonds which states have issued to finance their infrastructure improvements and industrial development projects: revenue bonds and their variants.

Revenue bonds, initially used to finance state-owned and state-operated projects retired from revenue generated by the project, had been legislatively modified and judicially legitimized in three important ways by 1980. First, state courts have approved legislation providing for the use of industrial development bonds which were retired from the rentals paid by the private corporation. Tennessee used these local bonds to finance the entire Nissan facility, while Kentucky used state bonds to finance the Toyota building construction.

Second, state courts have also upheld the use by public authorities, and also by state agencies in Ohio and Illinois, of revenue bonds which are retired from dedicated revenue sources. Michigan made the $21 million Mazda loan from economic development bonds which were retired from state oil and gas lease revenues and also financed $3.1 million in on-site railroad improvements from state gasoline tax proceeds. Kentucky also financed the road improvements with $47 million in road revenue bonds which will also be retired from state gasoline tax proceeds.

Third, state courts have accepted legislation authorizing the use of moral obligation bonds repaid by means of serial leases in circumstances in which a public authority would issue revenue bonds for a public project to which it holds title. The authority would then lease the project to a state agency which makes rent payments to the authority from its annual or biennial legislative appropriations. When the bonds were retired, then title to the project would pass to the state agency. This public project-based moral obligation bond and its serial lease repayment mechanism have undergone substantial modifications as a consequence of the Indiana and Kentucky industrial experiences of the 1980s.

In Indiana, Fuji-Isuzu nominally leases the Lafayette site from the Indiana Employment Development Commission (IEDC) which purchased the site with an Indiana Bond Bank loan which will be repaid with three general fund appropriations. When IEDC retires the Bond Bank notes, then Fuji-Isuzu is entitled to purchase the property for a nominal sum. The legislature is, of course, not legally obligated to appropriate the funds to retire the IEDC loan, but the note holders at least have a security interest in the improved property and a letter of credit.

In Kentucky, the moral obligation bond has been taken one step further. The State Property and Buildings Commission purchased the site with Economic Development Project (EDP) revenue bonds which the Commerce Cabinet will repay from successive biennial appropriations, but the Cabinet does not lease the property, nor does Toyota, even nominally, because the Commission does not hold title; Toyota does in fee simple. The legislature is not legally obligated to appropriate the funds, but the bond holders have no security in the property or letter of credit, only the promise of the state to repay. If the EDP revenue bond is the twilight of the revenue bond, it may also signal the appearance of the public junk bond. If that is true, then Justice Liebson may be correct that *Hayes* v. *State Property and Buildings Commission* is a watershed case in state constitutional law.

NOTES

1. These fiscal limitations were the product of two nineteenth century constitutional revolutions which occurred in response to state and local government financing of private economic development. The first began when state governments lent their credit and borrowed to finance canal and railroad construction in the 1820s and 1830s. The Panic of 1837 brought several states, including Indiana, near to bankruptcy and generated considerable popular resentment which resulted in the adoption of constitutional limitations on state financial powers by means of constitutional amendment or revision. The revised constitutions included those of Illinois (1848), Kentucky (1850), Michigan (1850), Indiana (1851), and Ohio (1851). After the Civil War, a second constitutional revolution occurred when municipalities, unencumbered by constitutional limitations on state government "freely granted favors to the railroads" (Bowmar, 1967: 864). The Panic of 1873 and the ensuing economic depression led states, once again, to amend or to provide in their rewritten constitutions, including the Kentucky Constitution of 1891, financial limitations on their political subdivisions.

2. The term incentive agreement is somewhat misleading. The Indiana Memorandum of Understanding is the only comprehensive document which addresses all the major incentives the state will provide to Fuji-Isuzu: property, acquisition, on-site improvements, off-site infrastructure improvements, and worker training (Memorandum of Understanding, 1986). The incentives provided by the other five states were not set forth in one document termed an agreement or memorandum of understanding, but were instead based on a collection of letters from state and local officials which made separate commitments.

3. The incentive package costs, reported in state government publications, newspapers, and professional journals are sometimes inaccurate, because they do not identify the precise local, state, and federal government funding source. The interest and production subsidy costs reported in this chapter have been verified by telephone conversations with economic development officials and agencies in the six states.

4. The six mid-American states have supplemented these tax-based training and infrastructure improvements, in part, with federal job training, community development, and highway funds, although there has been considerable variation in state use of federal funds.

Illinois, Indiana, and Ohio used no federal highway funds. In Michigan, federal highway funds paid $4.5 million of the $5 million for Mazda-related highway improvements. The remaining $500,000 came from an Urban Development Action grant (Lontz, 1989). In Tennessee, federal highway funds paid $5 million of the $23.7 million cost for Nissan-related highway improvements. In Kentucky, federal highway funds paid $5,171,000 for improvements to Interstate 75 and US 62 East (Kentucky Transportation Cabinet, 1989).

Federal Job Training in Partnership Act (JTPA) funds were not widely used primarily because the automobile manufacturers were unwilling to accept the conditions for their use. Michigan, Ohio, and Tennessee used no JTPA funds. Kentucky has not accessed its $22 million in JTPA funds for Toyota (Furr, 1989). In Illinois, only $1.4 million of the $40 million cost of Diamond-Star worker training has come from JTPA funds (Dennis, 1989). In Indiana, JTPA funds may provide up to $8 million for Fuji-Isuzu worker training.

5. The Cabinet is the term used to identify Kentucky's executive departments.

6. The following general funds were appropriated to the Ohio Industrial Training Program (OITP) for Honda worker training: 1984, $205,560 for the Anna engine plant; 1986, $36,274 for the Marysville auto plant; and 1987, $500,000 for Anna engine plant expansion. Total OITP funds: $741,834. (Honda-State Assistance, 1988.)

7. Honda could have used public financing. State and local government revenue bond financing was constitutionally permissible. Article 8, Section 13, added to the 1851 Ohio Constitution in 1966, provides that it is "a proper public purpose for the state or its public authorities . . . to issue revenue bonds [in order] . . . to create or preserve jobs and employment opportunities" (Ohio Constitution, Article 8, Section 13).

8. The $10 million for the purchase of the land and $25 million for the preparation of the plant site were part of $125 million in Kentucky interest and production subsidies to Toyota. A December 4, 1985 letter from Governor Martha Layne Collins and Secretary of the Kentucky Commerce Cabinet, Carroll Knicely, to Dr. Shoichiro Toyoda, President of Toyota Motor Corporation, set forth the Commonwealth's intent to convey the improved site: "The Georgetown site shall be conveyed without cost to Toyota . . . by a general warranty deed, with full covenants of title conveying an unencumbered marketable title in fee simple, free and clear of all liens and encumbrances." (Collins and Knicely, 1985: 1 and 2).

9. The Kentucky-Toyota Agreement formally commits the Commonwealth to submit legislation to finance the acquisition and improvement of the site and after the Project Improvements have been completed, provides that "the Commonwealth will forthwith convey the Project Site, as so improved, in fee simple" (Agreement, Section 5 and 7, 1986: 4, 5).

10. Senate Bill no. 361 became an addition to the State Property and Building Commission statute as Kentucky Revised Statutes Annotated, Section 56.440–56.590.

11. The State Property and Buildings Commission is the primary state revenue bond-

issuing agency, and it issues revenue bonds for various projects at the request of, for, and on behalf of various other state agencies.

12. The Kentucky-Toyota Agreement commits the Commonwealth "to take such actions as may be required for the validation through judicial proceedings of any legislation which may be enacted by the General Assembly . . . for financing of the Project Site and Project Improvements and the conveyance thereof to Toyota" (Agreement, Section 6, 1986: 5).

13. The intervenors sought unsuccessfully to make a broad-based constitutional challenge to all major features of the Kentucky-Toyota Agreement including the expenditure of general revenue funds which House Bill no. 398 authorized for the gas and water lines, employees training, and the local sewer treatment plant (*Maddox* v. *Mills, Complaint Seeking Declaration of Rights*, Franklin Circuit Court, Ky., 1986).

REFERENCES

Books and Articles

Benkelman, Susan. 1985. "Mazda Gets $21 Million State Loan." *Detroit News*, 4 April, 1A, 12A.

Bowmar, Robert H. 1967. "The Anachronism Called Debt Limitation." *Iowa Law Review* 52: 863–899.

Brammer, Jack. 1986. "Court Hears 'Toyota Deal' Challenges." *Lexington Herald-Leader*, 24 September, B-12.

———. 1987. "Incentives for Toyota Will Be Debated in High Court." *Lexington Herald-Leader*, 15 January, B-1.

Brammer, Jack, and Alecia Swasy. 1986. "Judge Rules $35 Million in Incentives for Plant Legal." *Lexington Herald-Leader*, 18 October, A-12.

Brammer, Jack, and John Winn Miller. 1987. "Toyota Incentives Legal, Court Rules." *Lexington Herald-Leader*, 12 June, A-1, 12.

Chellgren, Mark. 1986. "Wiggins, Allies Want Collins Impeached." *Louisville Courier-Journal*, 3 September, B-7.

Cohen, Ray. 1986. "Collins Testifies She Didn't Know Toyota Details." *Lexington Herald-Leader*, 2 July, B-1, 4.

Duke, Jacqueline. 1986. "State Files Test Suit on Toyota." *Lexington Herald-Leader*, 8 May, B-1.

Gelfand, M. David, and Peter W. Salsich, Jr. 1985. *State and Local Taxation and Finance*. St. Paul: West.

Gold, David M. 1985. "Public Aid to Private Enterprise under the Ohio Constitution: Section 4, 6, and 13 of Article VII in Historical Perspective." *Toledo Law Review* 16: 405–464.

Graves, W. Brooke. 1960. *Major Problems in State Constitutional Revision*. Chicago: Public Administration Service.

Gray, John, and Dean Spina. 1980. "State and Local Industrial Location Incentives: The Well-Stocked Candy Store." *Journal of Corporation Law* 5: 517–687.

Kline, John. 1985. "The Expanding International Agenda of State Government." *State Government* 55: 57–64.

Ledebur, Larry C., William W. Hamilton, and Stephen Rabinowitz. 1986. *State Constitutional Barriers to Economic Development*. Washington: Aslan Associates.

Marlin, Martin R. 1987. "Industrial Revenue Bonds at 50: A Golden Anniversary Review." *Economic Development Quarterly* 1: 391–410.

Note (Kelly Beers Rouse). 1988. "Facing the Economic Challenges of the Eighties: The Kentucky Constitution and Hayes v. State Property and Buildings Commission of Kentucky." *Northern Kentucky Law Review* 15: 645–656.

Pinsky, David E. 1963. "State Constitutional Limitations on Public Industrial Financing: An Historical and Economic Approach." *University of Pennsylvania Law Review* 111: 265–325.

Rasmussen, David W., Marc Bendick, Jr., and Larry C. Ledebur. 1984. "A Methodology for Selecting Economic Development Incentives." *Growth and Change* 15: 18–25.

Wilson, Dee. 1985. "Collins Unveils $125 Million Incentive Package for Toyota." *Louisville Courier-Journal*, 18 December, A-1, 18.

Government Documents

Illinois

Facts About the Diamond-Star Incentive Package. Undated. Illinois Department of Commerce and Community Affairs.

Smith-Hurd Illinois Annotated Statutes. 1988. Build Illinois Act. Chapter 127, Section 2701. St. Paul: West.

———. 1988. Build Illinois Bond Act. Chapter 127, Section 2801. St. Paul: West.

———. 1988. Build Illinois Fund. Chapter 127, Section 142z-9. St. Paul: West.

———. 1988. Constitution of the State of Illinois. Article 8: Finance and Revenue, Section 9. St. Paul: West.

———. 1988. Large Business Development Act. Chapter 127, Section 2710. St. Paul: West.

Indiana

Burns Indiana Statutes Annotated. 1978, 1988. Constitution of the State of Indiana, Articles 10 and 11. Indianapolis: Bobbs-Merrill.

———. 1978, 1988. Creation and Use of Industrial Development Funds. Sections 4–4–8–1 to 4–4–8–12. Indianapolis: Bobbs-Merrill.

———. 1978, 1988. Indiana Bond Bank. Sections 5–1.5–1–1 to 5–1.5–9–10. Indianapolis: Bobbs-Merrill.

———. 1978, 1988. Indiana Employment Development Commission. Sections 4–4–11–1 to 4–4–11–36.5. Indianapolis: Bobbs-Merrill.

———. 1978, 1988. Indiana Employment Development Commission Law: Definitions. Sections 4–4–10.9–1.5 to 4–4–10.9–27.7. Indianapolis: Bobbs-Merrill.

Indiana Bond Bank and Indiana Employment Development Commission. June 1, 1987. Purchase Agreement.

Indiana Employment Development Commission and the Indiana Bond Bank. June 1, 1987. Pledge Agreement.

Indiana Employment Development Commission to the Indiana Bond Bank. June 1, 1987. Promissory Note no. R-001.

King, J. B. June 2, 1987. Letter to Board of Directors, Indiana Bond Bank. "Special Counsel Opinion of Barker & Daniels."

Memorandum of Understanding Which Sets Forth the Understanding of John M. Muntz, Lieutenant Governor, on Behalf of the Executive Branch of the State of Indiana, and Fuji Heavy Industries, Ltd. and Isuzu Motors Limited. December 1, 1986.

Kentucky

Collins, Martha Layne and Carroll Knicely. December 4, 1986. Letter to Shoichiro Toyoda, Re: Conveyance of the Georgetown Site to Toyota Motor Corporation and Site Preparation Improvements.

Commonwealth of Kentucky. General Assembly. March 10, 1986. Senate Bill no. 361.

Commonwealth of Kentucky. Transportation Cabinet. February 28, 1989. Toyota Access Roads Costs through 2/28/89.

Commonwealth of Kentucky and Toyota Motor Corporation. February 25, 1986. Agreement By and Between the Commonwealth of Kentucky and Toyota Motor Corporation, a Japanese Corporation.

Hamilton, William W. September 3, 1986. Affidavit, State Property and Buildings Commission of Kentucky v. Hayes, No. 86-CI–0884 (Franklin Circuit Court, Kentucky. October 21, 1986).

Kentucky Revised Statutes Annotated. 1973, 1988. Constitution of the Commonwealth of Kentucky, Sections 3, 49, 50, 171, 177. Indianapolis: Bobbs-Merrill.

———. 1973, 1988. Kentucky Development Finance Authority. Section 154.701 to 154.705. Indianapolis: Bobbs-Merrill.

———. 1973, 1988. Property and Buildings Commission. Chapter 56. Indianapolis: Bobbs-Merrill.

———. 1973, 1988. Revenue Bonds for Miscellaneous City or County Projects: Issuance of Bonds. Section 103.210. Indianapolis: Bobbs-Merrill.

———. 1973, 1988. Roads, Waterways, and Aviation: Turnpike Revenue Bonds. Chapter 177.450. Indianapolis: Bobbs-Merrill.

Ledebur, Larry C. September 2, 1986. Affidavit, State Property and Buildings Commission of Kentucky v. Hayes, No. 86-CI–0884 (Franklin Circuit Court, Ky. October 21, 1986).

Michigan

Mazda Summary. Undated. Michigan Department of Commerce.

Michigan Compiled Laws Annotated. 1985, 1988. Constitution of the State of Michigan. Article 9. St. Paul: West.

———. 1985, 1988. Michigan Strategic Fund. Section 125.2001 et. seq. St. Paul: West.

Michigan Public Acts. 1982. Economic Development Act. Act 70. 1982. St. Paul: West.

Ohio

Honda-State Assistance. 1988. Columbus: Ohio Department of Development.

Page's Ohio Revised Code Annotated. 1979, 1988. Constitution of the State of Ohio. Article 8. Cincinnati: Anderson.

Tennessee

Burnett, Wilton. January 23, 1981. Nissan Budget. Nashville: Department of Economic and Community Development.

Industrial Development Board of Rutherford County, Tennessee and Nissan Motor Manufacturing Corporation, U.S.A. October 13, 1980. Memorandum of Agreement.

Industrial Development Board of Rutherford County, Tennessee and Nissan Motor Manufacturing Corporation. October 12, 1980. A Resolution Authorizing the Execution and Delivery of an Inducement Contract By and Between the Industrial Development Board of Rutherford County, Tennessee and Nissan Motor Manufacturing Corporation, Ltd. U.S.A.

Tennessee Code Annotated. 1980, 1988. Constitution of the State of Tennessee. Article 2. Charlottesville: Mitchie.

Cases

Albritton v. City of Winona, 178 S. 799 (Miss. 1938).

American National Bank and Trust Company v. Indiana Department of Highways, 439 N.E.2d 1129 (Ind. 1982).

Bazell v. City of Cincinnati, 233 N.E.2d 864 (Ohio 1968).

Blythe v. Transportation Cabinet of the Commonwealth of Kentucky, 660 S.W.2d 668 (Ky. 1983).

Dyche v. City of London, 288 S.W.2d 648 (Ky. 1956).

Eaves v. State Bridge Commission, 269 N.W.2d 388 (Mich. 1936).

Edwards v. Housing Authority of City of Muncie, 19 N.E.2d 741 (Ind. 1939).

Ennis v. State Highway Commission, 108 N.E.2d 687 (Ind. 1952).

Faulconer v. City of Danville, 232 S.W.2d 80 (Ky. 1950).

Guthrie v. Curlin, 263 S.W.2d 240 (Ky. 1953).

Hayes v. State Property and Buildings Commission, 731 S.W.2d 797 (Ky. 1987).

Industrial Development Authority v. Eastern Kentucky Regional Planning Commission, 332 S.W.2d 274 (Ky. 1960).

In Re Request for Advisory Opinion Enrolled Senate Bill 558 (Being 1976 P.A. 240). 254 N.W.2d 544 (Mich. 1977).

J. D. van Hooser & Co. v. University of Kentucky, 90 S.W.2d 1029 (Ky. 1936).

Kauer v. Defenbacher, 91 N.E.2d 512 (Ohio 1950).

Maddox v. Mills, No. 86-CI-0084 (Franklin Circuit Court, Ky. 1986).

Marshall Field & Company v. Village of South Barrington, 415 N.E.2d 1277 (Ill. App. 1981).

McConnell v. City of Lebanon, 314 S.W.2d 12 (Tenn. 1958).

McGuffey v. Hall, 557 S.W.2d 401 (Ky. 1977).

Northern Securities Co. v. U.S., 193 U.S. 197 (1904).

O'Fallon Development Company v. City of O'Fallon, 356 N.E.2d 1293 (Ill. App. 1976).

Orbison v. Welch, 179 N.E.2d 727 (Ind. 1962).

People v. Illinois State Highway Commission, 120 N.E.2d 35 (Ill. 1954).

People v. McMackin, 291 N.E.2d 807 (Ill. 1972).

Preston v. Clements, 232 S.W.2d 85 (Ky. 1950).

Request for Advisory Opinion In Re Enrolled Senate Bills 1385 and 1387 (Being 1976 P.A. 295 and 1976 P.A. 297), 259 N.W.2d 129 (Mich. 1977).

Rosemont Building Supply v. Illinois Highway Trust Fund Authority. 256 N.E.2d 569 (Ill. 1970).

Schureman v. State Highway Commission, 141 N.W.2d 62 (Mich. 1966).

State v. Brand, 197 N.E.2d 328 (Ky. 1964).

State v. Griffith, 25 N.E.2d 847 (Ohio 1940).
State Property and Buildings Commission v. Hayes, No.86-CI-0884. (Franklin Circuit Court, Ky. 1986).
Steup v. Indiana Housing Finance Authority, 402 N.E.2d 1215 (Ind. 1980).
Turnpike Authority of Kentucky v. Wall, 336 S.W.2d 551 (Ky. 1960).

Interviews

Bratcher, David. Kentucky Development Finance Authority. February 3, 1989.
Cole, Roger. Kentucky Transportation Cabinet. March 15, 1989.
Dees, Daniel. Illinois Department of Transportation. February 3, 1989.
Dennis, Herbert. Illinois Department of Commerce and Community Development. January 6 and 31, 1989.
Dorman, Jeffrey. Indiana Agricultural Development Corporation. January 10, 1989.
Fraser, Robert. Michigan Department of Labor. January 31, 1989.
Furr, Charles. Kentucky Human Resources Cabinet. February 23, 1989.
Giscala, Jonathan. Illinois Department of Commerce and Community Development. January 25, 1989.
Hamilton, John. Illinois Department of Commerce and Community Affairs. January 10, 1989.
Hammond, Jerry. Kentucky State Buildings and Trades Council. October 17, 1988.
Lontz, William. Michigan Department of Commerce. February 24, 1989.
McGuire, Michael. Tennessee Department of Economic and Community Development. February 21, 1989.
Parsons, Robert. Tennessee Department of Labor. February 23, 1989.
Pentilla, Roy. Michigan Department of Commerce, February 28, 1989.
Pitcher, Eric. Illinois Department of Commerce and Community Affairs. February 3, 1989.
Preston, Charles. Indiana Department of Commerce. January 6 and February 3, 1989.
Ross, Read. Michigan Department of Commerce. January 20 and 31, 1989.
Sellers, William T. Attorney, Industrial Development Board of Rutherford County, Tennessee. January 5, 1989.
Wallace, William. Tennessee Department of Transportation. March 16, 1989.
Wickliffe, Charles. Kentucky Finance and Administration Cabinet. February 10, March 14, 1989.
Wise, Herbert. Ohio Department of Development. January 10 and 19, February 24, 1989.

Letters

Bachelor, Lynn. February 16, 1989. Letter to William Green, Re: Michigan financial incentives to Mazda.
Sellers, William T. January 6, 1989. Letter to William Green, Re: Revenue bonds issued by Industrial Development of Rutherford County for the Nissan Project.

PART II

MID-AMERICAN STATE PERSPECTIVES

4

Flat Rock, Michigan, Trades a Ford for a Mazda: State Policy and the Evaluation of Plant Location Incentives

Lynn W. Bachelor

The decision of Mazda Motors Corporation to locate its first U.S. automobile assembly plant in Flat Rock, Michigan, represented a major success for the state's economic development program. Mazda's modern assembly plant exemplified the themes of technological innovation and the "factory of the future" which have been central elements of Governor James Blanchard's industrial recruitment efforts. The plant is perceived as a milestone in reversing the negative image of a declining "Rustbelt" economy and in paving the way to cooperation between Japanese firms and unionized American workers. But, as with other major economic development projects, expectations exceeded initial impacts, and as Mazda Motors Manufacturing (U.S.A.) celebrated the first anniversary of the opening of its assembly plant in September 1988, criticisms of the policies used in attracting the plant persisted.

The incentive package developed by state and local officials for Mazda included loans and grants valued at $48.8 million and a local tax abatement estimated to be worth $87 million over a 14-year period. Major elements of the incentive package were:

—A training program for new Mazda employees, funded jointly by the state and the corporation, which included sending 300 supervisory employees to Japan to be trained and then to serve as trainers at the new plant. The State of Michigan's share of the $40 million program was $19 million.

—A low-interest, long-term loan to Mazda, covering part of the cost of construction of the $450 million plant. The Michigan Economic Development Authority provided a 20-year, $21 million loan at eight percent interest.

—Improvements to roads, rail lines, and sewers to serve the plant. Road improvements cost the state approximately $5.2 million, rail improvements were paid for by the state ($3.1 million) and the Grand Trunk Railroad ($4 million), and sewer development was paid for with $1.6 million in federal UDAG funds.

—A 100 percent tax abatement for 14 years (2 years of plant construction and 12 years of plant operations) from the City of Flat Rock, valued at $87 million. Under Michigan Public Act 198 (1974 rev.), if a plant is a "replacement facility," its assessment may be frozen at the assessed value of the facility it is replacing for up to the first 12 years it is in operation (a 100 percent abatement); a "new facility" may be granted a 50 percent abatement, in which taxes are paid on 50 percent of its assessed value, for up to 12 years. The Mazda plant was considered a "replacement facility" because it was built on the site of the obsolete Ford Michigan Casting Center.

Development of the Mazda package entailed complex intergovernmental relationships and required compromises among their interests. As a consequence, critics have charged that the City of Flat Rock was required to bear a disproportionately large share of the cost of the project by providing the 100 percent tax abatement (Hill et al., 1988: 85). The overall cost of the package was also criticized as excessive. For example, a newspaper editorial openly questioned "whether we can afford to put up $34,285 for every job we generate . . . the Mazda figure [is] based on 3,500 jobs for an incentive package of $120 million" (*Detroit News*, 31 May 1985). The Mazda project, however, has also been praised for its positive impact on the Michigan economy and the downriver area. A *Detroit Free Press* editorial titled, "Mazda: The Rising Sun Shines on a Rebounding Michigan," captured the essence of this perspective (*Detroit Free Press*, 31 May 1985). Through examining the policies and relationships which brought about the location of the Mazda plant in Flat Rock, this chapter will assess the validity of these competing assessments: did public officials pay too high a price when they traded a Ford for a Mazda?

Specifically, the objective of the chapter is to evaluate locational incentives and projected benefits of the plant in relation to the interests of Mazda and state and local officials. A central concern of the study is the use of economic development policy goals by state officials in formulating an incentive package which would also conform to corporate concerns. Development of the incentive package, however, was not without conflict, as it required intergovernmental coordination and negotiation to obtain the support of key officials and the funding sources required. Review of the perspectives of the actors involved reveals areas of agreement and disagreement on the costs and benefits of the project and suggests that state and local officials evaluate costs and benefits quite differently, and that both qualitative and quantitative factors play an important part in these evaluations.

Figure 4.1
Impact of Ford Plant on Flat Rock's Tax Base

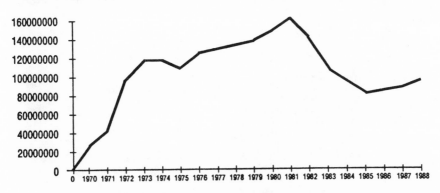

BACKGROUND

The Mazda assembly plant is located on a 400-acre site in Flat Rock, Michigan, 25 miles southwest of Detroit in Wayne County's "downriver" industrial corridor. The site formerly housed Ford Motor Company's Michigan Casting Center, which, prior to its closing in 1981, provided 67 percent of Flat Rock's tax base, with an assessed value of $97.9 million. After the plant closed, the reduction in Ford's assessment and taxes was phased in over a five-year period: in 1985, its state equalized value (SEV)[1] was $20.9 million and its base bill was $371,334 (compared with taxes of nearly $1.4 million in 1980). The public sector impact on the city of 7,000 was devastating: eight of its 53 full-time employees were laid off, including six police officers, and its bond rating was dropped from "A" to "Baa" by Moody's. Moreover, an inadequate local sewer system had resulted in an EPA moratorium on new construction, precluding diversification of the tax base or new residential development.

The impact of the Ford closing on Flat Rock's tax base is illustrated in Figures 4.1 and 4.2. In Figure 4.1, the opening of the casting plant in 1971 is shown to have brought about a marked increase in assessed values, which remain relatively steady until 1981, the year of the closing. The phasing in of the Ford assessment reduction is evident in the steady decline through 1985. Reassessment of land value for the Mazda site and the positive impact of the Mazda announcement account for a slight increase after 1985. Figure 4.2 illustrates the size of the plant's contribution to Flat Rock's tax base. Prior to 1981, its assessment (indicated by the solid bars on the graph) represented more than two-thirds of the city's total. As the decrease in Ford's assessment was phased in after the 1981 closing, both the plant's share and the total SEV declined steadily. Because the tax abatement granted to Mazda froze its assessment at the 1985

Figure 4.2
Ford/Mazda Share of Assessed Property Value, as Measured by State Equalized
Value (SEV)

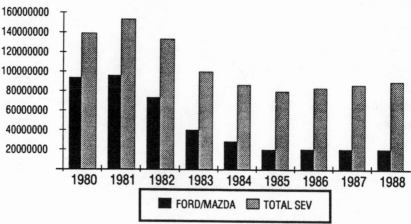

Ford value, Mazda's share of the tax base (1986–1988) has remained much smaller than Ford's had been prior to 1981.

The downriver area had been hard hit by plant closings in the late 1970s, due to cutbacks in automobile manufacturing and related industries. Employment levels of the region's 15 largest employers declined from 36,269 in July 1979 to 13,899 in February 1983, a decline of 61 percent; these figures include the 4,600 jobs lost by the closing of the Ford casting plant (Pruchaska, 1985: 6). The unemployment level for Wayne County in 1982 was 15.8 percent. In this context, the Downriver Community Conference (DCC), a regional association of area municipalities, identified economic development as its top program priority and obtained federal and foundation grants to establish a demonstration retraining program for laid-off autoworkers and to provide technical assistance to small businesses to improve their access to federal defense procurement contracts (Henry, 1988). In response to a study by economic strategy consultants, DCC's economic development program sought to increase diversification from basic manufacturing into more "technologically oriented" industries and to counteract the area's "Rustbelt" image. The uniqueness of the Ford facility precluded any attempts to find a new use for the casting plant site.

At the same time, officials of the Michigan Department of Commerce were in regular contact with Mazda and other Japanese firms, circulating general information on the state's advantages as a U.S. plant site. There were no serious or detailed discussions with Mazda, or about the Flat Rock site, however, until early 1984. Such discussions with the Japanese were consistent with the state's economic development objectives of expansion of the economic base through attraction of major manufacturing facilities and development of advanced, automated manufacturing. This strategy is perceived as building from the strengths of the state's economy—manufacturing and a skilled work force—to reestablish Michigan's position as a center of complex manufacturing through encouraging technological advances by existing industries and attraction of technologically sophisticated firms (Osborne, 1988: 153).

An additional consideration in state policy has been maximization of economic impacts resulting from a new plant. These economic impact analyses were generated from a model developed by the Michigan Department of Commerce and the University of Michigan Institute of Labor and Industrial Relations (Fulton et al., 1984). The model projects secondary development and jobs generated by a particular industrial facility, and is used by state officials to assess appropriate levels of financial incentives for a developer by weighing the long-term gains against short-term costs. One deficiency of the model, as applied to the Mazda case, is that gains are measured for the state economy (suppliers locating anywhere in Michigan are counted as an economic gain), while costs may be concentrated in a particular locality (e.g., the municipality granting a tax abatement). Former Deputy Commerce Director Peter Walters summarized this relationship with the observation that "positive economic impact is less closer to the plant" (Walters, 1988).

Determination of appropriate development incentives also requires estimation of the state's advantages and disadvantages in relation to other potential plant locations and a firm's primary locational concerns. The ILIR/Commerce Department study, utilizing an extensive data base on industrial profiles, concluded that Michigan was "very well situated in terms of resource availability for auto assembly" but found "distinct cost disadvantages to producing in Michigan" (Fulton et al., 1984: 11). The main focus of its comparisons was on the states of Nebraska and South Carolina, which had been identified as potential sites by Mazda. Michigan's primary advantages were identified as its substantially higher internal supply percentage for automobile production, the diversity and capacity of the state's supplier base, and its large pool of qualified workers (Fulton et al., 1984: 20). Its cost disadvantages were found to be the result of significantly higher wage costs in the state.

GENERAL ISSUES IN STATE ECONOMIC DEVELOPMENT POLICY

Michigan's economic base, long dominated by durable goods manufacturing and related services, underwent significant transformations in the early 1980s. Most visible were the inroads made by foreign competition in the automobile, primary metals, and machine tool industries, which began in the late 1970s and were triggered by the Arab oil embargo's reduction of consumer demand for traditional large cars. Not surprisingly, Ford's Flat Rock casting plant, a facility producing large (V-8) engines, was a victim of this shift, as its production levels far exceeded demand for large cars (Pruchaska, 1985: 8). During the same period,

evolution of the auto industry to more standardized means of production contributed to a shift of jobs to less skilled, lower-wage labor in Sunbelt states.
Nevertheless, some Michigan manufacturing firms grew during this period. One
study characterized this growing segment as newer, smaller, and more reliant
upon technological advances in production methods (Jackson, 1988: 98) and
compared this phenomenon with the process of innovation in methods and products in existing industries which had allowed the state's economy to adapt and
expand in response to earlier transformations.

State policy responses to the economic changes of the early 1980s evolved
from a focus on maintenance of existing industries to an emphasis on fostering
the creation of new industries through the birth of new firms and the transformation of existing ones; less emphasis has been placed on recruitment of firms
from other states (Jackson, 1988: 112). The shift to an "industry-creation"
strategy was evident in "The Path to Prosperity," a task force report prepared
in 1984 for Governor James Blanchard, who used this approach as the basis of
his administration's initiatives (Jackson, 1988: 121).

Although preparation of "The Path to Prosperity" coincided with Commerce
Department discussions with Mazda, the report was not merely a justification
of these initiatives. Its recommendations were based upon a detailed review of
both the causes of the state's economic difficulties and its competitive advantages.
Noting that past economic growth in Michigan resulted from innovation and
transformation of existing industries, it recommended this principle (a "get
smart" strategy) as a foundation for future policy over the strategic alternatives
of wage reduction ("get poor") or a shift away from durable goods manufacturing
("get out") (Ross, 1984: 51–52). The rationale for this recommendation may
be summarized as follows: (1) the central focus of state economic development
policy should be expansion of the state's economic base because such industries
produce goods and services which are exported and thus provide both direct and
indirect employment, as well as generating jobs in the local market sector through
wages paid to their employees; (2) manufacturing firms are central to Michigan's
economic base; (3) the state's competitive advantages are derived from its manufacturing position—a workforce skilled in durable goods production, a "vast
industrial infrastructure" for manufacturing, a broad network of durable goods
suppliers, and universities with strong resources and programs in industrial technology (Ross, 1984: 7, 8, 53). State policy, the report contends, should maximize
these strengths through fostering a "culture of innovation" in which base industries incorporate new production technologies and workers develop new and
more diversified skills (Ross, 1984: 57–59, 65). Such a climate would be con-
ducive to entrepreneurial efforts to establish new firms and attractive to out-of-
state firms. Recruitment of out-of-state firms, then, is sanctioned, provided the
firm in question meets the conditions of innovativeness and relationship to economic base. On the other hand, strategies should emphasize business services
(job training programs, infrastructure support) rather than tax abatements (Ross,
1984: 89). Recognizing that this recommendation might be interpreted as a

criticism of the tax abatement included in the Mazda package, the report included the following caveat: "rare but important exceptions to the use of tax incentives [include] a Japanese auto firm that uses advanced technology and will employ laid off Detroit auto workers" (Ross, 1984: 89).

With the exception of the tax abatement, the Mazda package is quite consistent with state policy guidelines. Mazda is a firm which utilizes new technology in manufacturing a durable good, employing a skilled workforce, and drawing upon the state's industrial infrastructure and supplier networks. The incentives offered were primarily related to business services—job training, road and sewer construction, and assistance in obtaining necessary construction permits—and the process by which the package was developed incorporated state and local, public, and private institutions.

In this context, the tax abatement is a troubling inconsistency and may be interpreted as a remnant of the earlier maintenance and recruitment strategies based in interstate competition. The $87 million cost of the abatement was really double the value of other public sector incentives, but it was spread over 14 years, and the money would not have been available unless the new plant were built. For these reasons, as well as its inconsistency with state economic development policy, the importance of the abatement was discounted by state officials, who characterized it as secondary to the locational advantages of a skilled workforce and a supplier network. Local economic development officials at the Downriver Community Conference, however, interpreted the abatement as a key "demand" (Wild, 1988). The disagreement provides support for a hypothesis that the Mazda tax abatement might comprise a "corporate surplus"— a locational incentive beyond the minimum necessary to attract the facility (Jones and Bachelor, 1984).

Whether the tax abatement was necessary to attract Mazda was not a consideration in the input-output model used by state officials to assess the appropriate level of incentives to attract the facility. Rather, this model compared the long-term multiplier effects of a facility on earnings, jobs, and state and local tax revenues with its short-term public costs in incentives or subsidies (Jackson, 1988: 125). The model was formulated in two stages: the first, which preceded the Mazda decision, projected multiplier effects on jobs and wages; the second, formulated after the Mazda decision, estimated state tax revenue returns on funds invested over a 10-year period (Lontz, 1988). Summarizing the application of the model to the Mazda project, one policy analyst noted: "The state promised Mazda subsidies in the form of lower taxes, worker training, and investments in infrastructure developments after determining that, in the long run, the benefits from the Flat Rock plant would exceed the cost of the subsidies" (Jackson, 1988: 125).

The model's projections are based on an assumption of 2,500 auto assembly jobs in two shifts of 1,400 and 1,100 workers, beginning in 1986, and an expected annual output of 240,000 units at full production. The number of indirect jobs generated is estimated from national input-output coefficients for affected sectors, adjusted for the percentage of demand in each sector satisfied within the state. Jobs and income generated by construction expenditures were estimated from an assumed expenditure of $200 million spread over three years (Fulton et al., 1984: 30–31). The model used a multiplier of 2.10 for construction-only employment in 1985, increasing to a high of 5.01 in 1988 as auto assembly became the dominant source of direct employment; a lower long-term multiplier of 4.88 was used after 1988, "because higher wage levels, resulting from the increased demand for labor, encourage the substitution of capital for labor, as well as causing relative production cost disadvantages with other regions" (Fulton et al., 1984: 34–35). These figures yield projections of more than 12,000 jobs generated by the 2,500 assembly jobs for the years 1986–1990. More than half of these jobs would be in manufacturing, primarily auto supplier industries. Of the remainder, most are in services and retail trade, while 500 additional governmental jobs were projected on the basis of an assumed increase in demand for government services. The model projects that these new jobs would result in an increase of $682 million (in current dollars) in personal income for residents of the State of Michigan in 1990, although the basis for this figure is not explained.

Although this model is considerably more sophisticated than that used by the City of Detroit to project the anticipated economic impacts of the General Motors "Poletown" plant, it suffers from some of the same deficiencies identified by David Fasenfest (1986) in his critique of that project. The Detroit projections did not make clear whether personal wage projections were in discounted or undiscounted dollars, and no estimates of public sector costs were included. Fasenfest's revisions of the Detroit projections incorporating these considerations led him to conclude that the more than $200 million public cost of that project exceeded its probable benefits (1986: 112–114). More significant here is his implicit criticism of both his own and the City of Detroit analysis (which may apply as well to the Commerce Department's analyses). For, as he acknowledges in his conclusion, benefit-cost analysis, is "an easily manipulated form of analysis" because the assessment of the worth of a project depends upon the assumptions on which it is based (1986: 120).

Judgments on the merits of a project, however, involve qualitative judgments as well as quantitative assessments. The ILIR/Commerce Department impact analysis concluded that the Mazda plant's benefits for the state's economy and residents included: (1) its use of new production techniques with an American workforce and local suppliers, which would aid in assessing the "factory of the future" concept; (2) spinoffs from Mazda's introduction of new production techniques which could assist the state in its transition from traditional manufacturing to new methods; and (3) the likelihood that Mazda would prosper in a period of restructuring due to its greater efficiency, innovativeness, and use of new technologies in producing a product for which there would be a continuing demand (Fulton et al., 1984: 47–48).

Governor James Blanchard, who played a key role in both the formulation of state economic development policy and the effort to attract Mazda, characterized the plant as a "major transformation" that altered negative perceptions of the state's economic climate (Osborne, 1988: 167). Officials of the Downriver Community Conference (DCC) who participated in formulation of the Mazda package credit the plant with having a similar impact on that region's image (Henry, 1988). While these intangible benefits are likely to pay off in future business investment and jobs, they are not amenable to cost-benefit analysis. Nevertheless, for the officials involved in developing the Mazda package, they augmented the financial benefits projected for the plant.

POLICY FORMULATION FOR MAZDA

Policy decisions which would culminate in the construction of the Flat Rock Mazda plant were made months and even years in advance of the discussions specific to the project. To state officials, the agreement with Mazda represented the first fruit of economic development initiatives aimed at promoting techno- logical innovations in manufacturing base industries and fostering a new, less conflictual style of labor-management relations.

Mazda's decision to locate in Flat Rock, however, had its origins in the corporation's interest in expanding the U.S. market for its product. Studies by the corporation as early as 1981 had indicated that this effort required producing cars in the United States (Uchida, 1988). Production schedules for introduction of the models to be built at the U.S. plant set the timetable for the locational decision to be made by late 1984. Deputy Commerce Director Peter Walters first learned of Mazda's interest in a U.S. site from a Ford Motor Company official in early 1984, but Ford, despite its 25 percent ownership of Mazda and interest in having the plant located at the Flat Rock site, was not directly involved in the location decision. In February 1984, Mazda officials met with Governor Blanchard and Commerce Director Ralph Gerson to discuss incentives and labor and environmental permit concerns. Subsequent discussions were conducted with attorneys from the New York law firm of Webster, Sheffield, who represented Mazda. Rumors that the Flat Rock site was under consideration by Mazda surfaced in March, 1984, when corporate officials were quoted as citing supplier access, product distribution networks, labor relations, government grants, and tax incentives as factors in site selection (Lienert, 1984a).

Meanwhile, Mazda initiated feasibility studies to evaluate these and other factors affecting the profitability of a U.S. plant. A key element in these analyses was the relationship between the company and the UAW. In contrast to other negotiations in Japanese auto firms, discussions with the union preceded the locational decision. Discussions between Mazda and the UAW were held throughout the spring and summer of 1984 and were viewed by participants as providing each side with a better understanding of what the other wanted to accomplish. The tone of the discussions was summarized in a letter of intent signed by both parties. While the letter was not legally binding, it set the basis for future negotiations of the first Mazda-UAW contract. It expressed the themes of mutual cooperation and respect between the union and the corporation and established broad agreement in principle on the installation of Japanese production systems in the new plant. To Mazda, the most important elements of that agreement were the use of single-job classification (where each worker receives cross-training and has multiple skills), the concept of production teams, and the adoption of productivity increases. Also addressed in the agreement were preference for laid-off Ford workers in the application process and start-up wages slightly below those of other Ford employees (Hennigar, 1988).

The Mazda-UAW initiative indicates that the corporation was seriously considering Michigan before specific governmental incentives had been offered. A Mazda official later reflected that Michigan was a "good candidate" because of its skilled work force and component suppliers to serve a "just in time" assembly operation. On the other hand, he observed that governmental assistance was also an important issue, describing Michigan's incentives as "very generous." He also alluded to Ford's behind-the-scenes role: because of the Mazda-Ford relationship, Mazda was able to get "a good deal" from Ford on the vacant Flat Rock site, ($14 million, according to Commerce Department officials). Another factor which promoted Mazda's focus on Michigan was a concern about unemployment in the United States and a desire to be a good corporate citizen by locating in an area of high unemployment such as Detroit (Uchida, 1988). Thus, although reports circulated that South Carolina and Nebraska were under consideration by Mazda, and these states were evaluated in the ILIR/Commerce Department study, Mazda does not appear to have been involved in the sort of interstate competition that characterized the Saturn project (in which governors made pitches on a television talk show) or the General Motors Poletown plant (in which the corporation threatened to locate elsewhere if Detroit failed to meet its demands). For Mazda, the major issue was whether, not where, to build a plant in the United States. According to former Deputy Commerce Director Peter Walters, this issue so divided corporate leadership that a change in top officials coincided with announcement of the plant location (Walters, 1988). He characterized the preparation of the incentive package as a process in which the state "replied to Mazda's concerns," instead of competing with other states.

This description of policy formulation should not be taken to mean that the process was not a complicated one. Action by local, state, and federal agencies was needed to provide the infrastructure improvements, training program, governmental services, and funding mechanisms comprising the incentive package. Development teams were set up to focus on particular elements of the package. Moreover, each team incorporated representatives of affected governmental bodies: road and rail improvements necessitated participation by the state Department of Transportation and the Grand Trunk Railroad; the Governor's Office of Job Training assisted in the preparation of a job training program; a funding source had to be identified for Mazda's request for assistance with project financing; the Downriver Community Conference acted as an intermediary with local governments, coordinating federal funding applications and assisting in preparation of various technical studies; review of the tax abatement request by the Attorney General's office was needed; and approval of the abatement by the City of Flat Rock had to be secured. These arrangements, as well as the agreement with the UAW, were formulated in less than a year in order to meet Mazda's decision deadline of late 1984, which was necessitated by its production schedule.

Firm commitments on all components of the package were not in place at the time of Mazda's announcement on November 30, 1984. The first threat to the project came from Flat Rock Mayor Ted Anders, who took issue with the guarantee of preference to laid-off Ford workers included in the Mazda-UAW letter of intent. Anders charged that this guarantee violated a commitment of jobs for unemployed Flat Rock residents that had been requested by the city in return for granting the tax abatement, and threatened to withdraw the abatement offer (Lienert, 1984b). Two months later, a compromise was reached in which city residents were given preference for nonunion jobs and the Flat Rock City Council voted to permit the abatement, valued at more than $70 million. Mazda also pledged to pay Flat Rock $100,000 annually in lieu of taxes for the term of the abatement and to provide the city with two new police cars (Katz, 1985).

In March 1985, the project was jeopardized again when federal funding fell short of the $20 million in construction financing assistance requested by Mazda (Benkelman and Higgins, 1985). Application had been made by the City of River Rouge for a $20.3 million Urban Development Action Grant (because Flat Rock did not qualify for the program), which would then be loaned to Mazda at 8 percent interest. HUD approved only a $2.5 million grant, explaining that the request far exceeded the minimum assistance needed for the project to be viable (Benkelman and Higgins, 1985). Arrangements were made by Commerce Department officials to provide the required assistance through a $21 million, 20-year loan from the Michigan Economic Development Authority to Mazda at 8 percent interest (Benkelman, 1985). Net cost to the state of the loan was estimated at $2 to $6 million, because the state would borrow against Mazda's annual $2.14 million payments at a slighter higher interest rate (Benkelman, 1985).

Sewer facilities for the plant posed another problem, due to the inadequacy of the Flat Rock wastewater system and delays in construction of a new Huron Valley interceptor and treatment plant to serve Flat Rock and three adjacent communities. Unable to obtain a guaranteed opening date for the new system from Wayne County, state officials secured an agreement from the adjacent City of Rockwood, which had an excess capacity in its treatment plant, to accept Mazda's sewage until the new system was completed. Urban Development Action Grant Funds of $1.5 million were used to build a connector to the Rockwood plant (Lontz, 1988). Mazda will pay usage fees to Rockwood and will pay Flat Rock's share of the cost of connections to the new system.

The negotiations and policy revisions which permitted the package to survive these potential roadblocks are indicative of the commitment of all parties involved to bringing the project to fruition, and a willingness not to sacrifice it on the altar of their own self interests. Reflecting on his own involvement, Mayor Anders captured this spirit, when he commented, "Rather than jeopardize the plant on the issue of [union] jobs, we backed down" (Katz, 1985). Anders's earlier confrontational stance reflected a feeling that the city was being treated as a less-than-equal partner in the formulation of the incentive package and that its concerns were neglected by the state, DCC, and Mazda. Flat Rock's current mayor, Richard Jones, who made the tax abatement a key issue in his campaign against Anders, believes an earlier agreement between Ford, the city, and the Flat Rock school district set the stage for the discussions with Mazda. This prior agreement established a five-year phasing in of the reductions in the assessed value of the casting facility. The value of the Ford plant at the end of the five-year period was used for Mazda's assessment under the tax abatement agreement (Jones, 1988).

According to Richard Jones, the actual value of the property and equipment remaining on the site in December 1984 (which would have applied to the February 1985 council vote on tax abatement) was $36.5 million; using the lower Ford agreement value, he contends, saved Mazda $300,000 in property taxes. Jones also questions the legality of the "replacement facility" status granted to Mazda that allowed it to receive the 100 percent abatement under P.A. 198 because the old plant is not being used for manufacturing by Mazda. (It is presently used for a variety of activities, including hiring and training, air conditioner subassembly, and an employee fitness center.) If Mazda had received the 50 percent abatement permitted for new facilities, its property taxes would have been nearly 10 times their current level, based on a December 1987 state equalized value of $340 million (Jones, 1988).

The tax abatement, however, was not an issue for the state officials who coordinated the elements of the incentive package, whose primary objective was to comply with Mazda's requests. DCC officials, closer to the concerns of local governments, were bothered by the 100 percent abatement but were afraid that testing how important it was to Mazda would risk loss of the plant and the badly needed jobs for their constituents. In hindsight, one official reflected that "we might have given them too much" and wondered if a commitment from Mazda about supplier firms might have been possible in return for the 100 percent abatement (Henry, 1988). The DCC, however, was more involved in implementation than in formulation of the incentive package and devoted considerable attention to such qualitative factors as overcoming Japanese anxieties about living in the Detroit area and working with the UAW and demonstrating an interest in Japanese culture. These "supportive services" were perceived by former DCC Director Dewitt Henry (1988) as equal in importance to Mazda as the remainder of the incentive package.

How important the 100 percent abatement actually was to Mazda, however, is unclear. The corporation's requirements were presented by its attorneys, who were in a position to assess whether the plant qualified as a replacement facility under P.A. 198. The corporate philosophy, with its emphasis on employee involvement, work force quality, and cooperation between workers and management, is more closely linked to provision of a training program and the formulation of an agreement on principles with the UAW, than to tax reductions and other financial inducements. That the cost of the training program was split between the State of Michigan and Mazda is indicative of the corporation's willingness to pay for the training it required of its workers. From Mazda's perspective, the central provisions of the letter of intent dealt with mutual cooperation, cross training of workers, and a single job classification system for production workers. Nevertheless, profitability was Mazda's primary objective, and lower taxes mean more profits.

CONCLUSIONS

Mazda completed its first year of production in Flat Rock on September 1, 1988. Total employment at the plant was 3,300, of which 2,800 were production workers. The work force included 116 Flat Rock residents (office and production) and approximately 250 Japanese, who will stay two to five years (Hennigar, 1988). Its assessed value was $21 million, due to a reassessment of land values, generating approximately $373,000 in taxes plus an "in-lieu" payment of $100,000 per year. The Flat Rock and Gibraltar school districts, the boundary of which runs through the plant site, continue to receive reimbursement through the state school aid formula for their shares of the abatement, a combined total of nearly $7 million annually. A tax increment financing district has been established for the Mazda site and adjacent Gateway Commerce Park, in which increased tax revenues from both facilities must be used for improvements within the district, dimming prospects for increased tax revenues when the abatement expires. The one office building in the commerce park has only one tenant, but a feasibility study has reported good prospects for a hotel and convention center. The expectations of nearby Mazda suppliers have not materialized: only paint and painting tape are produced in Flat Rock, though Japanese-owned Penstone, a glass supplier, is located in Rockwood, and Delta, a seat manufacturer, has a plant a few miles south in Monroe. Reports have circulated that Mazda may build an engine or transmission plant near the assembly plant (Lupo, 1988) to obviate its prevailing policy of importing engines and transmissions from Japan.

Flat Rock officials estimated that the Mazda plant would necessitate hiring additional policy and public works employees, purchasing additional police and firefighting equipment, and constructing a larger water service tap line for the plant (Pruchaska, 1985; Jones, 1986). They projected salary, equipment, and construction costs of nearly $650,000 through 1987, more than Mazda's tax payments up to that time, even if the donated police cars are subtracted from city costs. From this short-term perspective, the city's costs exceeded its benefits. But these costs should also be compared with the alternative of a still-vacant casting facility, generating no jobs and minimal tax revenues, unsuited to other industrial activities. It is difficult to imagine any financial benefits from this scenario, even if it generated no costs. In this context, the costs associated with Mazda may be perceived as an investment in Flat Rock's future.

It is too early in the operation of the plant to pass judgment on its profitability or efficiency. Initial reports indicated that efficiency compared favorably with other U.S. plants, but that employee turnover and quality control problems existed (Lupo, 1988; Lupo and Lippert, 1988). Company officials attributed both turnover and quality problems to adjustment difficulties of employees inexperienced in auto production; a UAW official and an American former administrator at the plant, on the other hand, cited cultural differences as a contributing factor (Lupo and Lippert, 1988). Expectations are that these problems will decline in subsequent years; if not, productivity and profitability could suffer.

For Mazda, as for public officials, the Flat Rock assembly plant was a risk. It required severe cultural adjustments and reliance on a unionized work force alien to Japanese production methods. The payoff lies in the future, in the expansion of Mazda's share of U.S. auto sales; the size of that gain depends upon unpredictable intervening factors. Mazda and the State of Michigan are exploring new territory with this project, and Mazda's relative success or failure may be interpreted as indicative of the state's ability to promote a technological transformation of its economic base. When one is building a factory of the future, the price may be higher, but the benefits are not limited to the tax revenues and jobs generated by a single plant. Examination of the process by which the Mazda incentive package was developed and the criteria which guided participants in that process indicates that qualitative impacts of the plant received considerable attention and probably weighed more heavily in their final decision than a quantitative evaluation of costs and benefits. While the outcome may have been costly in the short run for the City of Flat Rock, its ultimate impacts, while difficult to quantify or predict, should be more positive. The City of Flat Rock and the State of Michigan did more than trade a Ford for a Mazda—they traded the past for the future.

NOTE

1. State Equalized Value represents the assessed value of property in a municipality, as equalized among jurisdictions in each county and among counties, to adjust for valuation of property at less or more than true cash value. The assessed value of each piece of property cannot exceed 50 percent of its true cash value: Ford's $20.9 million assessment translates to a cash value of $41.8 million (Michigan Compiled Laws Annotated, Sec. 211.24, 211.34 and Michigan Constitution, Article 9, Sec. 3).

REFERENCES

Benkelman, Susan. 1985. "Mazda Gets $21 Million State Loan." *Detroit News*, 4 April, 1A, 12A.
Benkelman, Susan, and James V. Higgins. 1985. "U.S. Funds for Mazda Plant Cut." *Detroit News*, 29 March, 3A, 4A.

Fasenfest, David. 1986. "Community Politics and Urban Redevelopment: Poletown, Detroit, and General Motors." *Urban Affairs Quarterly* 22 (September): 101–123.

Fulton, George A., Donald R. Grimes, and Alan L. Baum. 1984. "Industrial Location Decisions and Their Impact on the Michigan Economy: The Mazda Automobile Assembly Case." Paper presented at 32nd Annual Conference on the Economic Outlook, Ann Arbor, Mich., 15 November.

Hennigar, N. 1988. Interview with Nancy Hennigar, Manager, Public Relations, Mazda Motor Manufacturing (USA) Corporation, 6 September.

Henry, D. 1988. Interview with Dewitt Henry, former Director, Downriver Community Conference, 28 July.

Hill, Richard C., Michael Indergaard, and Kuniko Fujita. 1988. "Flat Rock, Home of Mazda: The Social Impact of a Japanese Company on an American Community." Paper presented at Eighth Annual International Automotive Conference, Ann Arbor, Mich., 22–23 March.

Jackson, John E. 1988. "Michigan." In R. Scott Fosler, ed., *The New Economic Role of the American States*. New York: Oxford University Press, 91–137.

Jones, Bryan D., and Lynn W. Bachelor. 1984. "Local Policy Discretion and the Corporate Surplus." In Richard D. Bingham and John P. Blair, eds., *Urban Economic Development*. Beverly Hills, Calif.: Sage, 245–267.

Jones, Richard. 1986. Letter to Michigan Department of Commerce, 21 May.

———. 1988. Interview with Richard Jones, Mayor of Flat Rock, Michigan, 6 September.

Katz, Diane. 1985. "Tax Deal Approved for Mazda." *Detroit News*, 20 February, 1A, 6A.

Lienert, Paul. 1984a. "Flat Rock Could be Mazda Site." *Detroit Free Press*, 16 March, 8B.

———. 1984b. "State and UAW Downplaying Mayor's Threat to Mazda Plant." *Detroit Free Press*, 14 December, 16C.

Lontz, W. 1988. Interview with William Lontz, Deputy Director, Manufacturing Development Group, Department of Commerce, State of Michigan, 26 July.

Lupo, Nunzio. 1988. "Mazda Sets its Sites on Possible Engine Plant Near Flat Rock." *Detroit Free Press*, 19 July, 9C.

Lupo, Nunzio, and John Lippert. 1988. "Flat Rock Mazda Aims for Tune-Up." *Detroit Free Press*, 26 August, 1A, 17A.

"Mazda: The Price of a Job." 1985. *Detroit News*, 31 May, A18.

"Mazda: The Rising Sun Shines on a Rebounding Michigan." 1985. *Detroit Free Press*, 31 May, 8C.

Osborne, David. 1988. *Laboratories of Democracy*. Boston: Harvard Business School Press.

Pruchaska, Michael. 1985. "Environmental Assessment: Mazda Motor Manufacturing (USA) Corporation Final Assembly Plant, Flat Rock, Michigan." Ann Arbor, Mich.

Ross, Doug. 1984. "The Path to Prosperity: Findings and Recommendations of the Task Force for a Long-term Economic Strategy for Michigan." Lansing: State of Michigan.

Uchida, M. 1988. Interview with Matsuhiro Uchida, Executive Vice President, Mazda Motor Manufacturing (USA) Corporation, 6 September.

Walter, P. 1988. Interview with Peter Walters, former Deputy Director of Commerce, State of Michigan, 25 July.
Wild, William. 1988. Interview with William Wild, former administrator of Downriver Community Conference. 28 July.

5

Economic Development and Diamond-Star Motors: Intergovernmental Competition and Cooperation

Nancy S. Lind

As increasing numbers of Japanese automobile companies set up joint ventures with American automobile companies, the competition to lure them has intensified. Recent negotiations between state and local governments and these companies has led to a "war between the states" (Milward and Newman, 1988: 2). At the same time, though, there are concerted team efforts on the part of city and state officials in recruiting new industries to the area (Erickson, 1985: 52). So long as states and localities continue to possess a high degree of autonomy, there will be both competition and cooperation (Kenyon and Kincaid, 1988: 12). This chapter describes both approaches, and uses them to examine the siting of the joint Chrysler–Mitsubishi Diamond-Star Motors plant in Bloomington-Normal, Illinois.

Competition is a major characteristic of state and local governments efforts to promote development. Interstate "bidding wars" for automobile plants and other investments are well-documented (Kenyon and Kincaid, 1988: 12). In response to closing factories and regional distress, governors have initiated programs to improve the competitiveness of their economies (Osborne, 1987: 2). These state efforts have been labeled industrial policies or "competitiveness strategies" (Osborne, 1987: 2). States have been creating economic development policies to address the demands of their residents and to increase the viability of their region.

This state level phenomenon has occurred partially because the federal government has failed to act (Osborne, 1987: 3), and this has led to a battle between states to attract new industries (Schmidt, 1989). The arms race model (Peretz, 1986) contends that states match and raise incentives as they compete for limited opportunities (Grady, 1987: 87). This rationale begins to identify the forces driving economic development competition between states.

The federal government has shown little interest in inducing interstate cooperation and hence competition continues. This competition to attract new industries requires states to pay higher costs than might otherwise be required by foregoing taxes and other revenues in the expectation of receiving appreciable future benefits. Unfortunately, this competition may cost state and local governments more than they stand to gain. The closing of the Volkswagen plant in Pennsylvania is a recent and dramatic example of this risk. One suggestion is that, to alleviate this problem, the federal government should forbid states to offer incentives or, alternatively, require states to negotiate interstate agreements within regions. These alternatives would, in effect, neutralize intraregional competition (Grady, 1987: 93).

The second approach, cooperation within states and between states improves the prospects for outside investments. However, states can intervene to encourage cooperation among local governments. In the case of Diamond-Star, the State of Illinois competed vigorously with other states but encouraged its local governments to cooperate in site selection. Further, states themselves are proposing "industrial disarmament" whereby regional accords have been proposed rather than state versus state wars (Schmidt, 1989). States are beginning to recognize that not all competition is healthy.

The location of Diamond-Star provides evidence of both approaches to economic development. At the interstate level, competition was the predominant approach. The rivals for the Diamond-Star plant included Illinois, Indiana, and Michigan. At the intrastate level, cooperation occurred at the initiative of the Illinois Department of Commerce and Community Affairs which required local governments to cooperate with each other in order to become eligible for consideration as a site for the automobile plant.

INTERSTATE COMPETITION

The search for effective economic development incentives has led states to adopt several methods for aiding industries willing to locate within their boundaries. At the time of the offer to Diamond-Star, incentives included gifts of land, tax abatements, and industrial revenue bonds. Where industrial revenue bonds could be issued, the cost of most of the development effort could be shifted to the federal government. Tax abatements, gifts of land, and other incentives, however, result in direct costs to state and local government.

During the 1980s, most states have prepared economic incentive packages to attract new industries. As a consequence, the advantages some states may have over others are negated or reduced. Some states, for example, lose their appeal by not having an income tax when other states offer income tax abatements as part of their economic development packages. Competition for industries intensifies as a result of the near parity that economic development packages can create.

The State of Illinois, the City of Bloomington, and the Town of Normal believed that the key to attracting new industry centered around the development of an incentive package. Like other state and local governments, they created innovative programs to "establish a competitive advantage over other states in the battle to attract new industry" (Gray and Spina, 1980: 528).

The location of Diamond-Star in Illinois exemplifies the role that competition played in the development of economic incentive packages. In recent years, Illinois has experienced a proliferation of programs and policies designed to stimulate economic development and improve the climate for new and existing businesses (*Illinois Economic Development Program Inventory*, 1988). Income and sales tax exemptions have been enacted, and tax abatements have provided relief for corporations. Illinois has also expanded its business, financial, and technical assistance programs. For Illinois, "economic development has been the buzz-phrase of the Eighties" (*Illinois Economic Development Program Inventory*, 1988). Although more than 20 separate state agencies claim some form of economic development activity, the Department of Commerce and Community Affairs was created in 1979 by Executive Order no. 3 on March 31, 1979, to consolidate over 40 community and economic development programs. Proponents argued that the new agency would improve coordination for federal and state development programs (*Illinois Economic Development Program Inventory*, 1988).

Since the end of the 1970s, economic development has been a top priority for the legislative and executive branches. The creation of the Department of Commerce and Community Affairs (DCCA) was followed by the enactment of several pieces of legislation, perhaps climaxing with the Enterprise Zone Act in 1982 and the Build Illinois Act in 1984.

The Enterprise Zone Act is intended to attract businesses to economically depressed or failing areas by offering state incentives to industries locating within a zone. Since the enterprise zone incentive already existed in over half of the states by 1982, the Illinois statute, which allowed DCCA to designate 67 enterprise zones statewide between 1983 and 1988, may be viewed as an attempt to keep Illinois competitive.

The Build Illinois Act is designated to finance infrastructure repairs. It authorizes the state to issue, sell, and provide for the retirement of limited obligation bonds to be issued for the construction and improvement of state infrastructure, business enhancement and development, the development and improvement of educational, technical, and vocational programs, and for protection, restoration and conservation of environmental and natural resources.

While Michigan and Indiana do not wish to reveal the exact economic development package offered to Diamond-Star, a perusal of the available incentives suggests the range that was available.[1] However, any in-depth analysis of state economic development is limited by the paucity of data made available. Government agencies are reluctant to provide the details of their incentive package for "fear of negative ramifications or providing too much information to competing states" (Milward and Newman, 1988: 5). Within those constraints, a second alternative is an examination of the incentives given to the Japanese automobile plants that located in Michigan and Indiana.

Michigan has invested heavily in economic development in the last several years, concentrating on creating jobs and new investment and preparing its citizens for the future (*Illinois Economic Development Program Inventory*, 1988). Michigan has attempted to improve the business climate by reducing unemployment insurance taxes, cutting worker's compensation costs, and containing medical care costs. The state has an overall goal of making a business climate which is "cost competitive within the region" (*Illinois Economic Development Program Inventory*, 1988). The state expansion of small business services attempts to increase the success rate of small businesses and entrepreneurs. The Michigan Strategic Fund provides additional financial support to Michigan entrepreneurs.

Mazda Motor Manufacturing Corporation built a new plant in Flat Rock with the state providing as incentives: $19 million in worker training, $5 million in road improvements, $500,000 for water system improvements, and a $21 million economic development loan. A pollution control bond for $32 million was also posted by the state (Milward and Newman, 1988: 3).

In Indiana, the story appears to be much the same as in Michigan and Illinois. Similar to Illinois, the State of Indiana is authorized to establish enterprise zones, though a maximum of only 10 zones is permitted. Within the Indiana enterprise zone, many incentives can also be offered. In terms of tax credits, property tax credits can be offered as well as 5 percent tax credits on interest from loans to firms in the zone, 10 percent credits on employer's income taxes, and equity investment credits of up to 30 percent of stock purchases. Also available are tax increment financing districts, low interest loans to various businesses, and priority for neighborhood assistance funds (National Association of State Development Agencies, 1986: 185).

In Indiana, the Corporation for Innovation Development supplies venture capital to new and existing small businesses in the state. Loan guarantees can be granted to any manufacturing enterprise. The Industrial Development Infrastructure Program exists to assist communities in attracting and supporting new business investment. The assistance, in the form of either grants or loans, can be supplemented with Industrial Development Grants for financing public infrastructure improvements and Industrial Development Bonds which provide tax-exempt financing to private businesses (National Association of State Development Agencies, 1986: 179–181).

A joint Fuji-Isuzu venture located in Lafayette, Indiana provides an indication of the incentives offered to Japanese automobile plants in that state, albeit not specifically to Diamond-Star Motors. The Fuji-Isuzu project was divided into two phases with the state providing $55 million in state funds, $3 million in water system improvements, $2 million in highway improvements, and $26 million in federal subsidies in Phase I. An estimated $25 million in additional support will be provided for Phase II (Milward and Newman, 1988: 3).

While this list of incentives is by no means exhaustive, it provides some indication of the economic development tools available in Michigan and Indiana, and it gives some indication of the incentives offered by these states to other Japanese automobile ventures. The incentive package offered to Diamond-Star Motors undoubtedly fell somewhere within this range of choices. The critical point to remember is that Indiana was competing against Michigan and Illinois in developing a package of incentives presumed to be attractive to Diamond-Star.

The 1985 announcement that the Diamond-Star automobile plant would be located in Bloomington-Normal, Illinois, ended the jousting match between the states. What tipped the balance in Illinois' favor? One possibility is that DCCA presented an incentive to Diamond-Star that already contained agreements between Bloomington-Normal and Illinois. The state had taken the responsibility to secure cooperation between the local governments and itself in providing incentives to the automobile industry. Thus, the automobile industry's negotiators dealt only with State of Illinois officials who also spoke for local government officials. This package may have been attractive to Diamond-Star representatives since they did not have to worry about quarrels between the local governments and were instead assured of their joint cooperation. If this assured cooperation was also provided by Indiana and Michigan, a second possibility simply suggests that Mitsubishi officials had ruled out states where other Japanese automobile companies already had plants. Mazda was slated to begin production in 1987, so Michigan might have been ruled out on those grounds. Walt Sorg of the Michigan Department of Commerce suggested a third possibility. "Michigan dropped out of the running," he said, "because Mitsubishi sought more inducements than the state was willing to offer, more than Michigan offered for Saturn and for the Mazda Flat Rock facility" (Johnson, 1985). Finally, Mitsubishi reportedly favored the Illinois site because of its proximity to Chicago, its attraction to Illinois State University in Normal, and the superconducting facilities available at the University of Illinois at Champaign (Johnson, 1985: 2).

THE SPIRIT OF COOPERATION

The cooperation which may have contributed to giving Bloomington-Normal the Diamond-Star plant had its roots in an agreement between the local governments and DCCA. The requirements stipulated by DCCA and the ensuing cooperation resulted in an incentive package that "blended state and local resources" (Elder and Lind, 1987: 37). The state provided an incentive package valued at $83.3 million, including commitments of $17.8 million for road improvements, $11 million for site acquisition, $14.5 million for infrastructure development, and $40 million for worker training (Elder and Lind, 1987: 35). Additional incentives which were to be offered had to be drawn from the local governments. Three primary means used to develop the incentive package for presentation to Diamond-Star—the Illinois Enterprise Zone Act, the home rule provisions of the Illinois Constitution which permitted the development of a metro zone, and the Build Illinois Act—all relied upon intergovernmental cooperation.

The Enterprise Zone

Under the provisions of Illinois' Enterprise Zone Act, local governments may make a joint application to DCCA for designation as an enterprise zone. The City of Bloomington, the Town of Normal, and McLean County made such an application which was approved for the period of July 1, 1985, through December 1, 1988. Subsequently, the State of Illinois and the local governments united to offer incentives to industries locating in the zone.

The Enterprise Zone Program provides numerous state incentives to encourage industries to locate or expand in enterprise zones. Currently, the following incentives are available: sales tax exemptions, income tax deductions, tax credits, and business financing.[2] The incentives publicly offered to Diamond-Star included highway improvements, site acquisition, water system improvements, and worker training. Loans were also provided for business financing.

Local governments may also provide a variety of incentives to further encourage economic growth in the enterprise zone. The choice of these incentives is determined by the local governments. In the Diamond-Star case, local governments added to the state incentive package a 10 percent sales tax exemption, property tax abatements, land write-downs, reduced fees, and industrial revenue bonds.[3]

The incentives offered to Diamond-Star under the Enterprise Zone Act cost Bloomington and Normal each approximately $1.08 million. Additional costs borne by the county and special districts the first year brought the total local cost to approximately $3.6 million. In sum, the use of the enterprise zone in the Diamond-Star case demonstrates the level of cooperation which can be achieved when the state government stipulates the conditions for its local governments' participation in industrial recruitment activities (Randall, 1987).

The Metro Zone

In order to facilitate cooperation with each other, Bloomington and Normal used home rule powers to create a metro zone in 1986. The 1970 Illinois Constitution in Article VII, Section 6, grants local governments the authority to enter into contracts with each other. Article VII, Section 10, further authorizes local governments to contract or associate among themselves to exercise jointly any powers which may be exercised by any municipality individually.

The Bloomington-Normal Metro Zone was established to aid in the "orderly and planned growth and development of an area designated as an Enterprise Zone" (Metro-Zone Master Agreement, 1986). Five primary areas of agreement exist with respect to the metro zone: land acquisition, infrastructure improvements, revenue, services, and liability. The agreement provided that the cost incurred by a municipality in acquiring property or making infrastructure improvement within the zone would be shared equally between the parties, but costs of improvements attributable to areas outside the metro zone were not subject to this cost sharing. Payments for such infrastructure improvements could be made by cash, by an allocation of metro-zone revenue, or as offset against other infrastructure improvements by the other municipality. Municipal revenues—excluding water use charges necessary to pay the actual cost of providing treated water, hotel and motel taxes, and revenue from the sale of certain types of property—were also shared on an equal basis unless provided for otherwise. The costs of providing municipal services within the metro zone were shared on the basis of provisions of separate agreements. Finally, the city and town agreed to share equally in the payment of any judgments against the other in favor of third parties for liability as a result of metro zone activities (Master Agreement, 1986).

In sum, the Bloomington-Normal Metro Zone designates a portion of the enterprise zone as an area to be jointly administered by the two governments. The master agreement and thirteen specific agreements ranging from administrative services to policy and fire protection are binding upon both parties. The specificity of the agreements is designed to reduce conflict and competition between the two communities (Randall, 1987; Dirks, 1987).

Build Illinois

High demands for water and sewer facilities as well as requirements for heavy-duty roads into the auto plant would have probably been too expensive for the local government alone, especially in view of the costs of local tax abatements and the loss of fee income (Elder and Lind, 1987: 35). In creating the incentive package, therefore, funds from the Build Illinois Act were earmarked to ensure provisions of these services to the auto plant.

From the Build Illinois Act, the state paid $7.2 million of a total of $10.2 million to buy land, part of which was given to Diamond-Star. Local governments committed $1.5 million to upgrade and build roads to the plant, and the state paid approximately $18 million. Grants to the sanitary district and the provisions of small business loans also came from the Build Illinois Act (Lind and Elder, 1986: 23; Connor, 1988).

Summary

The Enterprise Zone, Metro Zone, and Build Illinois programs collectively illustrate the effective powerful cooperation that can result from requirements issued by DCCA. It also provides an indication of the level of incentives available to industries who enter into agreements with various levels of government. Specifically, the following incentives are currently available to Diamond-Star as a result of this cooperation: property tax abatements, $64.78 million;[4] training and education, $40 million; road improvements, $20 million; land acquisition, $7.63 million; water and sewer improvements, $13 million; development fee reductions, $2.4 million;[5] and federal import duty reductions, $29.7 million. The total of these incentives amounts to $177.51 million, and the total does not include savings available through the state-wide Investment Tax Credit Program, the statewide exemption of manufacturing equipment and machinery from sales tax, and the enterprise zone abatement of sales taxes on building materials. The impact of Diamond-Star Motors on Illinois is projected by DCCA to increase new personnel income and new taxes generated for every year over the next decade: from $7 million in 1986 to $62 million in 1990 to $98 million in 1995.[6] Thus the State of Illinois admits that there are costs involved in the attraction of Diamond-Star, but they also forecast rather substantial monetary benefits accruing to the state.

COSTS OF COOPERATION AND COMPETITION

Despite advances toward economic development and industrial recruitment provided by the cooperative and competitive approaches, neither approach comes without costs. While it has been argued that cooperation among state and local governments can generate benefits (Bucks, 1988: 1), there are also potential costs to cooperation.

Cooperation

Cooperation may make the negotiations process easier for industry and more difficult for state and local governments. Diamond-Star was delivered a package by the State of Illinois that had already reduced many of the concerns of the local governments. Rather than promising benefits to both Bloomington and Normal, Diamond-Star merely had to promise benefits to the state which were based on cooperation with local governments. Similarly, cooperation may drive up the incentives offered to the industry. For example, the Toyota plant in Georgetown, Kentucky made it known that unless they reached satisfactory agreement, "the automaker would close a deal with a neighboring state" (Miyauchi, 1987: 27). Playing state against state, the automobile company was able to achieve a powerful bargaining position.

Further, if the private company knows that intergovernmental cooperation raises their incentives, they are likely to promote this behavior. If all units of government can be forced to contribute to the incentive package, the industry will undoubtedly be offered more than any single unit of government could have offered. The blended package of incentives offered to Diamond-Star furnishes an example. The state had the funds and ability to finance major capital improvements projects that went beyond the reach of local governments. The local government, on the other hand, controlled property taxes and such services as waste disposal and water provision. Collectively, the cooperation led state and local governments to offer a very broad incentive package to Diamond-Star.

Local governments depend heavily upon the property tax for a large share of their revenue. Thus, when state governments require cooperation from local governments in property tax abatements, the local governments have more to lose than do the states. Cooperation may shift the burden of fiscal responsibility from one level of government to another. Granted, local governments may gain from the economic development investments, but it is ironic that both their gains and losses may come about due to "required activity," short of voluntary cooperation.

Finally, cooperation may also make it easier for any of the involved governments singly to estimate perceived costs conservatively and perceived benefits optimistically. Since costs are shared, government officials can stress their distributive effect and the minimal burden placed on any one level of government. Since benefits tend to be uncertain, all governments can predict numerous future advantages. Further, the perceived need for industrial recruitment influences the likelihood of decision makers succumbing to pressures to overestimate benefits and underestimate costs (Elder and Lind, 1987: 31).

In the Diamond-Star case, there was clearly a difference between the state and local governments along this dimension. Local governments limited their liability to recoverable costs while the state was more willing to incur higher costs with higher degrees of uncertainty (Elder and Lind, 1987: 37). To justify such a position, the state had to generate more optimistic estimates of expected benefits. The obvious cost incurred is directly tied to the accuracy of estimates and the willingness/reluctance to entertain optimistic benefit estimates.

As an additional cost, albeit perhaps a less tangible one, Diamond-Star was at the center of a dispute over who would benefit from taxes generated by the automobile plant. The town of Normal and the Towanda Community Fire Protection District entered a court battle over who would receive the fire protection taxes. The land had been owned by Towanda prior to Normal's annexation of the enterprise zone land. The McLean County Circuit Court ruled that the taxes would go to Normal. An Illinois Appellate Court overruled that judgment finding that the land annexed by Normal would hinder the Towanda District's ability to furnish fire protection to the rest of the district. The Illinois Supreme Court refused to hear Normal's appeal (Haake, 1988: 23).

The most recent cost directly revolves around cooperation. A dispute currently exists between the Town of Normal, the City of Bloomington, Dry Grove Township, McLean County, and Diamond-Star over the assessed valuation of the plant. The final valuation will determine Diamond-Star's tax payments to these governments. The governments hope to convince tax assessors to set the plant's assessment higher than the current $60 million figure used by Diamond-Star, because these governmental units will receive only 50 percent of their tax bill from Diamond-Star until 1998.

Competition

The woes of competition are probably better documented than those of co-operation. Arguments against competition range from the creation of unjustified inequities in taxation through inverse relationships between taxation and economic growth to outright harmful economic effects (Bucks, 1988: 1).

Tax competition creates inequities in taxation by enabling some businesses to shift their taxes to others. Tax benefits given to corporations are often at the expense of citizens. Not only is there lost revenue, but citizen attitudes are likely to reflect their belief that if tax breaks can be given to new industries, there is not a need to raise taxes. Since the building of Diamond-Star, voters resoundingly defeated at least one referendum calling for tax increases for the building of new schools and meeting the rising operational costs of public education. Whether this is a direct consequence of Diamond-Star or a reflection of prevailing national attitudes is uncertain.

As early as 1967, the Advisory Commission on Intergovernmental Relations concluded that "efforts by states to attract new businesses by competing through tax policies result in a self-defeating cycle of competitive tax undercutting" (Bucks, 1988: 2). There is no reason to think that the effects of tax abatements are any different today.

A few recent studies suggest that greater tax incentives positively affect a state's economy. For years, however, a consensus has existed that state and local taxes have little effect upon business location decisions (Bucks, 1988: 2). Newer studies challenge that consensus but often provide contradictory evidence. One study claims that higher corporate taxes have a negative effect on investment decisions (Bartik, 1985), while another finds no effect (Wasylenko and McGuire, 1985). Thus, there is not agreement about whether increased tax incentives will have any influence at all on economic growth.

Competition can also increase the level of benefits available to industries. The industries expect some incentives, but ironically their level is pushed upward by the state and local governments themselves. Economic development has become increasingly competitive as states seek to provide unique incentives or attempt to maintain parity in their quest for economic development. Moreover, competition exists both among states and between communities within a state. This situation has led to the suggestion that by competing with each other, state and local governments may be "giving away the store" (Gray and Spina, 1980), a problem which could be exacerbated if industries leave the area after the incentive packages expire. Perhaps the most important lesson is provided by the closing of the Volkswagen plant: "all economic development deals, no matter how large, still involve risk" (Fulton, 1988: 37). Finally, governors seeking new industries must realize that the chase burns up a multitude of resources, running the gamut from staff time to the limited pot of resources available for other other economic development efforts (Fulton, 1988: 37).

CONCLUSION

The story of Diamond-Star Motors is an excellent case study of two facets of intergovernmental relations: cooperation and competition. In the former, it provides an example of what can happen when state and local governments cooperate in creating a package of incentives to offer an industry. The state and local governments were partners in negotiating with the corporation. It was in the interest of both levels of government to have the Japanese corporation locate in the state. The Diamond-Star experience also illustrates the types of incentives that are likely to be offered when states are competing against each other and the fact that, with increasing competition and increasing expectations by automobile companies, the level of incentives offered is likely to grow.

Cooperation and competition, however, are not always beneficial nor always harmful. This study of the Diamond-Star case has assessed both the costs and benefits associated with each of these approaches to economic development. It demonstrates that actions by another level of government are often necessary for encouraging the cooperative approach. The State of Illinois required cooperation before cities would be considered for the siting of the automobile plant. Competition between states is provoked by the lack of intervention by the federal government. If cooperation is to be added to the more commonly employed competitive approach to economic development, the federal government may need to get involved. Not unlike European nations, the federal government could require a cartel of states to negotiate with industries and not allow single states to reap all of the benefits or pay all of the costs. At a minimum, the equalization could occur at a regional level where states which did not receive new industries would be rebated a proportion of their taxes from the federal government. While either suggestion for federal involvement is counter to the tradition of federalism, it opens up options rarely explored.

Indeed, the lesson to be learned from the Diamond-Star case may be that cooperation, not competition, is a key to improved economic performance. The United States must recognize that to compete effectively on an international scale, states must cooperate at home (Bucks, 1988: 3). States, while still battling to attract Japanese automobile plants, are beginning to recognize their need to develop industrial policies rather than just chasing smokestacks (Schmidt, 1989). States are beginning to cooperate in the name of regional cooperation. And, as

Jack Russell of Michigan's Technology Institute suggests, "there will be episodic skirmishes between states" but they must recognize that "regions, rather than states, are the architectonic plates of an economic world" (Schmidt, 1989). Unfortunately, however great the need, the basis for interstate cooperation for economic development is tenuous. The prevailing ethic is interstate competition rather than cooperation (Ledebur and Barnes, 1988: 24).

NOTES

1. Detailed information on the incentive packages offered to Diamond-Star by Michigan and Indiana was unavailable to the author, an Illinois legislative commission, and the Illinois Governor's Office.

2. The following incentives are available under provisions of the Illinois Enterprise Zone Act: sales tax exemptions, income tax deductions, tax credits, and business financing. A five percent state sales tax exemption is permitted on building materials used in the zone. Exempted purchases must be made from within the county or municipalities that have established the zone.

Three prongs exist with regard to the income tax deduction: (a) dividend interest income: individuals, corporations, trusts and estates are not taxed on dividend income from corporations doing substantially all their business in a zone; (b) interest deductions: financial institutions are not taxed on the interest received from loans for development within a zone; (c) contribution deductions: business may deduct from taxable income double the value of in-kind contributions to an approved project in a zone.

An investment tax credit, in addition to the 5 percent available statewide, is allowed in the form of an additional 5 percent to taxpayers who invest in qualified property in a zone. Further, the Enterprise Zone Job Tax Credit allows a business a $500 credit on Illinois income taxes for each job created in the zone for which a dislocated worker or disadvantaged individual is hired.

Finally, the Illinois Development Finance Authority set aside $100 million of its lending authority for use exclusively in enterprise zones. In addition, all DCCA administered business financing programs are available to companies in the zone (*Illinois Enterprise Zone Annual Report*, 1988).

3. The Town of Normal, City of Bloomington, and McLean County approved a 1 percent local exemption of the Retailer's Occupation Tax for building materials used for real estate within the zone. Purchases had to be made from retailers within the above three jurisdictions. The Bloomington Sanitary District offered a 25 percent property tax abatement. A 50 percent abatement of property taxes was offered by the City of Bloomington, Town of Normal, McLean County, School District Units no. 5 and 87, and the Bloomington-Normal Airport Authority. The school districts have also agreed to abate their taxes through 1995, and other taxing bodies will abate through 1998. Publicly owned land, independently owned by the Town of Normal or the City of Bloomington, was made available at prices below market value. Finally, the City of Bloomington, Town of Normal, and McLean County offered a 50 percent reduction of all development and permit fees related to the development of the zone and also agreed to issue Industrial Revenue Bonds for the development of the enterprise zone to the full extent permitted by the Internal Revenue Service (*Enterprise Zone of City of Bloomington, Town of Normal, and McLean County, Illinois*, 1985).

4. The property tax abatements were offered through the Bloomington-Normal/McLean County Enterprise Zone Program.

5. The development fee reductions were offered through the Bloomington-Normal/ McLean County Enterprise Zone Program.

6. The projections for new taxes generated by Diamond–Star for each year over the next decade are the following: 1986: $7 million; 1987: $9 million; 1988: $34 million; 1989: $56 million; 1990: $62 million; 1991: $69 million; 1992: $77 million; 1993: $84 million; 1994: $91 million; 1995: $98 million. (Automotive Center of Illinois. Insert. Undated.)

REFERENCES

Books and Articles

Automotive Center of Illinois. Insert. Undated.

Bartik, Timothy. 1984. "Business Location Decisions in the United States: Estimates of the Effects of Unionization, Taxes, and Other Characteristics of States." *Journal of Business and Economic Statistics* 3: 14–22.

Bucks, Dan R. 1988. "Tax Competition: Patent Medicine for Economic Anxiety." *Multistate Tax Commission Review* 8 (May): 1–4.

City of Bloomington and Town of Normal, Illinois. 1986. *Metro-Zone Master Agreement.* 20 January.

City of Bloomington, Town of Normal, and McLean County, Illinois. 1985. *Enterprise Zone of City of Bloomington, Town of Normal, and McLean County.*

Elder, Ann H., and Nancy S. Lind. 1987. "The Implications of Uncertainty in Economic Development: The Case of Diamond-Star Motors." *Economic Development Quarterly* 1: 30–40.

Erickson, Richard. 1985. "Trends for Economic Development." *American City and County* 100 (October): 50–54.

Fulton, William. 1988. "VW in Pennsylvania: The Tale of the Rabbit That Got Away." *Governing* 2 (November): 32–37.

Grady, Dennis O. 1987. "State Economic Development Incentives: Why Do States Compete?" *State and Local Government Review* 19: 86–94.

Gray, John, and Dean Spina. 1980. "State and Local Industrial Location Incentives: A Well-Stocked Candy Store." *Journal of Corporation Law* 5: 517–587.

Haake, Dave. 1988. "Automaker in Middle of Political Pollution Squabble." *Pantagraph,* 10 November, 23.

Illinois Commission on Intergovernmental Cooperation. 1988. *Illinois Economic Development Program Inventory.*

Illinois Department of Commerce and Community Affairs. 1988. *Enterprise Zone Annual Report.*

Johnson, Richard. 1985. "Illinois Expected to be Mitsubishi Plant Site." *Automotive News,* 7 October, 2.

Kenyon, Daphne, and John Kincaid. 1988. "Rethinking Interjurisdictional Competition." *Multistate Tax Commission Review* 8 (October): 12–24.

Ledebur, Larry C., and William Barnes. 1988. "The Buck Starts Here." *State Government News* 31 (November): 24.

Lind, Nancy S., and Ann H. Elder. 1986. "Who Pays? Who Benefits?: The Case of the Incentive Package Offered to the Diamond-Star Automobile Plant." *Government Finance Review* 2: 19–23.

McCosh, Dan. 1985. "Iacocca Plans to Use Mitsubishi as a Spur." *Automotive News*, 14 October, 12.

Milward, H. Brinton, and Heidi H. Newman. 1988. "The Escalation of State Incentive Packages and the Japanese Auto Alley." *Review and Perspective* 12: 2–5.

Miyauchi, Takeo. 1987. "The Man Who Lured Toyota to Kentucky." *Economic Eye* 8 (March): 23–27.

National Association of State Development Agencies (NASDA). 1986. *Directory of Incentives for Business Investment and Development in the United States*, 2nd ed., Washington: Urban Institute Press.

Neenan, William, and Marcus Ethridge. 1984. "Competition and Cooperation Among Localities." In Richard D. Bingham and John P. Blair, eds., *Urban Economic Development*. Beverly Hills, Calif.: Sage, 175–190.

Osborne, David. 1987. *Economic Competitiveness: The States Take the Lead*. New York: Praeger.

Peretz, Paul. 1986. "The Market for Incentives: Where Angels Fear to Tread?" *Policy Studies Journal* 5: 624–633.

Schmidt, William. 1989. "What the States Are Doing for Industry." *New York Times*, 5 February, 4–2.

Wasylenko, Michael, and Therese McGuire. 1985. "Jobs and Taxes: The Effects of Business Climate on States' Employment Growth Rates." *National Tax Journal* 38: 497–510.

Interviews

Kevin Connor, Illinois Governor's Office, Springfield, Illinois. 12 March 1988.

Herman Dirks, Bloomington City Manager's Office, Bloomington, Illinois. 24 January 1987.

Scott Randall, Normal City Manager's Office, Normal, Illinois. 23 January 1987.

6

Japanese Automobile Investment in West Central Ohio: Economic Development and Labor-Management Issues

John P. Blair, Carole Endres, and Rudy Fichtenbaum

The Honda automobile facility near Marysville, which produces Civics and Accords, is the brightest star in a constellation of Japanese automobile-related facilities in West Central Ohio, a region on the leading edge of the internationalization of the American economy. The automobile complex did not emerge from a single decision but was the outgrowth of many decisions made over more than a decade. The development of the complex began in 1977 when Honda officials decided to locate a motorcycle facility near Marysville. Later, other Honda facilities and their parts suppliers were established in the region. Today, the Japanese automobile complex continues to grow. (See Table 6.1 for the milestones in Honda's growth and Figure 6.1 for Honda's investment pattern.) This chapter will examine the decisions made since 1977 which have created the West Central Ohio, Honda-centered automobile complex. The first section will examine the reasons for the emergence of the West Central Ohio automobile complex. Here, particular attention will be given to the role of state government and to local economic and quality of life factors. The second section will provide a detailed examination of the labor-management issues. The final section will extract some lessons for public and private policy makers.

Table 6.1
Milestones: Honda in Ohio

1977	Honda announces plans to construct $35 million motorcycle production plant in Marysville, Ohio.
1979	Production begins at Honda's Marysville motorcycle plant in September.
1980	Honda announces plans to construct $250 million auto plant of 1 million square feet next to motorcycle plant in Marysville.
1982	Production of Accord begins at Marysville auto plant in November.
1984	Honda announces expansion of Marysville auto plant, doubling its original size, to produce Civic 4-door sedans in 1986.
1984	Honda announces plans for $30 million motorcycle engine plant at Anna, Ohio.
1984	Honda announces construction of a $42 million plastics plant at its Marysville site.
1985	Honda announces plans for expansion of the engine plant to include Civic engine production in 1986.
1986	$10 million renovation of Marysville motorcycle plant begins in February.
1986	Expansion of Marysville auto plant to 2.2 million square feet is completed, permitting production capacity to reach 320,000 cars per year; plans also announced to increase auto production to 360,000 Accords and Civics.
1987	Honda announces plans to commence full-scale production of Accord and Civic auto engines, drive trains, and suspension and brake parts at the Anna engine plant. Plans call for a $450 million investment and a projected 800 new associates, with full-scale production to be in place in 1990.

EMERGENCE OF THE JAPANESE AUTOMOBILE COMPLEX

Several sets of factors have contributed to the development of the West Central Ohio Japanese automobile complex. These factors include the national and international business climate, the economic and political pressure for Japanese investment, prior Japanese manufacturing experience, and region-specific factors that favored development in West Central Ohio. Our analysis begins with an examination of the economic and political reasons for Japanese investment in the United States with specific attention to their impact on Honda.

The Decision to Invest in the United States

The United States market for automobiles is large and, although slower sales growth is anticipated, the Japanese are expected to capture an increasing share

Figure 6.1
Honda Investment in Ohio

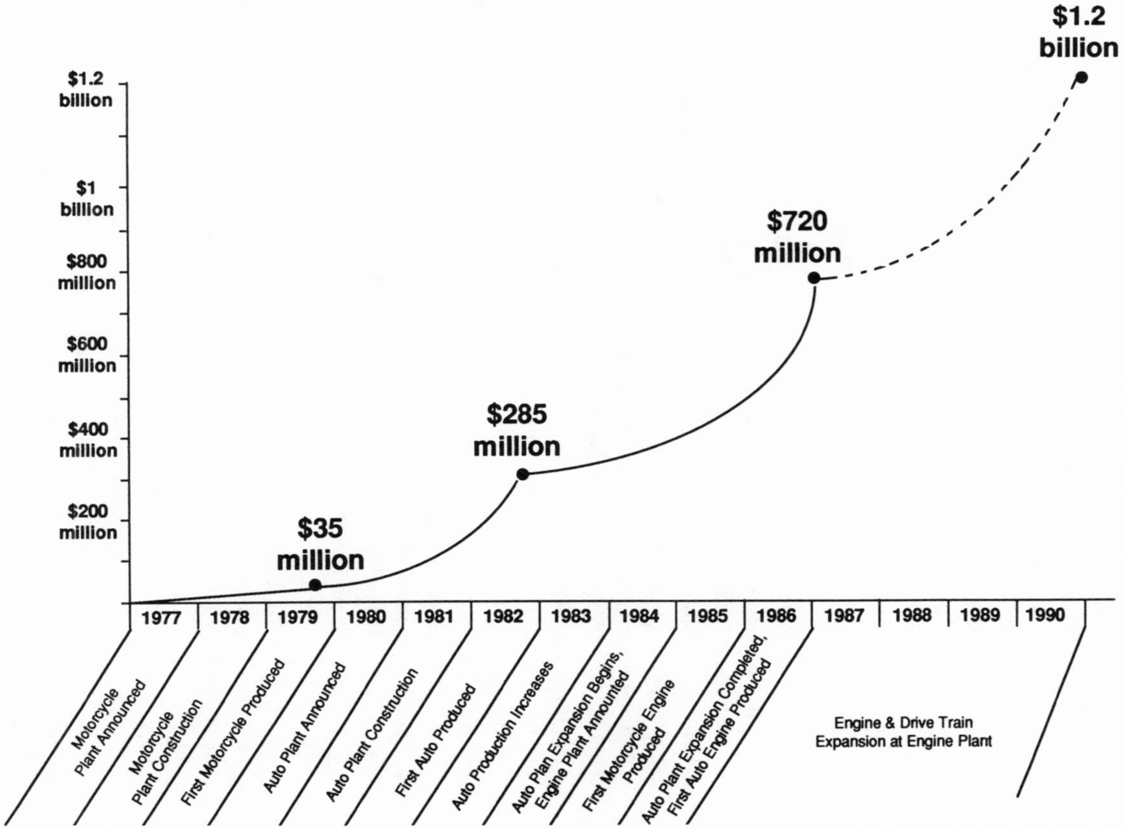

of the U.S. market (College of Urban Affairs, Cleveland State University, 1986: 40). Japanese companies believe that they can successfully compete in the U.S. market because of their managerial ability which enables them to supply high quality products at reasonable prices. A facility in the United States also positions a company like Honda to capitalize on changing U.S. market conditions. This advantage of being located in the markets that Honda serves is an integral part of their corporate philosophy.

Although the general corporate philosophy regarding the advantages of locating close to markets was a factor in Honda's decision to establish plants in America, the precipitating reasons were the collapse of the Bretton Woods agreement and the belief that the dollar was fundamentally overvalued. Significant declines in the value of the dollar since the mid–1970s had increased the cost of importing foreign-made cars into the United States and thwarted Honda's plans to gain a bigger share of the U.S. market. Even if the dollar had not been overvalued, fluctuations in exchange rates would have encouraged Japanese investment in the United States because the capacity to shift production from one country to another is useful in an era of exchange rate fluctuations.

American trade policies also have influenced Japanese automobile investment. Particularly since 1985, the threat of trade restrictions has tended to accelerate investment. While the Reagan administration was generally opposed to protectionist policies, there have been notable exceptions such as the imposition of quotas on motorcycles in order to protect Harley-Davidson. However, the decision to manufacture motorcycles near Marysville in Union County was made in 1977, prior to political pressures such as domestic content legislation, tariffs, or quotas that have stimulated growth of Japanese automobile facilities in the United States in more recent years. Consequently, Japanese manufacturers became increasingly concerned about further restrictive trade policies.

While the international financial climate contributed to Japan's decision to invest in the United States, more recent political factors have probably contributed to the growth of investment in Japanese establishments already in the United States. First, efforts to protect American firms from Japanese imports also protected Honda of America and other Japanese firms in West Central Ohio. Second, the threat of protective legislation may have accelerated the rate of Honda's investment in the United States as well as the rate of investment of Japanese suppliers. Third, declines in the value of the dollar relative to the yen since 1985 have lowered the cost of Japanese investment in the United States.

Japanese automobile manufacturers locating in the United States have also benefited from previous experiences in the U.S. market. Prior success in exporting has helped establish strategic market beachheads, provided a source of financing, and established working relationships with purchasers. In this regard, Honda's initial success in the U.S. market is due to its successful marketing of motorcycles. The company cleverly countered the black leather image of motorcyclists with an advertising campaign that pictured ordinary people riding motorcycles and the slogan, "you meet the nicest people on a Honda." The success in the motorcycle market was the basis for branching into the basic transportation segment of the automotive market.

The Decision to Invest in West Central Ohio

Ohio has been successful in attracting Japanese automobile and automotive component plants, ranking fourth among the states with the most Japanese automobile facilities. Excluding California, which has the largest number (88), the states with the most Japanese automobile-related facilities are in the traditional manufacturing region: Michigan (36), Illinois (36), and Ohio (35). There also has been a noticeable concentration of facilities south of the traditional manufacturing states in Kentucky (13) and Tennessee (9). In recent years, Ohio has achieved one of the highest growth rates for foreign investment in the nation (College of Urban Affairs, Cleveland State University, 1986: 18–27). Given the international and national investment climate, the question arises as to why the West Central Ohio region became a site for the Japanese-based automobile complex. Two sets of factors have been important: the State of Ohio's recruitment activities and the region's locational factors including both traditional economic conditions and the quality of life.

State and Local Recruitment Activities

Studies of major industrial location decisions indicate that states rather than local governments play the dominant role in developing the necessary subsidy packages to influence the locational choice. Such was the case with Honda and the West Central Ohio Japanese automobile complex. Under former Governor James Rhodes, the State of Ohio began efforts to attract Japanese transportation facilities in the early 1970s. Governor Rhodes visited Japan and built a personal relationship with several key Honda executives. Subsequently, he hosted a tour of several Ohio communities that were potential sites for Honda. The Governor also was interested in strengthening the automobile industry in Ohio. He proposed and helped establish the 8,000 acre Transportation Research Center testing facility that included a seven-mile test track in Union and nearby Logan County. Thus, the combination of a personal relationship and a site with automotive research facilities, available land for expansion, as well as approximately $16 million in state investment contributed to the establishment of the motorcycle plant in 1977 near Marysville.

Honda's investment of $61 million in the motorcycle plant has been dwarfed by later investments, but the motorcycle plant is important because it provided a foundation for an ongoing relationship between the State of Ohio and Honda. According to Governor Richard Celeste, previously developed cooperative relationships with Honda officials helped speed negotiations regarding Ohio's role in the establishment of Honda's second automobile facility in West Central Ohio (in Anna, about 20 miles from Marysville.) In effect, transactions or bargaining costs have been reduced because of the development of a variety of formal and informal communications channels between Honda and Ohio officials.

The cultivation of ongoing relationships is one of the key factors that distinguishes the development of the West Central Ohio automobile complex from an ad hoc locational choice. Honda officials have been explicit regarding the importance they place upon a continuing relationship with Ohio. Similarly, officials in the Ohio Department of Development have been clear about their intent to maintain and strengthen the working relationships with Honda. As Richard Celeste observed: "Far beyond the value of the incentive package, the spirit of cooperation between Ohio and Honda . . . has grown stronger and more secure as we have worked together over the past ten years" (Celeste, 1987).

The cooperative relationship with Honda has been based upon more than goodwill, however. Since 1977, Ohio has committed over $62 million to all Honda facilities and also has provided locational incentives to other firms to further strengthen the West Central Ohio automotive economy. (See Table 6.2.) At the same time, Ohio made clear that "no foreign company, not even Honda, was going to receive a better incentive package than that available to Ohio-based firms already operating here" (Celeste, 1988). For its part, Honda has never conducted an explicit and blatant bidding war in which Ohio was forced to compete with other states on the basis of the attractiveness of subsidy packages.

The continuing relationship between Ohio and Honda has paid off in an additional way. Ohio officials believe that Honda has helped introduce executives of other Japanese companies to Ohio economic development officials, making it easier for Ohio to attract other firms. The ability to attract Honda suppliers and ancillary producers is essential to the evolution of the automotive complex.

Local governments have played a subordinate role in encouraging Japanese automobile producers to locate in the region. In most of the small West Central Ohio communities where Japanese automotive facilities have located, local governments have provided only modest locational incentives. These partial tax abatements have exempted land or structures but still taxed equipment. However, local communities also have played an important role in creating a hospitable atmosphere. Paired family programs and cultural centers have helped smooth the relocation of some Japanese families. However, none of these programs are large scale because of the few Japanese employees at Honda sites.

Locational Factors

Duane Kujawa, in his study of Honda's choice of the Marysville site for its motorcycle plant, concluded that although Marysville is near a large market, the site was selected primarily because of the quality of the workforce, the proximity to local suppliers, and the existence of an efficient transportation system (Kujawa, 1986: 1).

The Marysville area labor force was considered work-oriented and appreciative of the opportunity to obtain relatively well-paying manufacturing jobs. Critics of Honda also contend that the area was not strongly influenced by labor unions

Table 6.2
Honda: State and Local Assistance

Project	Jobs	Investment	412	OITP	Highway	Local Assistance
1. Motorcycle Plant (Oct. (1977) Marysville/Union	400	$ 40,000,000	$3,610,595 (Attachment 1)	None	$11,100,000	100% tax abatement for 15 years on building. Union County
2. Honda Auto Plant (1981) Marysville/Union	2,000	$220,000,000	$1,668,909 (Attachment 1)	None	State committed to widen SR 33 to four lanes. 1987: $35,128,520	1) 100% tax abatement for 15 years on building. Union County 2) Marysville expanded sewer plant
3. Expand Auto Plant (Jan. 1984) Marysville/Union	500	$240,000,000	None	1986: $205,560	None	None
4. Engine Plant (March 1984) Anna/Shelby	200	$ 30,000,000	$1,000,000 On-site: –Road –Gas –Water –Sewer	$36,274	None	100% tax abatement for 15 years on building. Shelby County
5. Plastics Plant (Nov. 1984) Marysville/Union	140	$ 42,000,000	$1,500,000 On-site: –Electric –Gas –Rail Spur –Water Pump		None	100% tax abatement for 15 years on building. Union County
6. Expand Engine Plant and Foundry (Jan. 1987) Anna/Shelby	800	$450,000,000	$3,500,000 (Attachment 3)	$500,000	None	100% tax abatement for 15 years on building. Shelby County
GRAND TOTAL	4,040	$1.2 Billion	$11,279,504	$741,834 (Attachment 2)	$46,228,520	N/A

Source: State of Ohio, Department of Development.

as were nearby cities such as Dayton and Springfield. Lack of labor-management hostilities and bureaucratic procedures associated with unionization are critical to developing the kind of labor environment Honda desired.

The site also was chosen because of its proximity to local suppliers. The Japanese-style, just-in-time delivery inventory system makes proximity to suppliers more important than in the past because the automobile plants hold fewer inventories to reduce carrying costs and, thus, depend upon quick delivery to avoid parts shortages. The Honda facilities in West Central Ohio are close to local automobile suppliers and have excellent access to the interstate highway system including the I–75 "auto alley" corridor that links Detroit to Dayton and the Midsouth.

In addition to the factors cited by Kujawa, the availability of land was a key locational factor according to Honda and state officials. Honda officials, like representatives of other Japanese firms, wanted "greenfields" in which to build the kind of facility they wanted and in order to have room for future expansion. Consequently, building a manufacturing facility from "the ground up" allows the Japanese to design the internal floor space so as to maximize the advantages of their production methods. Revamping an existing building would not allow them that freedom. The desire for sites with ample land for the present and the future has contributed to the rural orientation of many Japanese facilities in West Central Ohio. As described above, the State of Ohio played an important role in providing suitable land.

A further analysis of why Japanese companies have located in West Central Ohio is presented in the Community Factor's Evaluation Project which included a survey of eighteen Japanese companies with plants in West Central Ohio. The survey was conducted, in part, to identify and evaluate factors the companies considered in making locational decisions (Wright State University and Area Progress Council, 1987). Seven of the eighteen companies provided usable responses and the results provide insights about making locational decisions even though the number of respondents is small. The results are summarized in Table 6.3. First, the importance of hard-cost factors was compared to the local living environment. Only one company described hard-cost factors as the only locational consideration. Two companies stated that hard-cost factors dominated their decision but the quality of the local living environment was given some consideration. The quality of the living environment was rated equal to, or more important than, hard-cost factors by four of the transplants.

Second, the survey respondents were asked to evaluate several specific locational factors. As shown in Table 6.4, the most important locational determinant of foreign-based companies was the availability of international education for the children of Japanese employees. International communications was the second most important locational factor with international travel opportunities, international media coverage (i.e., world financial news), and access to business services in Japan also considered important.

All of these international factors involve services that generally can be obtained

Table 6.3
Importance of Life Quality and Hard-Cost Factors

Number of Responses	Type of Factors
1	hard cost factors are the only consideration
2	hard cost factors are dominant but the local living environment is also considered
2	hard cost factors and the local living environment are about equal
2	hard cost factors are less important than the local living environment

Source: Wright State University and the Area Progress Council, *Community Factors Evaluation Project*, 1988.

Table 6.4
Importance of Specific Locational Factors

Locational Factor	Locational Importance
International Air Passenger Service	6.9
International Communications	8.0
Cultural Diversity	5.9
Community Hospitality Towards International Residents	7.6
Centrality to U.S. Markets	7.3
Dayton's Visibility in Other Countries	3.7
Downtown Amenities	5.4
International Education for Children	8.3
Presence of Other International-Based Companies of Similar National Origin	6.4

0 indicates least importance and 10 indicates most importance

Source: Wright State University and the Area Progress Council, *Community Factors Evaluation Project*, 1988.

more readily in metropolitan areas, which may explain why the Japanese automobile complex is located near the metropolitan areas of Columbus and Dayton. Marysville officials reported that most Honda executives have chosen to live near Columbus and commute to the plant because of the importance of urban access. Thus, urban pull is a significant factor in location decisions in addition to the orientation towards smaller towns because of labor supply and land considerations. But, since downtown amenities were ranked near the bottom of the list of locational factors, the responses suggest that most of the advantages of metropolitan locations can be obtained in the suburbs. This finding reinforces the view that quick access to the central city is decreasing in importance especially for manufacturing-oriented firms.

Community hospitality towards international residents was considered important as was the presence of other Japanese companies in the area. The presence of Japanese firms is likely to have a cumulative effect tending to reinforce the locational strengths of the region.

Agglomeration and Coevolutionary Development

The ability to take advantage of agglomeration economies is another important locational factor in the development of the automobile complex. Agglomeration economies refer to the lowering of production costs that occur because production is carried on to a substantial degree in one place (Isard, 1975: 113). For instance, if producers of a similar product locate near each other, suppliers of required inputs may be attracted to the area, and the entire business complex may benefit. Agglomeration economies are generally believed to be more important to firms located in metropolitan areas than to firms located in rural areas. However, the West Central Ohio Japanese automobile agglomeration is located in a region geographically wider than economists normally envision when discussing agglomeration economies. The West Central Ohio automobile agglomeration suggests that with the development of interstate highways and improved communications, agglomeration linkages may be effective throughout a large geographical region that includes several major cities and their hinterlands.

More recently, economists also have begun to draw upon the concept of coevolution to further explain the development of economic relationships. The development of the West Central Ohio automotive complex can be understood as a product of coevolution (Norgaard, 1984). The coevolutionary model, borrowed by development economists from ecological scientists, suggests that a new firm may modify its activities to fit or take advantage of characteristics of the local economy. At the same time, the local economy will change to better accommodate and exploit opportunities created by the new firm. The links between the firm and the local environment strengthen over time. Accordingly, the firm will become more dependent upon the local economy and hence less footloose while the local economy becomes more dependent upon the firm.

According to the coevolutionary model, Honda's original motorcycle plant can be understood as a first step in the development process. The state, other businesses, workers, and communities made adjustments to accommodate or exploit the facility. Local accommodations to Honda include the location of suppliers and the further development of the automotive complex, changes in labor force skills and attitudes, and the development of a better understanding of Japanese traditions by local residents. These and other changes made the area more attractive for further investment. The development of trust between Honda, public agencies, and private suppliers is another aspect of the coevolutionary process. Trust is an important element in Japanese-style negotiations and decisions (Sullivan and Peterson, 1982). Hence, the stronger the trust between Honda and other parties, the stronger the economic linkages and the greater the potential for coevolutionary development.

Local Economic Impacts

Honda has had a substantial economic impact on Marysville, Union County, and the West Central Ohio region. The total employment in the country's transportation manufacturing sector increased by 3325 employees between 1979–1986. Honda's expansion was particularly important during the 1979–1983 recession because the region was experiencing skyrocketing unemployment and cutbacks by other major employers such as Goodyear and Nestle. But for employment growth among automobile manufacturers, regional employment would have actually declined between 1979 and 1986. However, since Honda was expanding during a period of national recession, it was able to absorb displaced workers. Growth during the national recession enhanced Honda's reputation as a stable employer.

Honda operations propelled average income in Union County upward. Between 1985–1986, incomes increased 6.4 percent in Union County, well above the Ohio average. In fact, in 1986, Union County had a higher average income, $23,294, than any other county in Ohio. Until recently, Honda limited its employment pool to residents within 30 miles of the plant. This policy concentrated the economic benefits of Honda within Union County. After September, 1987, the hiring radius was expanded to 40 miles, so income and employment benefits have become more diffuse.

Another consequence of Honda's activities has been greater local awareness of international economic interdependence. Local business representatives have become much more aware of community economic linkages with the rest of the world. Chamber of Commerce officials include in their promotional literature a list of internationally based firms with local branches.

In contrast to the substantial impact on employment and jobs, Honda's impact on cultural activities has been less dramatic. Although many American workers at Honda take lessons in Japanese language and culture, and high performers have opportunities to travel to Japan, a substantial Japanese cultural presence in Marysville is not evident. There is virtually no Japanese presence in Marysville because Japanese executives gravitate toward Columbus to shop. However, Honda contributes to local civic projects similar to other major corporations. Union County officials also credit the economic growth attributable to Honda with stimulating a sense of optimism and civic interest. They point to passage of school bond issues and other successful community projects as events that were spurred by the revitalization of the local economic base.

LABOR-MANAGEMENT RELATIONS

One of the most widely publicized labor-management issues has been the unsuccessful attempt by the United Auto Workers to organize Honda production workers. Although the UAW has neither officially nor permanently given up unionization efforts, their attempts have been discontinued indefinitely because of the lack of support among Honda employees. One of the primary reasons for the failure of unionization efforts was Honda's good labor-management practices.

Japanese culture, which has been molded by a long history and deep-rooted traditions, dictates a paternalistic and collectivity-oriented management style. Because of these traditions, Japanese managers have been able to generate a high level of motivation and loyalty from their employees. Consequently, labor-management practices are based in Japanese culture and embodied in the "Associate System."

The Associate System is predicated upon the idea that everyone in the company is a colleague. Efforts are made to avoid invidious distinctions between labor and management. For instance: everyone wears similar uniforms and eats in the same cafeteria, there are no reserved parking spaces, and executives do not have separate enclosed offices. The former President of Honda Manufacturing of America (Shoichiro Irimajiri) used the term "togetherness" to describe the Associate System. Five areas important to the operation of the Associate System are: (1) employment security, (2) recruitment, (3) job duties, (4) training-promotion and (5) compensation.

Employment Security

Large Japanese corporations in Japan offer lifetime employment to certain segments of their workforce. However, Honda does not offer lifetime employment to its U.S. associates and for legal reasons does not intimate any tenure commitment. Still, workers have the impression that their jobs are more secure than comparable jobs in American automobile facilities even though no contractual obligation exists. Why do Honda employees feel so secure? First, the Honda plant has not had to lay off workers even during employment cutbacks in the automobile industry (nor has Honda worldwide). A bonus system helps ensure wage flexibility so that declines in product demand are felt in the form of lower compensation (a lost bonus instead of an actual reduction in the hourly rate) rather than layoffs (Weitzman, 1984). Second, Honda management has created an atmosphere that suggests a long-term commitment towards its employees. The tree planting ceremony is an example of a symbolically rich practice that contributes to the sense of employment permanence. New employees plant a tree on the company grounds with their names attached to it (Bowman, 1986). The ceremony implies that, like the tree, Honda will nurture the employee and the employee will sink roots into the Honda organization. The long-term commitment also is suggested by the corporate training programs for production associates (workers), as described below. Third, the Associate System drastically reduces distinctions between labor and management. Thus, production associates are more likely to view managers as colleagues sharing similar problems in the event of potential layoff. In contrast, traditional American firms make a sharp distinction between how hourly and salaried workers will be treated in the event of sales declines. Layoffs of hourly employees is one of the first responses to sales declines in most American manufacturing companies. As one Honda associate said, "Sure, I suppose we could demand more money right now and take a chance that we'd be out of work in ten years. . . . I'd rather see us reinvest than pay it all out. Job security is important to me" (Merwin, 1986: 105).

Recruitment

Honda, unlike most American manufacturing companies, deliberately attempts to build a corporate culture on the shop floor as well as in the executive suite. Recruitment policies and procedures are used to help select employees who will contribute toward the atmosphere the company is trying to create. Therefore, when hiring an employee, the company emphasizes personal and intellectual abilities, including the ability to learn, flexibility, group cohesion, honesty, and company loyalty much more than job specific skills and experience. Personnel officials at Honda believe that recruiting employees with these attributes will reduce absenteeism and enhance efficiency.

The employment selection process centers around the interview where executives and production associates interview groups of three or four prospective employees simultaneously. This mini-assessment center approach allows Honda officials the opportunity to present real-life scenarios or problems that could occur during the production process. In this way, the interviewing panel can assess a prospective associate's attitude toward teamwork, group problem solving, initiative, creativity, and flexibility. A rigorous, extensive recruitment process is a rational management policy given their desire to build and maintain a cooperative corporate culture and their commitment to avoid layoffs. "The recruitment effort reflects the importance that the Japanese attach to personal relationship . . . but there is also a practical necessity . . . to do with the way Honda makes cars" (Bowman and Caison, 1980: 25). The match of employees appears excellent since the turnover rate at Honda is only 1.1 percent compared to a national average for manufacturing firms of approximately 12 percent.

Until recently, Honda limited the hiring range to a radius of 30 miles around where the facility was located. This policy is consistent with several goals. First, and perhaps most practical, the company required some method for limiting applications. Based upon the ratio of applications to job openings, one observer noted that it was harder to get a Honda job than to get into an Ivy League college (Schook, 1988: 169). Second, by helping the local economy, Honda could secure a more prominent place in the region. Third, the geographic limits also may contribute to a workforce that suits Honda's corporate culture. The largely white rural workers may have work attitudes different from urban workers who may have union backgrounds. Finally, the geographic limits allowed the company to become an important part of the associates' nonwork environment. Following Japanese practice, Honda attempts to treat their associates as "whole persons," not nine-to-five sellers of labor. The closer associates live to the plant, the more easily they can participate in corporate recreation and social events.

However, union officials and others have charged that Honda's recruitment processes screen out blacks and other urban minorities. Efforts to hire locally and "to eliminate personalities that would clash with the cultural norms of the company" (Behr, 1987: 4) may have resulted in unlawful discrimination. The Equal Employment Opportunity Commission found merit in a discrimination charge against Honda. As part of a settlement, Honda agreed to pay $6 million in monetary compensation and seniority adjustments to 370 individuals (*New York Times*, February 24, 1988: 12). Japanese firms are particularly vulnerable to discrimination charges because Japan has deliberately maintained a homogeneous population and is viewed as intolerant of blacks by many Americans.

Job Duties

Employees at Honda are required to be flexible in their work assignments. Consequently, production is organized around groups of workers rather than around individual skills and has resulted in fewer clear-cut job specifications and job duties.

In describing the advantages of flexible job categories, Peter Drucker said:

In all the hundreds of books, articles and speeches on American competitiveness—or lack thereof—work rules and job restrictions are rarely mentioned. Such rules forbid a foreman to do any production work, whether taking the place of a worker who goes to the restroom, repairing tools or helping when the work falls behind. They forbid electricians to straighten a stud when installing a fuse box. They forbid workers moving from one job to another, thus restricting them to narrow, repetitive tasks. . . . Yet, the evidence indicates that work rules and job restrictions are the *main cause* of "the productivity gap" [emphasis added]. (1988: 7)

Union representatives, particularly UAW officials, often opposed job flexibility. They argue that with fewer job classifications, working conditions will deteriorate, employees will be subject to line speed ups, and fewer employees will be required. Since the trust level between management and employees of American-owned companies is often low, employees rely on these rigid delineations for job protection.

However, at Honda there are no job descriptions, and production associates are encouraged to be output- rather than task-oriented. For instance, one person moves parts from inventory to the production line where assembly workers pull them up as needed. If additional tasks need doing, the associates will pitch in. In contrast, the 1986 UAW contract with AMC Jeep Division near Toledo called for three workers, each with a different job description, to move parts to the assembly line. By working outside a specific classification, Honda employees can better understand the company. This structuring of the work leads to organizational, not functional, experts and also avoids the "that's not in my job" response prevalent in many American-owned manufacturing companies.

To encourage teamwork, quality circles are formed around specific production problems, and associates are encouraged to participate based on their interests and experience without regard to job title. Edward Demming's (1986) approach, especially his idea that all levels of employees should actively be concerned about quality, is part of the corporate culture at Honda.[1] A saying at Honda is, "There is more knowledge in the factory than in the office." The answers to problems and improvements in quality often come from the associate most directly involved.

Honda employees also are expected to participate in the decision-making processes. For Japanese, few decisions are too critical to forego reaching a consensus (Keys and Miller, 1984). Even if the consensus decision is mediocre, it will have the support of the employees, their knowledge of the decision parameters, and their commitment to successful execution. Thus, the decision will be able to withstand the uncertainties of implementation better than some decision imposed from above.

James Swaney (1981) provided a general theoretical framework that helps explain why a less rigid, informal set of job duties and decision-making processes may be more efficient than the carefully defined bureaucratic structure that characterized market transactions. He suggested that a sense of community can reduce negative spillovers (externalities) that are a major problem in market economies:

The following argument suggests that the particular habits of thought and mind nurtured and instilled through the domination of economic decision-making by the market mechanisms are partly to blame for the rapid growth of externality . . . [and] the gradual erosion of community responsibility, caused by the domination of the market mentality, is a major cause of externality. (Swaney, 1981: 617, 624)

A similar theoretical perspective may apply to the production process. If every rule must be spelled out, slight, unanticipated disruptions in the work routine may create spillovers in other aspects of the production process. In contrast, if a sense of community exists in the work place, individuals may be willing to pitch in to help smooth unanticipated events. Thus, a sense of community may contribute to greater production efficiency.

Training and Promotion

Honda recently built a $3 million center to provide a home for education, training, and quality circle groups. In addition to technical training, Honda offers some classes in more general or academic subjects such as Japanese language classes. Honda also sends hundreds of its employees to Japan for training and to present innovative production ideas developed by quality circle groups. The heavy investment in training supports the impression that production associates are part of a corporate team and that the company has a commitment to the individual.

Honda is committed to promoting from within. Again, this practice is an outgrowth of their philosophy about how to treat people. As previously noted, Honda expends tremendous effort to hire individuals who fit their corporate culture and who are eager to grow with the company. It only makes sense to promote employees who share Honda's vision. Many of the executives at the Marysville plant have not risen through the ranks because the facility is too new to have a pool of experienced insiders. However, throughout the worldwide organization, the vast majority of senior managers began their careers with Honda at entry level positions. A Honda manager said that it was a sign of failure when a company must appoint outsiders to executive positions (Schook, 1988: 172). The practice of internal promotion helps maintain morale and insures that executives have shop-floor experience.

Compensation

At Honda, the spread in total compensation between the executives, middle managers, and the production associates is significantly less than at other U.S. automobile companies. The smaller spreads reflect the Japanese practice of having smaller salary differentials and fewer pay classes as well as Honda's smaller size compared to its U.S. competitors. In either case, the smaller spread probably helps reduce a substantial barrier to the development of a team spirit between labor and management.

Currently, compensation for production associates is roughly equal to compensation of employees at other U.S. automobile facilities. However, Honda employees have less experience and seniority. Consequently, Honda officials claim that the total benefit package is above that offered elsewhere when age and experience factors are considered. (See Table 6.5.)

Compensation at Honda was below the industry standard prior to 1986. The compensation gap recently closed not merely because of increases in Honda's compensation, but also because UAW workers have not received large pay increases in recent years. In turn, the slow increase in UAW compensation can be attributed to restructuring within the automobile industry and to nonunionized plants such as the Honda facilities that have weakened union bargaining power.

POLICY IMPLICATIONS

The success of West Central Ohio Japanese automobile agglomeration has important implications for public development officials, corporate managers, union leaders, and Japanese executives operating in the United States.

First, state and local development officials should distinguish between one-shot efforts to attract potential employers and ongoing efforts required to develop an industrial agglomeration. Although the initial effort to successfully attract a

Table 6.5

Wages and Benefits at Honda of America Manufacturing*

Wages (production)	$13.20 after 18 months
Bonuses	Attendance, $80 – $104; Annual, 2.25% of regular earnings; Bonus Sharing, $5.86 per point (November 1987)
Shift Premiums	$.60 to $.70 per hour
Paid Days Off	13 Holidays, 4 plant shutdown days, vacation, personal leave (more paid time off than union workers in the auto industry)
Health Insurance	Hospital and surgical, weekly sickness and accident ($250), supplemental accident, major medical, long-term disability ($4,000/mo)
Pension	Benefits exceed other auto industry pension plans
Additional Benefits	Safety shoe allowance (2 prs./$25 per pair), uniforms, dental, educational assistance program, prescription drug coverage, bereavement pay, etc.

*Wages and benefit level as of March 1988

Source: Honda of America Manufacturing, Inc.

firm to an area is important, additional benefits may accrue through the development of an industrial agglomeration. Ohio has successfully institutionalized what was initially a personal working relationship between Honda officials and Governor Rhodes. In the long run, a policy designed to establish working relationships with Japanese firms in the United States may help stimulate regional development more than efforts that end when a locational agreement has been reached. Follow-up and concern for expansions are important to the coevolutionary process. Attracting suppliers and related firms can help existing industries and regional employment, thus contributing to agglomeration economies. The potential for attracting other firms also should be considered in determining what industries to initially recruit. Moreover, government officials should appreciate the substantial geographic scope of agglomeration economies.

Many Japanese firms seek locations that provide both a good life quality and low production costs. Sites on the fringe of urban areas appear to offer a suitable tradeoff between desirable urban amenities and low production costs. Development planners may want to highlight such areas in their attempts to attract Japanese firms. Marysville representatives have created a hospitable atmosphere without altering local culture or customs in any significant way.

The Honda experience also has important implications for U.S. management practices. The principal challenge to U.S. management is to develop an efficient work atmosphere. The sense of "community" that appears to exist at the Honda facilities is efficient but rare. Developing such an atmosphere will be difficult because of the substantial barriers that exist between management and production workers in the United States. Many of these barriers are systemic to U.S. management style. The "associate system" is a model that will work in the U.S. labor environment as evidenced by the current 5800 American associates who work for Honda in Marysville. U.S. managers may wish to modify existing practices to capture the efficiencies associated with a more cooperative work environment.

The success of Honda's motorcycle and automobile facilities is a challenge to industrial unions. Production employees at Honda rejected UAW organizing efforts in large part because they feared a conflict-oriented style that would lead to inefficiencies and job loss in the long run. Honda's collegial treatment of Production Associates and the attitude of teamwork has made unionization difficult. Union leaders must develop a representational model that will avoid unnecessary conflict and inefficient work rules while protecting workers.

Finally, there are lessons for Japanese companies locating in the United States. Particularly in their hiring practices, Honda appears to have failed to appreciate the importance of nondiscriminatory hiring procedures. Dexter Dunphy (1987) made the following generalization about Japanese practices that is illustrated by the Honda case: "When operating overseas, some Japanese companies have failed to appreciate that key stakeholder relationships (e.g., government) are different in the U.S. and have ended with major lawsuits against them" (Dunphy, 1987: 454).

In addition, the changing demographics of the workplace will present challenges to Japanese management practices. As Honda's work force ages, the sense of community and teamwork may be threatened. Employees may not feel as grateful for their jobs as they do now, and they may become more cynical toward concepts of teamwork and cooperation. In addition, union representatives claim that the current line speed will become difficult for older workers to maintain, so the potential for labor management conflict will increase. Whether the associate system can deal successfully with these potential challenges is an open question.

NOTE

1. Quality control circles, now commonly called "quality circles," are a problem-solving method whereby small groups of employees regularly meet to develop methods that will solve problems relating to production, quality, cost, and the organizational environment.

REFERENCES

Behr, Peter. 1987. "Honda is Rolling Success Off Its Ohio Assembly Line." *Washington Post*, 3 May, 4.
Bowman, James A. 1986. "The Rising Sun in America." *Personnel Administrator*, September: 63–67.

Bowman, James S., and Frederick K. Caison. 1980. "Japanese Management in America: Experts Evaluate Japanese Subsidiaries." *Advanced Management Journal* 51: 22–28.

Celeste, Richard. 1987. "Remarks: Honda Announcement." Mimeo, 17 September.

———. 1988. "How Honda and Ohio Grow Together." *Ohio Business* 5 (February): 2.

College of Urban Affairs, Cleveland State University. 1986. *Targeting Japanese Automotive Investment Opportunities for the State of Ohio*. Cleveland, Ohio: Cleveland State University.

Demming, W. Edward. 1986. *Out of Crisis*. Cambridge: Massachusetts Institute of Technology, Center for Advanced Engineering.

Drucker, Peter. 1988. "Workers' Hands Bound by Tradition." *Wall Street Journal*, 2 August, 7.

Dunphy, Dexter. 1987. "Convergence/Divergence: A Temporal Review of the Japanese Enterprise and Its Management." *Academy of Management Review* 12: 445–459.

"Honda Agrees to Pay $6 Million in Discrimination Settlement." 1988. *New York Times*, 24 February, 12.

Isard, Walter. 1975. *Introduction to Regional Science*. Englewood Cliffs, N.J.: Prentice-Hall.

Keys, J. Bernard, and Thomas R. Miller. 1984. "The Japanese Theory Management Jungle." *Academy of Management Review* 9: 342–353.

Kujawa, Duane. 1986. *Japanese Multinationals in the United States*. New York: Praeger.

Merwin, John. 1986. "A Tale of Two Worlds." *Forbes* 137 (16 June): 101–106.

Norgaard, Richard B. 1984. "Coevolutionary Development Potential." *Land Economics* 60: 160–173.

Schook, Robert L. 1988. *Honda: An American Success Story*. Englewood Cliffs, N.J.: Prentice-Hall.

Sullivan, Jeremiah, and Richard B. Peterson. 1982. "Factors Associated With Trust in Japanese-American Joint Ventures." *Management International Review* 22: 30–40.

Swaney, James A. 1981. "Externality and Community." *Journal of Economic Issues* 15 (September): 615–627.

Tolchin, Martin, and Susan Tolchin. 1988. *Buying into America*. New York: Time Books.

Weitzman, Martin L. 1984. *The Share Economy*. Cambridge, Mass.: Harvard University Press.

Wright State University and Area Progress Council. 1987. *Community Factors Evaluation Project*. Dayton, Ohio: Wright State University.

7

Local Images of Japanese Automobile Investment in Indiana and Kentucky

Robert Perrucci and Madhavi Patel

The past decade has seen a substantial increase in foreign investment in the American economy. A prominent element of this foreign investment has been associated with the construction and operation of assembly plants by Japanese automobile corporations. Their plant location decisions have been embedded in intense competition among states and regions for the new plant sites. How have states competed for foreign capital? Promoting the general quality of life of an area, such as its climate, culture, educational system, and leisure activities, is part of routine state industrial recruitment efforts. Robert Goodman in *The Last Entrepreneurs* (1979) also suggests that states offer relaxed environmental pollution standards, an antilabor climate, and economic incentives. A significant feature of this interstate competition is the use of tax abatements, land, job training, and low cost loans, all of which often involve the offer of millions of dollars in public funds to multinational private enterprises.

When Goodman's book appeared, Pennsylvania had been the only state to use an economic incentive package to attract foreign automobile investment. The state had provided Volkswagen with $71 million in low interest loans, rail and highway improvements, job recruiting, and tax abatements for the construction of a $200 million plant which began operation in 1978. Since then, there have been six major Japanese automobile ventures financed with state economic incentives including Toyota's $800 million plant in Georgetown, Kentucky, built with a $125 million state incentive package, and Subaru-Isuzu, a $500 million plant in Lafayette, Indiana, built with $83 million in state incentives.

State government leaders who have negotiated these incentive packages with Japanese automobile executives have done so believing that the new assembly plants will produce substantial economic benefits in the form of jobs and taxes. They have, however, encountered opposition from environmentalists concerned about damage to air and water quality and from taxpayers fearful about the cost of the incentive and the need for increased taxes to provide the infrastructure of roads, schools, recreation, and police and fire protection generated by the new plant. Given this great potential for public controversy and community conflict, what has been the role of local newspapers in these state economic development activities? How have they presented the state government's use of public monies to attract foreign automobile manufacturers? Do they seek to shape public awareness and public opinion? If so, do they take a critical independent stance or do they function as part of the state government's legitimation process?

This chapter will explore these questions by analyzing the amount and type of coverage the *Lafayette Journal and Courier*, the *Louisville Courier-Journal*, and the *Lexington Herald-Leader* have provided their readers about the establishment of the Subaru-Isuzu and Toyota assembly plants. We begin with the assumption that local newspapers are the principal source of information for citizens about the general issues of growth and development and about specific efforts by their state governments to use economic incentives to attract Japanese auto plants. We expect that local newspaper portrayals of the auto plant recruitment efforts will reflect the structure of community influence, be it the views of economic elites, diverse interest groups, or dominant political coalitions.

NEWSPAPERS AND COMMUNITY STRUCTURE

The special status of newspapers in American society is based largely on an ideology which extols the values of objectivity and impartiality. The press does not reflect the views of any particular segment of society but provides a balance of perspectives that "satisfy the public's need to know" (Drier, 1982; Schudson, 1978; Tuchman, 1978). This view of newspapers dovetails with the pluralist theory of community influence which sees a community as composed of competing interest groups pursuing narrow interests. The press, through its balanced coverage of issues and its editorials, is the guardian of the public interest against the misuse of power by government or by special interests. At its best, therefore, newspapers represent a reformist influence and the voice of the community at large.

An alternative view argues that while newspapers attempt to present a pluralistic view of issues, their economic underpinnings are probusiness and procapital (Murdock, 1980, 1982). A newspaper has a direct interest in growth, because it is a business whose financial status is related to the size of the local community and its aggregate growth (Molotch, 1976). As the city expands, a newspaper, which benefits primarily from increased ad lines and circulation, will be able to increase its customers, revenues, and profits. Newspapers also have strong institutional links with the dominant centers of power and use their influence to legitimate the existing political and economic structures of society (Drier, 1982) and to maintain and bolster the predisposition for general economic growth (Logan and Molotch, 1987).

Since newspapers' interests are tied to growth, we would expect them to provide coverage of topics that are favorable to business interests and to avoid those that might be critical of growth strategies. We would also expect them to be very supportive of efforts by state and local government to provide economic incentives to attract foreign capital including Japanese automobile manufacturers. As a consequence, their support will be reflected in the particular images of community growth which are presented in editorials and news accounts about the new automobile plants.

IMAGES OF COMMUNITY GROWTH

News accounts about a new automobile plant are not so much a matter of reporting events that have occurred, as they are creating and shaping readers' perceptions of and experience with the new plant. Newspapers have a special opportunity to influence attitudes and opinions about economic growth, because they can frame growth questions in terms of new jobs or new problems. Thus a newspaper's selection, construction, and orchestration of editorials and articles will be able to create a general image of why growth is occurring and with what consequences. We believe that there are three images that newspapers can present: a growth-elitist image, a political-pluralist image, and an ecological image.

Growth-Elitist Image

"A city and, more generally, any locality, is conceived as the areal expression of some land-based elite" (Molotch, 1976: 309). Those with ownership rights to land seek profits through expanded demand for the holdings that they control and compete to have resources that will contribute to growth applied to their areas of control. Local business elites with practical interests in the use of land and buildings, such as developers, landlords, and savings and loan officials, are the major participants in urban politics. They build their fortunes by managing cultural institutions, promoting urban growth, and influencing urban governments (Molotch and Logan, 1984). The role of government in this institutional system is to promote the growth process. Cities function, in effect, as "growth machines" (Molotch, 1976). They compete with other local governments to attract capital and, thereby, intensify returns on land, buildings, products, and services.

The most common effort of local leaders hoping to improve employment and income in their community is the pursuit of new basic employers: those industries that produce goods and services for which payments are received from outside the community (Pulver, 1979). The rationale is that basic industries will more fully utilize local resources, which in turn will bring income into the community to be dispersed among its citizens. Through the multiplier effect, this income will be spent on goods and services in the community, producing still more income and employment. Support for the growth machine hypothesis is provided by Larry Lyon et al. (1981), who found that the power of the business sector of a community was directly associated with greater local population growth.

A number of options are available to policy makers interested in attracting new employers. None will ensure that new employment occurs unless the policy makers themselves initiate the development. Most of the options propose action aimed at the creation of an atmosphere that provides positive incentives for new businesses: the development of industrial sites; the extension of sewer, water, rail, and power lines; investments in speculative buildings; and labor force surveys. None guarantees new industry, but each facilitates movement to the community and, at minimum, evidences community interest (Pulver, 1979).

With rare exceptions, one issue consistently generates consensus among local elite groups and separates them from people who use a city principally as a place to live and work: the issue of growth. For those who count, the city is a growth machine, one that can increase aggregate rents and trap related wealths for those in the right position to benefit (Molotch, 1976). The desire for growth creates consensus among a wide range of elite groups, regardless of their stand on other issues. It does not even matter that elites often fail to achieve their growth goal; with virtually all players in the same game, some elites will inevitably lose no matter how great their effort (Logan and Molotch, 1987). But more importantly, elites use their growth consensus to eliminate any alternate vision of the purpose of local government or the meaning of community. The ability of the business elite to dominate a community's agenda is found in the multiple positions held in major community organizations and their interlocking business and social ties (Perrucci and Lewis, 1989).

Political-Pluralist Image

In the 1950s and 1960s, the study of urban politics was embroiled in a debate over the degree of concentration of power in American communities. One perspective—the elitist tradition—maintained that community life is dominated by a relatively small group of persons with economic and political power who initiate, direct, and resolve that level of decision-making which has a major bearing on the body politic (Hunter, 1953; Miller, 1958; Form and D'Antonio, 1959). A second perspective—the pluralist view—found power to be distributed among a number of organized community groups, with influence shifting according to the issues rather than domination by a single power faction across all community issues (Dahl, 1961; Wolfinger, 1960; Polsby, 1963).

In an effort to move beyond the case studies of single communities that fueled the elitist-pluralist debate, Terry Clark (1968) initiated a program of comparative studies in which he attempted to link centralization of power and decision-making to specific community characteristics. Decentralized and pluralistic power structures are expected in larger, more heterogeneous communities with a diverse economy. Other community characteristics that are linked to pluralism include the extent of unionization and the existence of strong extralocal ties, as in absentee ownership of businesses (Trounstine and Christensen, 1982). The emphasis of this research on broad comparisons using archival data resulted in less attention to the basic questions of "power, inequality, and the workings of the political process" and more attention to a "wide assortment of variables relating to community structure and policy outputs" (Walton, 1976: 298–299). Thus, power came to be viewed as the exercise of influence over a series of loosely related discrete decisions in a variety of issue areas.

The pluralist perspective sees the community as composed of interest sectors having different views of what is best for the community, for example, political, industrial, banking, labor, commercial, religious, and education sectors. These sectors are interest groups that develop out of concern for protecting their own "territory." For instance, the industrial sector is constantly trying to promote industrial growth and will lobby for or against community decisions that will enhance or threaten their success; the other sectors follow likewise. Any empirical evidence of visible cleavage, such as disputes on a public issue, has been accepted as evidence of pluralistic competition.

Many sectors emerge in a community when the issue of growth is presented. These different sectors are vying for economic growth which will be most suitable to their interests. This inevitably motivates each sector to take a stand either for or against the issues of growth. For instance, with the opening of the Subaru-Isuzu auto plant in Indiana, there are certain sectors of the community that are apprehensive, such as the parents of school-age children and school teachers who have voiced their concern about the Japanese children adjusting to the system. Similarly, the labor community is concerned about whether it will have more jobs available and whether there will be a unionized or nonunionized work force.

Each unit of the community will strive, at the expense of others, to enhance the land-use potential of the parcels with which it is associated. Hence, the political-pluralist image is that which stands for all the different sectors of society which have a say in the issues of economic growth. If the *Lafayette Journal and Courier*, and *Louisville Courier-Journal*, and the *Lexington Herald-Leader* are embedded in a pluralist model of influence, they will voice the views and interests of different sectors of their respective communities, be they the commercial, labor, religious, or educational sectors.

Ecological Image

The classical school of human ecology explains urban development in terms of biotic determinism (Molotch, 1976). Like all living things, human beings must find a spatial niche in the larger habitat. This gives rise to competition between the different types of land users with each type seeking out a location to which he or she is most adaptable. Since land is a scarce resource, there is competition among land users for the most desirable space. Winners and losers in this competition find their place within the human ecological community and, in their own way, contribute to the sustenance of the total habitat (Hawley, 1950). The resulting patterns of adaptation produce a city with distinctive areas, each with its own types of land use, structures, and transportation patterns.

The ecological image views economic development in a community as part of a natural process that determines the relative desirability of particular locations and the resulting patterns of development. The image also embraces a free market concept in which buyers and sellers compete to satisfy the space needs of consumers. In this view, trying to resist the natural processes of industrial and population growth in a community would be as pointless as trying to deter the adaptation of particular plants to changes in the natural environment. If growth is prevented in one location, it will simply occur in the next most suitable location.

Among the more significant consequences of this natural struggle for space is an inevitable inequality and differentiation within and between cities. According to Amos Hawley, inequality among places is even more explicitly construed as a natural consequence to differentiation. Certain activities carried out in a particular location (for example, location of needed raw materials) will give that place greater power in relations among differentiated units. Differences between cities are based on a functional symbiosis that distributes growth and development across regions (Duncan et al., 1960). Cities thus grow because they are able to make a positive contribution in the larger system of cities.

Contemporary human ecologists use an ecosystem perspective that gives central attention to the interdependence of ecological forces that shape a community (Hassinger and Pinkerton, 1986). A change in a community's population, for example, reverberates throughout the ecosystem to produce changes in social organization, in the natural environment, and in the technology used by a population. The ecosystem perspective is also part of the way that environmentalists think about the mutually dependent relationships between groups in a community, and the necessity of human communities to be sensitive to their impact on the natural environment.

NEWSPAPERS AND COMMUNITY GROWTH IMAGES

The three images of community growth hypothesize different functions for local newspapers. A newspaper which employs the elitist-growth image would stress the views held by the community's business and economic elites. In this case, a newspaper would cover growth issues as if they were in a win-win situation. Stories would emphasize the advantages of having a $500 million automobile plant in the community: the creation of more jobs, the possibility of new supplier industries, and the likely economic growth of the community. This type of coverage would also carefully sidestep, counter, or dilute potential negative issues and, thereby, diffuse any anti-Toyota or anti-Subaru talk.

If a newspaper followed the political-pluralist image, we would expect a wide variety of news accounts about the actions and opinions of different leaders and interest groups about the new automobile plant and its impact. Here stories would provide a broad representation of opinions about the costs and benefits from increased employment, the demand for public services, and the general economic growth of the community.

A newspaper's use of the ecological image would result in stories examining alternative patterns of community development and give voice to concerns about the social and environmental consequences of an automobile assembly plant. Stories would examine the plant's impact on the social and natural environment. They would, for example, focus on the problems of increased traffic, the influx of foreign students into local schools, the use of agricultural land for industrial purposes, population pressure on housing, and the environmental pollution due to the operation of the new plant.

Which of these images of economic growth will newspapers use to report the events concerning new Japanese automobile plants in Kentucky and Indiana? The general hypothesis we examine is that the coverage and dominant themes of newspaper articles on Toyota and Subaru-Isuzu automobile plants will be likely to support the growth-elitist image. We will also examine three specific hypotheses. First, the news coverage will emphasize growth themes over pluralism and ecological themes. Second, the news accounts will focus primarily on economic and political figures as compared to persons from the religious, educational, labor, environmental, and social service sectors of the community. Third, the news coverage will present a predominantly positive view of the new plant, thereby diffusing any criticism which could arouse anti-Toyota or anti-Subaru-Isuzu sentiment.

Finally, we provide an intrastate comparison of coverage provided by the Louisville and Lexington newspapers. Louisville is approximately 80 miles from the Toyota plant site, and the newspaper is oriented toward statewide and national events. Lexington is 12 miles from the plant, and the *Herald-Leader* is the major *local* newspaper reporting the Toyota story. This will permit us to see if the local newspaper provides coverage that is more sensitive to the social and environmental impact of the plant, while the statewide newspaper gives more attention to economic growth.

Method

We will conduct a content analysis of material from three newspapers, the *Lafayette Journal and Courier*, the *Louisville Courier-Journal*, and the *Lexington Herald-Leader*. The unit of analysis will be the newspaper clipping. We collected every item which mentioned Toyota or Subaru–Isuzu during the thirteen months after the first story about Toyota's choice of the Georgetown site and Subaru-

Isuzu's choice of Lafayette. The sample includes 139 *Courier-Journal* and 60 *Herald-Leader* clippings from December 1985 to December 1986, and 236 *Journal and Courier* stories from December 1986 to December 1987.

The clippings from the three papers are primarily news stories, 86 percent in the *Journal and Courier* and 95 percent in the *Courier-Journal* and *Herald-Leader*. The remainder are editorials or letters to the editor. Although the number of *Journal and Courier* news clippings devoted to Subaru-Isuzu is considerably greater than those of the Kentucky newspapers, the amount of space provided by the three papers does not follow this pattern. A total of 8,695 square inches of coverage (or an average of 62.6 inches per article) was provided in the *Courier-Journal* as compared to 5,776 square inches (96.3 inches per article) in the *Herald-Leader* and 5,520 square inches (or an average of 23.4 inches per article) in the *Journal and Courier*.

These clippings were analyzed by reading and coding them for their specific content including, for example, the number of political leaders, the rise in housing and land values, and the prospects of attracting additional new industries. Some of the categories are descriptive, identifying, for instance, the number and length of articles, editorials, and letters. Other categories are analytical, based on the three ideal types of community growth images. Analytical categories include articles about the costs and benefits of the new plant, the state's incentive package, and the views of community sectors represented in the articles.

The coding categories take into account the themes of each clipping, whether the issues appear, the frequency of coverage of certain categories, and the amount of space in square inches devoted to each case.[1] Reliability estimates for coding the *Journal and Courier* articles were obtained by having an independent person code a sample of the articles.[2] Ten percent, or 23 of the 236 clippings were randomly selected and then coded in terms of 43 categories for a total of 989 codes. Thirty-one coding differences occurred for an overall coder reliability of .96. Since these differences were minor and distributed evenly over all the categories, the same codes were applied, without reliability testing, to the *Courier-Journal* and *Herald-Leader* articles.

NEWSPAPER COVERAGE IN KENTUCKY AND INDIANA

The newspaper coverage of the Toyota and Subaru-Isuzu automobile plants provides the opportunity to examine our hypotheses about the amount and type of coverage devoted to the plant openings. In this section, we will analyze the persons, organizations, and topics mentioned in the news accounts and the amount of coverage that is positive or negative in its treatment of the subject. This analysis will identify the significant issues that dominate coverage about automobile plants and the consequential actors: those persons and organizations whose views should be taken into account because they are involved in dealing with issues related to community growth.

Table 7.1 contains information on the persons and organizations from different

Table 7.1
Persons/Organizations from Different Community Sectors Mentioned in News Accounts

Community Sector	Lafayette J&C No. of Mentions	%	Louisville CJ No. of Mentions	%	Lexington H-L No. of Mentions	%
Sector 1						
Labor Leader/Organization	6	1.0	164	20.0	23	15.0
Education Leader/Organization	60	9.9	40	4.9	12	8.0
Religious Leader/Organization	1	.2	--	--	--	--
Social Service Agencies	15	2.5 (13.6)	3	.4 (25.3)	--	-- (23.3)
Sector 2						
Business-Industry Leader	56	9.3	21	2.6	8	5.3
Professionals (attorneys, consultants)	47	7.8	85	10.4	19	12.7
Commercial Leader/Organization (e.g. Chamber of Commerce)	117	17.7 (34.8)	25	3.0 (16.0)	17	11.3 (29.3)
Sector 3						
Political Official – Local	146	24.3	82	10.0	19	12.7
Political Official – State	146	24.3	227	27.7	34	22.7
Political Official – National	14	2.5 (51.1)	93	11.3 (49.0)	8	5.3 (40.7)
Other	4	.7	81	9.9	10	6.7
	612	(100.2)	821	(100.2)	150	(100)

Table 7.2
Ecological Topics Mentioned in News Accounts

Topic	Lafayette J&C No. of Mentions	%	Louisville CJ No. of Mentions	%	Lexington H-L No. of Mentions	%
Land Use	34	30.6	23	11.6	3	5.8
Displaced Homeowners	30	27.0	46	23.1	2	3.8
Pollution	9	8.1	53	26.6	14	26.9
Traffic	8	7.2	10	5.0	2	3.8
Impact on Schools	7	6.3	6	3.0	3	5.8
Intergroup Tensions	20	18.0	17	8.5	8	15.3
Constitutional Questions	2	1.8	20	10.0	13	25.0
General Changes in Community	1	.9	24	12.1	7	13.5
Total Mentions	111	(99.9)	199	(99.9)	52	(99.9)
Mentions Per Article	.47		1.4		.87	

sectors mentioned in newspaper stories about the new automobile plants. A balanced dispersion of mentions across community sectors would suggest that the newspapers present a pluralistic image of the community, because different views about the auto plant are presented. Table 7.1 indicates, however, that most of the persons and organizations mentioned in news accounts are from the business and political sectors, and this is especially true in Indiana. In general, much less attention is given to labor, education, religious, environmental, and social service agencies. There are notable differences among the newspapers, in that the two Kentucky papers give much more attention to labor in their news accounts. But this is due primarily to the fact that labor representatives and organizations were involved in a dispute over hiring practices by the Ohbayashi construction firm which was building the Toyota plant. As a result of this dispute, labor initiated several legal actions involving constitutional and environmental issues which served to slow progress at the construction site until they were resolved. Thus labor's higher profile in the Kentucky newspapers was the result of its own efforts that were publicly visible and newsworthy and not because the newspapers took the initiative to advance the interests of labor.

In sum, the evidence in Table 7.1 supports the growth-elitist image of newspaper coverage of the new automobile assembly plants. The actors of consequence in the news accounts are drawn primarily from the political sector which was responsible for developing the economic incentive packages and from the business sector which will benefit from any economic growth that is generated by the new plants. Persons and organizations who will have to deal with the impact of the new plants on the environment, schools, housing markets, transient populations, and other aspects of community life have not been sought out by newspapers to provide their views on economic growth.

Table 7.2 summarizes those news accounts which present an ecological image of growth, in that they place the auto plant in a broader systemic context of interdependencies and consequences. The *Lafayette Journal and Courier* contained 111 mentions of such topics (.47 mentions per article). The majority of the topics involved land use issues ("Panel OKs Auto Plant Zoning Request" and "Recommendation: New Homes Go East of Auto Site") and displaced or disgruntled homeowners ("Mobile Home Park Fate in Limbo," "Path to Auto Plant Cuts Across Yards," and "Residents Fight Park Evictions"). The next largest category of topics involved tensions between Japanese and Americans because of the auto plant ("Auto Plant Dredges Up Ill Will" and "Fear of Racism Opens Rift Among Toyota Protesters").

The *Louisville Courier-Journal*, which contained almost 200 mentions (1.4 mentions per article), gave much more prominent coverage to ecological topics, with similar attention given land use topics, and to the state's acquisition of homeowners' property for road expansion and of farm land for the plant site.[3] A notable difference from the Lafayette paper's coverage was the greater attention given to concerns about environmental pollution and to questions about the constitutionality of the state's incentive package. In both cases, the coverage emphasizes the law suits initiated by labor and citizens groups to challenge actions undertaken by the state on behalf of Toyota.

The *Lexington Herald-Leader*, whose readers will be neighbors of the new auto plant, provided 52 mentions of ecology topics (.87 mentions per article). This "hometown" paper gave greatest attention to environmental pollution, constitutional questions, intergroup tensions, and the way the auto plant would change the community. The Lexington paper also gave prominent attention to the law suits initiated by labor and citizens groups.

Immediately after the state made public its economic incentive package ("Governor Collins Unveils $125 Million Incentive Package for Toyota"), constitutional lawyers raised questions about its legality ("State's Plan to Give Toyota Land May Be Unconstitutional") and labor leaders moved to test its constitutionality ("Two To Join Suit Over Toyota Plant Financing"). Local citizens concerned about environmental issues held public meetings ("Toyota Jobs vs. Environmental Impact Debates" and "Scott County Families Seek Aid to Ensure Clean Water"), and soon afterward union officials challenged the state's issuance of a permit for air pollution control facilities at the Toyota plant ("2 Protest Toyota Pollution Permit"). Although these legal challenges slowed legislative action on the incentive package and construction at the plant site ("Toyota Plant Euphoria Sagging Under Load of Legal Documents"), the courts eventually ruled in favor of the state and Toyota on all matters.

Table 7.3 contains a summary of growth topics from the Kentucky and Indiana newspapers. In each case, there is a heavy emphasis on jobs ("Toyota Provides 3000 Jobs," "More Jobs for State Expected," and "There's Still Time to Apply at Auto Plant"); spin-off industries ("Car Parts Firms Wheel Into State" and "Japanese Suppliers Interested in State"); and local economic growth ("New Shopping Plaza Planned," "Hotels, Eating Planned for Ind .26," and "Factory Sows Seeds of Growth"). These hard news stories about new jobs, new companies, and tax revenues, all of which stress benefits over costs, were accom-

Table 7.3
Growth Topics Mentioned in News Accounts

Topic	Lafayette J&C No. of Mentions	%	Louisville CJ No. of Mentions	%	Lexington H-L No. of Mentions	%
Boost Economy	17	11.8	26	11.9	14	17.5
New Jobs	65	45.1	64	29.4	26	32.5
New Buying Power	13	9.0	22	10.1	5	6.2
Spin-off Industries	18	12.5	32	14.7	14	17.5
Higher Land Values	2	1.4	4	1.8	2	2.5
Higher Standard of Living	2	1.4	6	2.8	2	2.5
Salary of New Workers	10	6.9	5	2.3	3	3.8
Tax Increase/Reduction	9	6.2	17	7.8	5	6.2
Experience of Other Communities	8	5.5	42	19.3	9	11.2
Total Mentions	144	(99.8)	218	(100.1)	80	(99.9)
Mentions Per Article	.61		1.57		1.33	

panied by soft news that was also very progrowth. These included human interest stories about Japanese families moving to Kentucky or Indiana ("New Life in Kentucky Not Without Its Problems" and "Japanese Family Enjoys New Life in Greater Lafayette") or half page "man on the street" stories which contained interviews with and photos of eight community residents under the headline "Auto Plant Gets Community Support."

The differences in the newspapers' coverage of growth topics are small, except for two topics. The two Kentucky newspapers gave less attention to topics about new jobs and more attention to the experiences of other states and communities that had attracted Japanese auto plants. The effort to look at other communities may appear to be an attempt to provide more balanced news stories, but such comparative articles generally have a progrowth emphasis. In sum, this analysis of news accounts, so far, indicates that the newspaper coverage of the new Japanese automobile plants and their potential impact is dominated by persons and organizations that are part of a growth coalition, and the topics covered give special attention to the economic benefits of growth.

Table 7.4 provides the final analysis of news accounts: the amount of coverage in square inches that the newspapers gave to stories about the Japanese auto plants. The space provided for articles is classified as unambiguously positive ("Hopes Ride High on Auto Plant"), negative ("Homeless: Auto Plant Causes Concern"), neutral ("Report Details Highway Project") or mixed ("Progress Takes Bit Out of Couple's Front Yard"). Our analysis also recognizes that two of these categories are often interrelated. Some neutral articles which are, for example, objective descriptions of progress on the building of the plant, details of employee recruitment, or discussions of the economic incentive package, are also positive accounts in that they will implicitly endorse or accept the states' and automakers' actions.

Positive articles in the Indiana paper and the *Louisville Courier–Journal*, as Table 7.4 reveals, were given substantially greater space than negative articles.

Table 7.4

Square Inches Devoted to Positive/Negative/Mixed Themes

Theme	Lafayette J&C Square Inches	%	Louisville CJ Square Inches	%	Lexington H-L Square Inches	%
Positive: e.g. new jobs, industries, economic growth	1,709	31.0	2,810	32.3	1,251	21.9
Negative: e.g. criticism of incentive package, law suits, intergroup tensions	465	8.4	1,680	19.3	2,539	44.4
Neutral: e.g. building site progress, employee selection plans, economic incentive package	1,512	27.4	2,357	27.1	1,174	20.5
Mixed: e.g. land use plan, assessments, easements/evictions, environmental impact	1,834	33.2	1,847	21.2	756	13.2
Totals	5,520	(100.0)	8,694	(99.9)	5,720	(100)

If the neutral articles are joined with the positive articles, the positive coverage was seven times greater in the *Lafayette Journal and Courier* and three times greater in the *Louisville Courier-Journal* than the negative coverage. The newspapers also presented the negative or critical information in terms of what Gaye Tuchman (1972) calls "objectivity rituals" or justifications based on a claim of professionalism.

In the *Lafayette Journal and Courier*, for example, there is a 43-square inch story about an out-of-state town with a new Japanese auto plant that is experiencing severe traffic problems and overcrowding in its schools. The article points to the failure of the state government to follow through on its commitment when the incentive package was developed to assist the community with these problems. Lafayette residents reading such an article might understandably raise questions about whether the Subaru-Isuzu plant is likely to have more problems than expected. In the same issue of the paper, however, there is a shorter article, 20-square inches, about why there should be fewer traffic problems or increased school enrollments as a result of the Lafayette plant. There was also a 44-square inch article about how to apply for one of the 1,700 new jobs at the plant where the "average worker will earn $30,000 a year." Thus a *Journal and Courier* article that was potentially critical of the new industrial venture was easily defused by the simultaneous publication of two additional items stressing the positive aspects of the new plant.

The *Louisville Courier-Journal* provides another example with a news item about a county official near the Toyota plant site who was opposed to the state's efforts to attract a second auto plant. The story carries the headline "Official Hopes Auto Plant Spurns His County" and is 98-square inches long. The officials is quoted as saying, "If they say we want this in Kentucky just to say 'We're bigger, we've got more industry here and we've got more jobs here,' but it's not doing you any good—how can you call it progress.'' This quote is followed by the statement, ''His is the lone voice of dissent among county and city leaders hoping to have the big Japanese car and truck assembly plant.'' Moreover, the dissident official's views are covered in 13-square inches with the remaining 86 square inches devoted to the views of eight state and local officials, business leaders, and economists which are different from or critical of the dissident.

A major difference among the newspapers, as can be seen in Table 7.4, is the *Lexington Herald-Leader*, which provides extensive coverage of negative topics. In contrast to the other two papers, negative and positive coverage in the *Herald-Leader* is about equal. The negative coverage clearly stems from the law suits initiated by labor and citizen groups. Since these suits dealt with matters that would directly affect citizens in the immediate vicinity of the plant, the local newspaper had greater reason to provide coverage than did the Louisville newspaper.

In sum, this analysis suggests that newspapers do attempt to shape public discussion of issues related to community growth. When they create stories about a new industry and about its contribution to the community's economic growth, they make choices about the points of view to be represented and what constitutes balance in the stories. Newspapers also make choices about whether to interview business leaders, union officials, or representatives of citizens groups in developing a story about the new plant and its economic impact. When newspapers report stories not of their making, such as a law suit by a labor union or environmental group, choices are made about how much coverage to provide, whether and how to balance the story with other points of view, and whether to develop follow-up stories. When individuals and organizations critical of the growth coalition become too loud to ignore, these dissident views are presented but countered by the presentation of alternative perspectives. Thus a newspaper is able to create a pluralistic community to counter views critical of the growth coalition.

CONCLUSION

This analysis of the *Louisville Courier-Journal*, the *Lexington Herald-Leader*, and the *Lafayette Journal and Courier* news accounts of Toyota and Subaru-Isuzu automobile plants supports our hypotheses about the role of newspapers in presenting a growth-elitist image. The newspapers are part of the growth coalition and see their own profit-oriented interests as aligned with similar interests in political and business communities. The accounts of the new automobile plants in the three newspapers stressed the views of public officials and business leaders and provided much less coverage of persons from other community sectors. Moreover, the topic content and coverage stressed the positive aspects of both general economic growth and these state-supported economic development activities. It is clear that the newspapers functioned as cheerleaders for their respective community's growth machine. In this regard, they did not take the initiative to present their readers with a broad range of questions about the costs and benefits of the new plant and about the wisdom of using public money to acquire and develop land for private corporations and to fund their recruitment and training programs. As a consequence, the newspapers failed to educate their communities about the reasons for Japanese automobile firms building assembly plants in mid-America, the wisdom of using public funds to subsidize them, and the significance of these plants for the economic life of their state and local communities.

NOTES

The authors thank Elizabeth Grauerholz and John Stahura for their helpful comments on an earlier draft of this paper, and Beverly Johns for assistance in coding. We are also indebted to William Green and Lucinda Zoe for assistance in obtaining clipping files from newspapers in Louisville and Lexington.

1. This measure of space was reached due to irregular size of column width.

2. It was decided prior to the reliability test that if more than a 10 percent difference occurred between the two coders, then the codes would be corrected.

3. Since more than one topic can be mentioned in a single article, the total number of topics mentioned can exceed the total number of articles.

REFERENCES

Clark, Terry N. 1968. *Community Structure and Decision-Making: Comparative Analysis*. San Francisco: Chandler.

Dahl, Robert. 1961. *Who Governs?* New Haven, Conn.: Yale University Press.

Drier, Peter. 1982. "The Position of the Press in the U.S. Power Structure." *Social Problems* 29: 298–310.

Duncan, Otis D., W. Richard Scott, Stanley Liberson, Beverly Duncan, Hal Winsborough. 1960. *Metropolis and Region*. Baltimore, Md.: Johns Hopkins University Press.

Form, William H., and W. V. D'Antonio. 1959. "Integration and Cleavage among Community Influentials in Two Border Cities." *American Sociological Review* 24: 804–814.

Goodman, Robert. 1979. *The Last Entrepreneurs: America's Regional Wars for Jobs and Dollars*. Boston: South End Press.

Hassinger, Edward W., and James R. Pinkerton. 1986. *The Human Community*. New York: Macmillan.

Hawley, Amos H. 1950. *Human Ecology: A Theory of Community Structure*. New York: Ronald Press.

Hunter, Floyd. 1953. *Community Power Structure*. Chapel Hill: University of North Carolina Press.

Logan, John R., and Harvey Molotch. 1987. *Urban Fortunes: The Political Economy of Place*. Berkeley: University of California Press.

Lyon, Larry, Lawrence G. Felice, M. Ray Perryman, and E. Stephen Parker. 1981. "Community Power and Population Increase: An Empirical Test of the Growth Machine Model." *American Journal of Sociology* 86: 1387–1400.

Miller, Delbert C. 1958. "Industry and Community Power Structure." *American Sociological Review* 23: 9–15.

Molotch, Harvey. 1976. "The American City as a Growth Machine: Toward a Political Economy of Place." *American Journal of Sociology* 82: 309–330.

Molotch, Harvey, and John Logan. 1984. "Tensions in the Growth Machine: Overcoming Resistance to Value-Free Development." *Social Problems* 31: 483–499.

Murdock, Graham. 1980. "Class, Power, and the Press: Problems of Conceptualization and Evidence." In Harry Christian, ed., *The Sociology of Journalism and the Press*. Totowa, N.J.: University of Keele.

————. 1982. "Large Corporations and the Control of the Communications Industries." In Michael Gurevitch, Tony Bennett, James Curran, and Janet Woolacott, eds., *Culture, Society, and the Media*. New York: Methuen.

Perrucci, Robert, and Bonnie Lewis. 1989. "Interorganizational Relations and Community Influence Structure: A Replication and Extension." *Sociological Quarterly* 30: 205–223.

Polsby, Nelson. 1963. *Community Power and Political Theory*. New Haven, Conn.: Yale University Press.

Pulver, Glen. 1979. "A Theoretical Framework for the Analysis of Community Economic Development Options." In Glen F. Summers and Arne Selvik, eds., *Non-Metropolitan Industrial Growth and Community Change*. Lexington, Mass.: D. C. Heath.

Schudson, Michael. 1978. *Discovering the News: A Social History of American Newspapers*. New York: Basic Books.

Trounstine, Philip J., and Terry Christensen. 1982. *Movers and Shakers: The Study of Community Power*. New York: St. Martin's Press.

Tuchman, Gaye. 1978. *Making News: A Study in Construction of Reality*. New York: The Free Press.

Walton, John. 1972. "Substance and Artifact: The Current Status of Research on Community Power Structure." *American Journal of Sociology* 71: 430–438.

————. 1976. "Community Power and the Retreat from Politics: Full Circle after Twenty Years?" *Social Problems* 23: 292–303.

Wolfinger, Raymond. 1960. "Reputation and Reality in the Study of Community Power." *American Sociological Review* 25: 636–644.

8

Problems of Coalition Building in Japanese Auto Alley: Public Opposition to the Georgetown/ Toyota Plant

Ernest J. Yanarella and Herbert G. Reid

In recent years, the appearance of six Japanese auto transplants in the American Midwest has made this area of the country—colloquially called, "Japanese auto alley"—a focus of increasing critical attention by scholars in a variety of fields. One of those locations, the site of an $800 million Toyota Camry plant in Georgetown, Kentucky, has received special interest due in part to the surfacing of considerable opposition from labor, environmental groups, and small business.

This chapter seeks to reconstruct the halting efforts by environmentalists and organized labor in Central Kentucky to achieve a working coalition in their contestations with the Toyota Corporation and its state and local allies over key constitutional, union labor, and environmental issues. Secondarily, it seeks to show the role played by the small business opposition in the ideological debate over state incentive packages. By comparing this case with an earlier, more successful environmentalist and citizen action group struggle in Georgetown, Kentucky, we hope to: (1) define the critical stakes involved in building coalitions around union representation and environmental issues to forestall the development of a "united front for capital accumulation" among groups and classes (e.g., blacks and nonunion workers) under the banner of policies supposedly promoting "economic development" and "reindustrialization"; (2) isolate the imposing obstacles inhibiting coalition-building across class lines; (3) delineate the strategy followed in the Georgetown case; (4) illuminate its larger significance for the incorporation of local economies like Georgetown into the international political economy; and (5) disclose certain individual and joint actions which organized labor and predominantly upper-middle class environmentalists must take to promote union resurgence and environmental protection.

FREE-MARKET CAPITALIST NOSTALGIA: THE FLIGHT OF SMALL BUSINESS FROM GLOBAL ECONOMIC REALITIES

On December 5, 1985, Governor Martha Layne Collins announced the decision of the Toyota Motor Corporation to locate an $800 million auto assembly plant in Georgetown, Kentucky. This announcement marked the culmination of months of intense state government bargaining to woo this multinational automobile giant to the Commonwealth (Stewart, 1985). Within a few short weeks, however, public euphoria surrounding this announcement dissipated somewhat in the wake of disclosures that Toyota's choice of the Scott County location was heavily influenced by a $125 million package of economic incentives offered by the state administration (Wilson, 1985; Snyder, 1987). As further details of the state-corporate deal were revealed, economic analysts in and out of government began to project more sobering assessments of the ultimate public cost of the inducements, while other forecasters raised doubts about the magnitude of the benefits the state economy would eventually derive or the length of time it would take to recoup its initial investment (Cross, 1987; Milward, 1986; Swasy, 31 October 1986). In addition, important legal questions were voiced by legislators and citizens alike as to the constitutionality of some or all the provisions in the state incentive package.

Over succeeding months, major public opposition to the Georgetown/Toyota project was expressed in three definable quarters: among environmentalists, who voiced alarm at the possible environmental consequences to the air and water which might attend the construction of the huge auto assembly plant; among organized labor, who objected to the choice by Ohbayashi Corporation (Toyota's construction management firm) of nonunion labor to build the facility; and among small business owners in the Georgetown and Lexington communities, who criticized the legality of state subsidies to Toyota.

One of the most vocal opposition forces to the Georgetown/Toyota project has taken the form of a political group of Central Kentuckians organized around the banner, "Concerned Citizens and Businessmen of Central Kentucky." Led by Lexington realtor Don Wiggins, this citizens action group has demonstrated and lobbied throughout the Commonwealth in an effort to protest what it sees as the massive giveaway program by Governor Collins to Toyota Motor Company and to challenge the constitutionality of this public policy. Its membership has been drawn primarily from the ranks of small business owners in the Lexington, Georgetown, and other Central Kentucky communities. Its vocabulary is the familiar rhetoric of free-market capitalism and its enemy is the specter of socialism. Its goal has been to overturn the decision through public education and political pressure and, if possible, through the impeachment of the governor and some of her key aides who were party to the state–corporate negotiations (Chellgren, 1986; Swasy, 17 January 1986; and Wiggins, 1985).

To date, this small-business protest has yielded little in the way of political gains. Although the group's leader claims a membership exceeding two hundred and a saving to taxpayers of $135 million over the preceding five years through challenges to various government bond proposals, the group failed in sustaining its politico-economic vision in the public realm and mobilizing support in the larger public, the state legislature, or the mass media (Swasy, 17 January 1986). Indeed, the only dubious benefit of their efforts would seem to be the generation of anti-Japanese feelings and attitudes among some of the older segments of the Central Kentucky community through hypernationalistic and anti-Oriental appeals (Hoagland, 1987). Quoting from two extremist books, *The Japanese Conspiracy* and *The Invisible Hand*, at one public rally, Don Wiggins alluded to evidence of Japanese collusion and conspiracy in the United States and declared economic war against the Japanese. Similarly, the protest group's petition to the General Assembly calling for the impeachment of Governor Collins, her commerce secretary, and the legislative leadership of both houses for violating the Kentucky constitution netted the organization nothing but ridicule in the representative body (Wiggins, 1986; Chellgren, 1986). And, given its antipathy to organized labor in any form, the small business group remained aloof from the trade union's suit against the state grounded in the alleged unconstitutionality of the incentive package. (On the constitutional issues, see William Green's chapter in this volume). A summary of the historical roots and ideological place of small business in American history and political economy will show why small entrepreneurs cling to an outmoded form of economic analysis while periodically venting their pent-up anger against misplaced targets in the contemporary political world.

Some years ago, John Bunzel (1962) traced the tradition of the small entrepreneur in the United States to its agrarian basis in the early American republic. Indeed, in his historical study, he found that the agrarian capitalist foundations of early America blended the ideas of Adam Smith with a version of allegedly Jeffersonian principles (Bunzel, 1962: 13–84; Mills, 1956: 73ff.). Owing to the absence of a feudal heritage, the American middle class, unlike its European predecessor, "enter[ed] history as a big stratum of small entrepreneurs . . . exist[ing] before and outside the city" (Mills, 1956: 73). The hightide of entrepreneurial capitalism and the predominance of the small property owner and businessperson in economic relations occurred in the 1820s, when the yeoman farmer was joined by the urban capitalist to form a society populated by many relatively independent property owners. Yet, even then, the seeds of agrarian capitalism's transcendence were being planted in the cities, as the first factories symbolizing the beginning of industrial capitalism began to appear by 1830 (Bender, 1982).

After the Civil War and certainly by 1890, the ideal of a self-balancing economic system based on a competitive market of small firms and only a loose political authority promoting largely negative functions was being replaced by the dawning of the corporate state. As a new railroad network increasingly tied local economies to regional and then national markets, and economic concentration in the political economy grew and intensified, the independent business owner was soon subordinated and made dependent upon large corporations involved in production, distribution, and sales operations of national scope (Mills, 1956: 21; Chandler, 1977). In the process, the small business owners lost their original function and increasingly became instruments of larger economic units.

Despite the internal transformation of America's capitalist system and the crystallization of the corporate state, the old ideal of the independent entrepreneur was perpetuated in the America's mainstream ideology as if this economic remnant of an earlier stage of our political economy was still the main actor, and the social and economic relations supporting him remained preeminent. Though long overtaken by new institutions and changed circumstances, the ethos of small business continues to be salient due to the peculiarities of legislative representation in the American political system and because of the ideological value of this symbol of utopian capitalism to Big Business, as well as the nostalgia of much of the American public for small-town life.

While corporate capitalism in America has been economically cruel to small business, it has been ideologically overly generous. Small business now occupies a shrinking place in the largely antiquated quasi-free market level of a three-tiered political economy increasingly driven by techno-corporate imperatives. Under these circumstances, the small entrepreneur has largely taken on a politically regressive role in contemporary politics and policy debate. The small businessperson's role as principled defender of the free enterprise system, evoking longing for the clarity and simplicity of the bygone era of liberal capitalism, serves as a convenient ideological veil for the complicated realities of the corporate capitalist system (Mills, 1956; Zeigler, 1961). Thus, for example, in the Georgetown/Toyota dispute, the Wiggins-led group tried to galvanize opposition against the state inducement package by asserting the timelessness of laissez-faire capitalism's laws and verities against the unwarranted assumption and irresponsible power of Big Labor, Big Government, and Foreign Corporations, leaving immune from criticism the actions and strategies of our megacorporations in shaping the present contours of the corporate state (Wiggins, 1985; Wiggins, 1986).

On the other hand, in small communities in particular, small business often acts as a carrier of civic spirit, participating widely in public offices and seeking to benefit small town America by voluntary leadership in community affairs. Where the small business owner cum "town father" fails is in the deficiency of his ideological framework "to guide him through the maze of economic interdependence and political conflict that defines his social world" (Bellah et al., 1985: 170). This point is brought home to him whenever the larger institutions or more influential patterns or relationships in the wider social order intrude on his small community and "compel him to recognize his dependence on a complicated national and international political economy'' (Bellah et al., 1985: 176). For the most part, Georgetown's stratum of civic leaders and "town fathers" has not succumbed to the temptation to embrace a reactionary vision of the political economy. Still, recent reports of the resignation of one Georgetown mayor and the chronic stress and illness of another in the face of the demands and repercussions of the new plant suggest that the strains of ideology and reality have taken their toll.

This failure is compounded by the fact that the typical small business refuses to recognize that the more fundamental transformations of economy and society (and less so polity) are rooted in a continuing economic restructuring generated out of an earlier and partially transcended phase of capitalism which small businesses continue to preserve in idealized form. This blindspot makes them prone to mobilization from the political right which in American turns them into one of the "shock troops" in the battle against labor and big government and in other countries has prompted them to join nazi and poujadist movements (Bechofer and Elliot, 1981; Bunzel, 1962: 172, 225, and 257; Mills, 1956: 53). For the small businesses, the complex world of late capitalism presents itself psychologically as an object of anxiety, frustration, resentment, and pent-up emotion which mistakenly leads them to vent their anger on an overblown image of the political power of labor and on an ideologically warped conception of the state and its corporate-biased policies as socialistic. Lacking any clear prospect for an improvement in their condition, the small business owners more often engage in a politics of despair against more formidable forces they cannot accurately define, in defense of a golden age which can never be recovered. Given the tendency of small business *ressentiment* to take expression in hypernationalism and militarism, it should occasion little surprise that among the Concerned Citizens and Small Businessmen of Central Kentucky's recent actions was the sponsorship of a demonstration and spirited defense of Oliver North's role in the Iran-Contragate scandal.

With this analysis of the economic place and ideological and political legacy of the small entrepeneur in mind, a key question for us is whether the political volatility of small business might be redirected into a more fundamental critique of corporate capitalism and an agenda for political action in alliance with other oppositional forces. Even though the Wiggins group seems to offer little hope that its mythical worldview and antiquated critique of corporate capitalism will be overcome, the frustrations and resentments generated by the tendency of small business owners to inhabit a world seemingly irretrievably lost remains a potent political resource for continuing political reaction or possible future redirection.

THE UNCOORDINATED ENVIRONMENTALIST CHALLENGE: UPPER-MIDDLE CLASS ENVIRONMENTALISM AND UNION LABOR

The eruption of environmental protest over the construction of the Toyota plant in the Scott County's sparsely populated farmland should have occasioned little surprise within the community or across the state. An assembly plant encompassing so much acreage and destined to spew forth many tons of waste and toxic byproducts was bound to generate careful scrutiny among concerned residents of the Georgetown area. Increasing the likelihood of such a close monitoring of the plant's potential environmental impact was the fact that less than a decade earlier a dispute over the building of a coal gasification plant and industrial park near the community's historic Royal Spring had galvanized opposition by a well-financed and expertly led group of predominantly upper-middle class inhabitants (Yanarella and Reid, 1987). Also contributing to widespread sensitivity to the plant's social and environmental impact was Georgetown's tradition of controlled-growth planning of which the town officials and area residents have been justly proud.

When environmental opposition arose less than two months after the governor's announcement, it might have been expected that protesting environmentalists and the area environmental and land trust groups supporting their questions and concerns would possess certain built-in advantages and serve as a formidable force in delaying or halting the project. Instead, although these environmentalists won the battle, they appear to have lost the larger war.

The issue which sparked the environmental dispute was the plan to construct a wastewater treatment facility for the Toyota auto plant which would discharge some 2.2 million gallons of treated waste per day into a small creek. The specific form which this environmental protest took was criticism of the risks of well contamination, dead aquatic life, and noxious odors from the treated waste (Kaiser, 27 February 1986, 4 May 1986, and 28 May 1986). In addition, the effluent from the sewage plant would flow into Lane's Run basin and through the farm of William and Jane Allen Offutt, the former Georgetown residents who had spearheaded and financed the coal gasification protest in the late seventies (Atkinson, 1986; and Kaiser, 4 May 1986). Like the earlier environmental dispute, the terms of this controversy were initially fought over relatively narrow, technical issues concerning the toxicity of the waste water, its potential impact upon groundwater and wells, and the existence of sinkholes and underground flows which might endanger the secondary water reservoir serving Georgetown residents.

Then, in early spring, the opposition succeeded in pressuring Kentucky's Cabinet for Natural Resources and Environmental Protection to hold a public hearing on the discharge permit for the proposed sewage. There, the environmental spokespeople—many of whom were holdovers from the earlier dispute—sought to widen the review process by calling for an EPA-sponsored environmental impact study of the waste water treatment plant, arguing that NEPA guidelines require such assessments of federally permitted projects in registered historic districts (Cropper, 1986; and Kaiser, 28 May 1986). Yet, despite the increased support among other landowners for their concerns and preliminary geological evidence of one or more sinkholes along the creek basin, the state environmental protection agency and two administrative boards in Scott County insisted on the environmental soundness and safety of the treatment and disposal proposal (McCord, 1986). And, apparently due to considerable political pressure brought to bear on the EPA's Atlanta office from Kentucky's two senators, Sixth District congressman, and state administrators (Hammond, 1988), no authorization for a federal EIS was forthcoming from the Environmental Protection Agency.

The specific public forum within which this environmental controversy ultimately played itself out was the Scott County Board of Adjustments. A creature of the longterm efforts in the community to build a sensible structure for controlled growth and planning, the board became the focus of the conflict between the goal of the Collins administration to put the wastewater treatment plant construction on a fast-track schedule and the objective of environmentalists and landowners in the affected area to protect their property and, in some cases, the community water supply against possible toxic chemical and heavy metal pollution and/or the depreciation of their property value. Over three long and sometimes contentious meetings between mid-March and late June 1986, the board heard the property owners and their legal representatives contest the position of local water board and the state environmental protection division concerning the choice of the facility site, the safety of the means or route for transmission of the wastewater, and the permissible levels of potentially toxic materials carried in the wastewater for treatment.

Among the two key environmental advocates, the Offutt family and its lawyer pressed a variety of issues, including the laxity of the Natural Resources and Environmental Protection Cabinet in setting safe environmental standards, its uncooperativeness in responding to legitimate requests for public information concerning the proposed plant and those environmental safety criteria, and, more generally, the environmental risks and public safety hazards to Georgetown's secondary water supply and to the Lane's Run land and farm owners from the proposed open ditch transportation of the industrial waste. The other vocal environmentalist and Lane's Run landowner, Randy Maddox, emphasized the aesthetic and public health dangers of the wastewater's open trench transport. While calling for the resolution of the immediate environmental and public health risks stemming from the use of an enclosed pipeline to transport the polluted water, Maddox also joined with the two Kentucky State Building and Construction Trades Council representatives Jerry Hammond and Charles Hoffmaster in filing several civil and administrative suits against the state Cabinet for Natural Resources and Environmental Protection and Toyota. These civil and administrative actions not only challenged the ultimate agreement reached by the county board of adjustments on the conditional use permit; they also enlarged the scope of the environmental attack to include the air pollution standards set by the environmental cabinet and the construction of the wastewater plant itself.

By the end of June 1986, the Offutt-led environmental dispute over the water treatment facility had petered out because the county board of adjustments granted a conditional use permit allowing plant construction to begin—a decision based on a compromise reached between the city's municipal water and sewer service and the environmentalists and property owners in the Lane's Run area (Atkinson, 1986; Branham, 1986). Among other stipulations, this twelve-point agreement required: that the effluent be closely monitored for leaks with any serious breaches mandating the treatment plant's closure; that a state-funded $2.7 million pipeline be built that would carry the waste through the Offutt's farmland and release it at a point beyond known sinkholes or other potential environmental hazards; and that water lines be run to property owners whose wells would be threatened by the discharge (Atkinson, 1986: 40). Thus, while the earlier Offutt-led concerned citizens group was able to defeat the federally-supported joint state-developer project to build a coal gasification project, this effort by environmental forces guided by the same leadership netted far more meager prizes.

Why did their protest fail to escalate into a fullblown attack on the potential environmental consequences of the auto assembly plant and to ignite widespread area opposition to the Georgetown/Toyota project? Some of the reasons lie in the differences between this dispute and the earlier one. One obvious reason lay in the direct role played by the governor's office in negotiating the Kentucky-Toyota agreement and mustering impressive political and financial backing for the project. The dynamics of the earlier industrial development controversy were heavily centered in the local politics and area (Lexington) financial and corporate circles with government administrators and politicians in Frankfort and Washington, D.C., playing a weaker supportive role (Yanarella and Reid, 1987). The Collins-inspired plan effectively moved the field of political contest and policy decision-making away from the Georgetown community, where local opposition forces possessed inherent advantages, and defined the economic stakes in state-wide terms, where grassroots and citizens action groups are typically outgunned and outmaneuvered.

The gubernatorial factor might not have been so formidable if the earlier formed concerned citizens group had decided to develop a multicounty, multi-organizational coalition designed to monitor and respond to local and state economic development plans deemed inimical to the Central Kentucky region's environmental health and controlled growth orientation. That is, in the early stages of the coal gasification controversy, the Scott County group considered two possible avenues of protest: putting pressure on the city council or setting up an area-wide coalition of environmental, preservationist, recreation and tourist, and horse farm representatives. When Jane Allen Offutt decided to seek election to the city council, the political strategy of the group became set on the former course and the more promising, long-term approach to the more enduring problems raised by the controversy was dropped. In light of the Georgetown/Toyota project, this decision may have been a mistake—or, at least, terribly shortsighted. For in the absence of any Central Kentucky environmental–controlled growth alliance, only the small business remnants within the area have sought to mobilize public opinion against the largely state-directed action. This organizational hole in the Commonwealth's political landscape has meant that the Collins administration did not need to take into account in preliminary deliberations and later formal negotiations the potential environmental and socioeconomic impacts of such a major industrial development in this rural community (Yanarella and Reid, 1987).

The continuing "impact elitism" of these environmentalists and concerned citizens (Schnaiberg, 1980) also hobbled these opposition forces in both controversies. In the first dispute, this elitism was manifested in the citizen action group's use of environmental issues to cloak the class-biased concerns for socioeconomic impact and quality of life which motivated its key representatives. Neglecting the legitimacy of the interests and claims of the working class and black minority in the community, the group set upon an obstructionist course of political action intended to stretch out the environmental impact process and outlast its opponents. In the latest controversy, the Offutt-directed elements pressed a narrow, class-biased environmental issue until it played itself out and paid out modest material dividends to the property owners. For those upperclass environmentalists, environmental and human health stopped at the factory door.

When the state building and construction union picked up the environmental concern, these upper-middle class environmentalists entered into a tacit, behind-the-scenes coalition with organized labor. Part of the environmental contingent, the Offutts, withdrew from pressing the environmental issues in the courts and left the political battle to be fought by Jerry Hammond, secretary-treasurer of Kentucky trades union and candidate for the Congress. One of the other landowners in the Lane's Run basin, Randy Maddox, joined the state building trade union in its environmental and constitutional challenges while the Offutts sought other environmental issues to pursue. The Offutt's reluctance to "go public" in their support of these union initiatives was dictated partly by their long-term friendship and support of Larry Hopkins, the Republican Congressman whose seat Jerry Hammond was vying for. Besides the Offutts have never shown great interest or enthusiasm for labor or minority concerns, as witnessed earlier in their refusal to incorporate such issues into the earlier coal-gasification dispute. That is, despite a sizable lower-income stratum and a large black population (17 percent), controlled growth and quality-of-life concerns dominated the citizen's action group's arguments, leaving suspended the legitimate working class concerns for job opportunities and better income. As a consequence, the task of trying to forge a labor and environmentalist strategy was instead left to the strenuous efforts of a beleaguered construction trades union.

ORGANIZED LABOR UNDER SIEGE: AWAKENING TO THE POLITICAL AND CORPORATE OBSTACLES TO UNIONIZATION

In spite of the vociferousness of the small business group and the financially well-heeled and the media-grabbing nature of the environmentalist opposition, a review of the public challenge to the Toyota/Georgetown project underlines the political centrality of the organized labor protest. The involvement of union labor in the politics of this industrial development project was precipitated by the decision on the part of Toyota's construction management firm, Ohbayashi Corporation, to set up a "merit shop" agreement with the nonunion Associated General Contractors of Kentucky (Swasy, 5 October 1985, 16 November 1986). On this basis, this nationally affiliated building association would refer workers, regardless of union status, for hiring by Ohbayashi and its designated contracting firms during the construction phase of the project. The Kentucky State Building and Construction Trades Council, an affiliate of the national AFL-CIO, immediately took the stance that this agreement was biased against union labor, would depress wage rates for building workers on the project, and would sacrifice the quality of construction workmanship on the plant (Rugeley, 17 October 1986, 25 October 1986). It demanded that Ohbayashi reach agreement with union representatives on behalf of the trades council and that a union hall be used to hire all the plant's construction workers.

When Ohbayashi balked, the state construction and trades union—led by its secretary–treasurer, Jerry Hammond—took the offensive, adopting a multi-pronged strategy challenging the plant's construction on every front and esca-lating the scope of the dispute beyond regional and state boundaries. Over the course of the controversy, this strategy involved: contesting the constitutionality of provisions of the original state agreement and incentive package with Toyota (Brammer, 24 September 1986); suing the state for issuing permits for the waste water treatment plant and the air pollution control facilities (Cohn, 1986; Ru-geley, 17 October 1986; Swasy, 7 November 1986); pressing the labor, envi-ronmental, and constitutional issues in Hammond's campaign as Democratic challenger in Kentucky's sixth district house election (Rugeley, 25, October 1986); flooding the members of the mass media and Kentucky's legislature with educational packets informing them of the union's positions (Rugeley, 17 October 1986); holding demonstrations and leafleting in key Kentucky cities protesting Toyota's anti-union policies (Swasy, 29 August 1986); expanding organized protests to Washington, D.C., and New York City and incorporating national representatives and workers for the AFL–CIO and other large union organizations in the picketing and marches (Swasy and York, 13 November 1986; Ward, 22 November 1986); and, finally, threatening to hold a national demonstration against Toyota on Pearl Harbor Day (York, 18 November 1986).

The militance of the trade union's strategy was dictated by the recognition of its key spokesman, Jerry Hammond, of the state and national repercussions of this dispute. Vowing to "draw the line" in this dispute, Hammond continually argued that the outcome of this political embroglio would determine the shape and form of contracts negotiated for future construction projects in Kentucky (Rugeley, 25 October 1986; Swasy, 5 October 1986, 16 November 1986). Having been frozen out of preliminary discussions between the Kentucky governor's office and Toyota top management prior to the agreement, the union leader feared that accepting defeat in this contest would foreshadow further losses should additional auto and other industrial plants be subsequently built in Kentucky (Hammond, 1988). Moreover, he claimed that winning union rights in the new Kentucky plant was essential to the American labor movement, which has been losing ground in all industries across the country. Finally, he emphasized that the Toyota/Georgetown case set in sharp relief the issue of the role and impact of foreign investment for the future of the American economy and the livelihood of union workers in America (Swasy, 16 November 1986).

The vehemence and urgency with which the Kentucky construction and trades council pressed its challenge can be best understood against the background of the general decline in union representation in the United States over the last two decades and the dilemmas that unions have had to confront in these difficult economic times. Organized workers, as Thomas Edsall (1984) has observed, have been among the chief losers in the "new politics of inequality" spawned by the restructuring of the international and national political economies and the political responses to the apparent dawning of a "zero-sum society" in the United States. From a high point in 1945, when over 35 percent of American workers were union members, union representation of the American workforce has declined to 24 percent in 1979 and 18.8 percent in 1985 (Edsall, 1984: 142; Katznelson and Kesselman, 1987: 248). Equally troublesome, union victories in representation and decertification contests have fallen off nationally from 60.2 percent in 1965 to 48.2 percent in 1975 to 42.4 percent in 1985 (Ward, 1 September 1986: F1).

The causes of the accelerating decline of the labor movement are not hard to uncover. A recent sociological analysis of this trend by Rob Wrenn has delineated five basic causes: "(1) the recent recession and the cumulative effect of high unemployment in the past decade; (2) the international domestic non-union competition confronting unionized firms and plants; (3) the corporate 'counterattack' and management's new hard-line anti-union stance; (4) changes in government policy; and (5) organized labor's own failure to maintain and expand its membership" (Wrenn, 1985: 109–114; summarized by Katznelson and Kesselman, 1987). Edsall, among others, has also pointed to the weakening of the ties to labor within the Democratic party (1984: 162–163). Yet, organized labor remains crucial as a political force for the crystallization of a progressive agenda in American politics. For union labor is still "the major institution in theory most capable of pressing the interests of the working and lower-middle classes" (Edsall, 1984: 142)—although other social theorists, like Carl Boggs and John Keane, have placed increasing emphasis on the role of new social movements in promoting social change. This claim is supported by a recent study by David Cameron which shows a direct correlation in advanced Western capitalist societies between strong union movements and public policies in taxation, employment, and social spending beneficial to the working class (Cameron study cited in Edsall, 1984: 147; Stephens, 1980).

Unfortunately, one effect of labor's steady decline has been its tendency to adopt a defensive political posture. This defensive stance has not only prompted union labor in the auto industry and elsewhere to lobby for strong protectionist legislation; it has forced many union leaders to take a more "realistic" position on contract bargaining. As a result, workers have increasingly come to question the traditional advantages to union membership while much of the public has lost confidence in union labor's claim to represent a broad core of America's working and lower-middle class and instead has perceived it increasingly as a mere special-interest group promoting its own narrow interests in the zero-sum battles of a contracting political economy.

Far from seeing this dispute as an isolated and idiosyncratic bargaining contest, Kentucky construction union representatives and national union officials have defined the issues in dispute in the Toyota/Georgetown controversy in national and even global terms. When six months of negotiations between the management firm and the building trades union broke down, Hammond decided to take a page from the book of strategies and tactics written by big business in the reactionary seventies and early eighties by, among other things, getting his national office committed to a frontal attack on Toyota and by hiring a friendly consulting firm, the Kamber Group, to assist in devising a multifaceted campaign to impress upon Toyota the heavy political, legal, public relations, and other costs which would be exacted by continued opposition to unionization of the construction workers (Hammond, 1988). Rejecting the new labor-management strategy of cooperation and concession promoted by Big Capital, Hammond was especially impressed with the arguments advanced by students of the contemporary labor scene calling for the return of a more adversarial strategy for unions under siege (for example, Reisman and Compa, 1985). Included in this wide-ranging program was the preparation and public distribution of analyses by the Kamber Group of the overall costs and expected returns of the Georgetown plant to Kentucky citizens, as well as detailed studies of the environmental and constitutional issues flowing from the Kentucky-Toyota pact (Kamber Group, 1986a, 1986b, 1986c). Between June and November of 1986, the union forces waged an unceasing campaign against the Japanese automaker in an effort to overturn the original Ohbayashi decision (reconstructed in "The Toyota Campaign," n.d.; and the Kamber Group, 1986c). Then, when Toyota and its construction management arm, apparently stung by the effects of the union struggle upon its public image, showed renewed interest in serious bargaining, Hammond and his fellow union negotiators used the considerable knowledge they had gained from long study of Japanese culture, strategy, and philosophy to bring the bargaining sessions to a fruitful conclusion in late November 1986 (Brown, 1986; Prather, 1988; Hammond, 1988).

Whether the victory of the building and trades council in reaching agreement with Ohbayashi Corporation represents a signal of renewed militance and growth in union power and organizing is an open question (Kuttner, Winter 1987). The union's replacement of the nonunion association means that it will influence the hiring of all future construction workers on the site and raise the wage schedules of all workers involved in the plant's construction. Moreover, the agreement eventually paved the way for a union contract for construction workers at the engine plant site adjoining the Camry assembly plant which Toyota decided to locate there some months later. Still, the terms of the agreement were modeled after the accord reached at the Saturn plant in Spring Hill, Tennessee, which was molded, in part, by suggestions of the Business Roundtable, a big business coalition that studies business problems (Swasy, 26 November 1986: 10).

Among the more unfortunate repercussions of the Kentucky Buildings Trade-Toyota accord was the shattering of the union's informal and fragile alliance with environmentalists in the Georgetown/Toyota dispute. For, while earning the right to hire all future construction workers on the site and to represent them in new wage contracts, the union representatives agreed to dismiss all pending civil actions and administrative proceedings and to forego forever all claims, actions, demands, rights, and damages pertaining to those court cases (Settlement and Release Agreement, 1987). In response, the Offutts filed motions in mid-January 1987 to give them the right to intervene as plaintiffs in the cases, citing organized labor's failure to honor its prior pledge to continue to pursue the litigation of these environmental issues to their judicial conclusion as the reasons for their motion (U.S. District Court, 17 January 1987).

While the import of this union-corporate accord would seem to be problematic, the victory does seem to hold out the hope of the American labor movement shifting to a more aggressive strategy to win back some of the ground lost in the wake of the rise of the corporate intransigence, reactionary government policies, and new social inequalities. Perceiving the critical importance of information in a changing and more complicated national and global political economy and the pressing need to counterbalance the use of sophisticated computer technology to promote their profit-maximization and market control strategies, the building trades union has worked in recent months to create a Kentucky International Employers Task Force composed of representatives from diverse organizations and interest groups designed: (1) to commission "a preliminary audit and review of employment practices, management philosophy, and the corporate goals of foreign employers" in Kentucky; and (2) to "collect, collate, analyze, develop and publish information of general public interest pertaining to corporate relationships and activity" (Kentucky Building and Trades Council, 17 March 1988).

The next phase in the labor struggle in Georgetown will involve the efforts of the United Auto Workers to unionize the production workers at the Toyota auto assembly and engine plants. Whether the more cooperative, nonadversarial approach to union organizing and contract negotiations evidenced by UAW at the NUMMI plant in California will be a harbinger of its strategy in central Kentucky remains to be seen (Prather, 1988; Hammond, 1988). Whatever the case, the labor campaign will involve not only the effort to secure union and collective bargaining rights but also the need to confront new issues relating to the Japanese management techniques in the workplace. For as one recent study of Toyota's heralded management strategy and style has shown, "Toyotism" as a successor to Fordism has striven to intensify the Taylorist impulses toward "scientific management" by methods which further rationalize mental and physical labor on the production line in the cause of greater "economic efficiency" (Dohse et al., 1985).

CONCLUSION

With the end of post-war American economic and military hegemony, new and daunting forces have reverberated throughout the international arena, affecting all levels of political economy (Wolfe, 1981; more recently, Moffitt, 1987). The rise of Japan as an economic superpower, the emergence of newly developing nations in the Middle East and East Asia, and the proliferation of multinational corporations have all become new fixtures on the landscape of global politics and economic relations extending their influence far and wide, whether in sprawling urban centers or small rural communities. Domestically, the unfolding of a multitiered fiscal crisis of the state in concert with the reversion to the programs and policies of the reactionary right in American politics have precipitated new strains in the liberal efficiency-equity bargain begun in the New Deal and furthered during the New Frontier–Great Society era. These factors, too, have shifted the balance between the state's dual functions of system legitimation and capital accumulation heavily toward the latter, as more and more of the social surplus produced from the nation's economy has, through tax reforms and budgetary cuts, gone into the pockets of the rich and the bank accounts of the America's megacorporations and the world's leading multinational corporate giants.

Faced with a shrinking portion of world markets, a growing trade imbalance, and continuing $100 billion-plus budgetary deficits, the post-World War II growth coalition in America has tried to restore and refurbish the earlier hegemonic strategy of high economic growth at home and military and economic expansion abroad. Challenged by new international realities and confounding domestic problems, governing elites of the coalition have responded at the federal level with a confusing array of policies and strategems, leaving lesser governmental units throughout the United States to find their own means for staving off the mounting costs of slow economic growth, corporate flight, and federal budgetary starvation. Meanwhile, reminiscent of the 1890s, capital-rich corporations and conglomerates have been buying up other large corporations in a tidal wave of mergers and hostile takeovers. This case study of the Georgetown/ Toyota controversy has shown how these many powerful forces and conflicting trends have been refracted through the lives of individuals and groups in this small Central Kentucky community trying to make sense of a development promising dramatically to alter the geographic space, economic relationships, political institutions, and environmental setting.

The tenuous nature of the labor-environmental coalition in this dispute and its ultimate breakup suggest the need for serious rethinking on all fronts about the longterm strategies and tactics necessary to overcome the prevailing tendencies within the postwar growth coalition to speed up the "treadmill of production" (Schnaiberg's apt term, 1980: 208) by relaxing environmental regulations and maximizing labor and capital inputs. In a period where voter alienation and dealignment and party irresponsibility and symbolic politics threaten to turn the political arena into a media circus featuring snake oil con artists offering the spectator masses mere symbolic gratification, the great hope of the restoration of a progressive agenda lies in the rehabilitation of the labor movement, the continued flowering of citizen action groups, and the development of grassroots and regional coalitions uniting labor, people of color, environmentalists, women, the poor, and other disaffected groups reeling from the genuine pain, injuries, and insults of the preceding eight years or more.

This prescription will not be easy to accomplish nor is it sure to succeed. For all the potential constituent elements of this alternative alliance remain organizationally scattered and ideologically flawed. By comparison with their counterparts in Northern Europe particularly, the labor movement in the United States has often been a partner with big business and the state in the growth coalition, having largely pushed for a limited agenda of "economism" and thus being satisfied with contesting over the size and its share of the social surplus (wages and fringe benefits). Yet, the experience of Swedish and other Northern European labor movements, even in the era of global recession and heightened competition in the international marketplace, demonstrates that efficiency-equity-ecological bargains can be struck where neither economic competitiveness nor social welfare nor environmental protection need be sacrificed through supposed tradeoffs among goals or values. As Robert Kuttner (1984, 1987) has noted, the dilemma for American labor is that, in order to be able to strike the kind of deals their European union brothers and sisters have managed to forge, organized labor in this country must become a much larger proportion of the overall labor force and must gain a federal policy commitment to achieving and maintaining full employment. Currently, the union voice is weak and its embattled state seems to leave it with few options other than to take what it can get.

Yet, Japanese auto transplants and joint ventures in the United States, whether in Georgetown, Flat Rock, Smyrna or elsewhere, promise to raise a number of highly mobilizable political issues now and in the future. In addition to the hyperrationalized management and production system being installed in these plants, the Japanese commitment to the use of robotics and other forms of high-technology innovation on the production line will likely threaten worker interest in job security. In the absence of a national policy of worker retraining and referral akin to the sophisticated program now operating in Sweden to sustain full employment (see Kuttner, 1984), American workers in these plants, whether unionized or not, are likely to see the number of production line jobs decrease steadily over the years.

Environmentalists, too, will probably face tough times in the future to the extent that the growth coalition reacts to the continuing policy impasse by stoking the engines turning the production treadmill. Despite palpable dangers of the greenhouse effect and acid precipitation emanating from the burning of fossil fuels for energy and industrial production and other risks to our streams, lakes, and seas, the corporate-dominated political constellation may seek to pacify environmentalist concerns either by promulgating mere adaptive policies of a coalition uniting state administrative mechanisms and the middle class, promoting what Frederick Buttel and Oscar Larson (1980) call an "environmentalism of the right," or worse by moving toward authoritarian programs in the face of future ecological crises generated by an ecological Hobbesianism foreshadowed by Garrett Hardin (1972) and William Ophuls (1977). Meanwhile, continued adherence by the environmental groups to upper-middle class and upper class biases and legalistic and obstructionist tactics insensitive to the interests of the poor and minorities in environmental battles over industry site decisions and other economic concerns will only further alienate blacks and the working class from the environmental movement and delay the fashioning of a new language of protest and affirmation encompassing economic, equity, and ecological interests and the generation of a working coalition among these groups.

Still, the transformation of the pastoral landscape of many rural communities affected by new plant locations and the attendant environmental problems flowing from new industrial sitings will make these issues potential sources of new public debate. As many environmental analysts have argued, the best hope of checking the "grow-or-die" logic of advanced capitalism and for expanding the social constituency and political clout of the environmental movement requires at a minimum a multiclass strategy which incorporates organized labor, the poor, and blacks into the environmental fold and thus militates against their joining a "popular front for accumulation" with corporate elites and right-wing politicians (Schnaiberg, 1980; Yanarella, 1985; Yanarella and Reid, 1987). Without labor-environmentalist and black-environmentalist coalitions in local, regional, and national disputes, these battles are likely to yield a variety of possible options—defeat, political stalemate, interest-group brokering—which do little to advance a progressive agenda uniting environmental and quality of life concerns with equity issues. Despite their relatively brief lifespan, Environmentalists for Full Employment and the Citizen/Labor Energy Coalition point in the right direction for future coalitional activities by environmentalists.

Despite the enormous potential of the Rainbow Coalition for future American politics, blacks and other people of color must learn to take a more critical attitude toward the expansionist imperatives of the growth coalition and its treadmill of production. While the civil rights struggle in the sixties achieved many gains for blacks and other Americans, it completely neglected the issue of altering the forms of surplus mobilization and the organization of production in the private sector. Indeed, as Allan Schnaiberg points out, "labor and poor people's movements often attacked environmentalist proposals as too costly [and failed] to support the emergent movement for an alternative technology—an alternative form of surplus mobilization'' (1980: 239). Yet, environmental protection and alternative technology are part of the larger interests of black and other exploited groups precisely because the poor and racial minorities tend to be most vulnerable to environmental pollution and workplace health hazards and because labor-intensive production processes promoted by the alternative technology movement promise more jobs and a more benign work environment. In the case of Japanese auto investment, the obvious entree for civil rights protest linked to larger coalitional activities is evidence of racially-biased hiring practices by new Japanese automobile plants and auto parts manufacturers in the United States (Cole and Deskins, 1988).

Even though remnants of earlier phases and partially transcended levels of American capitalism have generally played a reactionary role in politics, their possible function in a changed political setting and a new economic agenda influenced by the growth and maturity of a broad coalition dedicated to a more decentralized democratically-planned economy cannot be discounted. As the philosophy of Ernst Bloch has taught, the radical task of active inheritance— understood as paying ''the debts of the past in order to receive the present'' (Howard, 1977: 78)—is to articulate the *futurity* contained in every value and ideal expressed by existing remnants of older economic being and political consciousness. In spite of the traditional conservatism of small businessmen, farmers, and historical preservationists, the nostalgic values and ideals they espouse carry within them a future expression which can only be truly realized in a more democratic, egalitarian society. Naturally, the elements of these non-synchronous contradictions are too few and too weak to form a critical mass adequate to precipitate a transformation in late capitalism. But, their neglect by the Left in the United States will only allow the New Right to assimilate these elements into its political coalition while corporate capitalism continues to dig their graves. Moreover, if some form of noncentralized, democratic political economy is ever to replace late capitalism, it will have to take shape out of native traditions like civic republicanism, democratic populism, and even market capitalism, albeit radically restructured and refunctioned.

No formal criteria nor programmatic formula exists for the construction of the new coalition envisaged above. The context of social choice and public decision will be built out of a combination of bold vision and intense political conflict. The main lesson the Georgetown/Toyota controversy is that while the political ingredients for the coalescence of such a movement are lacking, some of its essential elements are striving to assimilate the demands of a new and changing political and economic environment offering new risks and new opportunities for moving beyond the politics of industrial recruitment toward a new politics and a new efficiency-equity-ecology equation only faintly limned.

REFERENCES

Aronowitz, Stanley. 1973. *False Promises: The Shaping of American Working Class Consciousness*. New York: McGraw-Hill Book Company.

Atkinson, Morgan. 1986."Jane Allen Offutt versus Toyota: A Test of Mettle or a Case of Meddling?" *Bluegrass Magazine* 1 (September-October): 36–43.

Bechofer Frank, and Brian Elliot, eds. 1981. *The Petite Bourgeoisie: Comparative Studies of the Uneasy Stratum*. New York: St. Martin's Press.

Bellah, Robert N. et al. 1985. *Habits of the Heart: Individualism and Commitment in American Life*. Berkeley: University of California Press.

Bender, Thomas. 1982. *Toward an Urban Vision: Ideas and Institutions in Nineteenth Century America*. Baltimore, Md.: The Johns Hopkins University Press.

Bloch, Ernst. 1977. "Nonsynchronism and the Obligation to Its Dialectics." *New German Critique* 11 (Spring): 22–38.

Bluestone, Barry, and Bennett Harrison. 1982. *The Deindustrialization of America: Plant Closings, Community Abandonment, and the Dismantling of Basic Industry*. New York: Basic Books, Inc.

Brammer, Jack. 1986. "State to Pay Toyota Workers for 6 Months." *Lexington Herald-Leader*, 10 September, 1, 16.

―――. 1986. "Court Hears 'Toyota Deal' Challenges." *Lexington Herald-Leader*, 24 September, B1, 2.

Brammer, Jack, and Alecia Swasy. 1986. "Toyota Battle Shifts to Federal Court." *Lexington Herald-Leader*, 25 October, B1, 3.

Branham, Mary. 1986. "Permit Granted for Treatment Plant." *Georgetown News & Times*, 1 July, 1, 2.

Brown, Mike. 1986. "The Toyota Pact: Union Halls Pick Workers, and No Strikes." *Louisville Courier-Journal*, 27 November, B9.

Bunzel, John H. 1962. *The American Small Businessman*. New York: Alfred A. Knopf, Inc.

Buttel, Frederick H., and Oscar W. Larson III. 1980. "Whither Environmentalism? The Future Political Path of the Environmental Movement." *National Resources Journal* 20 (April): 323–344.

Chandler, Alfred D., Jr. 1977. *The Visible Hand: The Managerial Revolution in American Business*. Cambridge, Mass.: Harvard University Press.

Chellgren, Mark R. 1986. "Wiggins Allies Want Collins Impeached." *Louisville Courier-Journal*, 3 September, B7.

Cohn, Ray. 1986. "Suit to Halt Toyota Plant Thrown Out." *Lexington Herald-Leader*, 29 July, B1, 2.

Cole, Robert E., and Donald R. Deskins, Jr. 1988. "Racial Factors in Site Location and Employment Patterns of Japanese Auto Plants in America." *California Management Review* 31 (Fall): 9–22.

Cropper, Carol Marie. 1986. "State Urged Not to Build Sewage Plant for Toyota." *Louisville Courier-Journal*, 28 May, 12.

Cross, Al. 1987. "Study Says Toyota Growth Will Strain City, Schools." *Louisville Courier-Journal*, 20 January, 1, 8.

Dohse, Knuth, Ulrich Jurgens, and Thomas Malsh. 1985. "From 'Fordism' to 'Toyotism'? The Social Organization of the Labor Process in the Japanese Automobile Industry." *Politics & Society* 14: 115–146.

Edsall, Thomas. 1984. "Labor Unions and Political Power." *The New Politics of Inequality*. New York: W.W. Norton & Company, 141–178.

Garrett, Robert T. 1986. "Unions Say Toyota Deal to Cost State $200 Million." *Louisville Courier-Journal*, 12 September, 1+.

Goodman, Robert. 1979. *The Last Entrepreneurs: America's Regional Wars for Jobs and Dollars*. Boston: South End Press.

Hammond, Jerry. Interview. Versailles, Kentucky. October 17, 1988.

Hardin, Garrett. 1972. *Exploring the New Ethics of Survival*. New York: Viking Press.

Hoagland, Jim. 1987. "As Dollar Declines, So Do International Relations." *Washington Post National Weekly*, 9 February, 20.

Howard, Dick. 1977. *The Marxian Legacy*. New York: Urizen Books.

Kaiser, Robert. 1986. "Hearing Today on Toyota Plan for Waste Plant." *Lexington Herald-Leader*, 27 February, B1, 2.

———. 1986. "Sewage Plant Urged for Toyota Draws Fire." *Lexington Herald-Leader*, 4 May, 1, 10.

———. 1986. "Opposition to Sewage Plan Grows." *Lexington Herald-Leader*, 28 May, B1, 2.

Kamber Group. 1986a. "The Kentucky-Toyota Agreement: Costs and Returns." McLean, Va.: The Kamber Group.

———. 1986b. "The Sins of Omission." McLean, Va.: The Kamber Group.

———. 1986c. "Chronology of Toyota Incentive Package." McLean, Va.: The Kamber Group.

Katznelson, Ira, and Mark Kesselman, 1987. *The Politics of Power: A Critical Introduction to American Government*. New York: Harcourt Brace Jovanovich.

Kentucky Building and Construction Trades Council. March 17, 1988. "20/20/–2020 Project: Vision for the Future." Frankfort, Ky.: KBCTC publication.

Kuttner, Robert. 1984. "Labor." *The Economic Illusion: False Choices Between Prosperity and Social Justice*. Boston: Houghton Mifflin, 136–186.

———. 1987. "Will Unions Organize Again?" *Dissent* 34 (Winter): 52–62.

———. 1987. *The Life of the Party: Democratic Prospects in 1988 and Beyond*. New York: Penguin Books.

Magaziner, Ira C. 1981. "Japanese Industrial Policy: Source of Strength for the Automobile Industry." In Robert E. Cole, ed. *The Japanese Automobile Industry: Model and Challenge for the Future*. Ann Arbor: University of Michigan, Center for Japanese Studies.

McCord, Tom. 1986. "Official: Toyota Sewage Plant Won't Damage Environment." *Lexington Herald-Leader*, 22 September, B1.

Mead, Andy. 1986. "Inside Toyota's Showcase Factory." *Lexington Herald-Leader*, 21 April, 1, 8.

Mills, C. Wright. 1956. *White Collar: The American Middle Classes*. New York: Oxford University Press.

Milward, H. Brinton. 1986. "Can a Governor Determine the Location of Private Industry?" *Kentucky Economy: Review and Perspective*, 10 (Summer): 3–4.

Moffitt, Michael. 1987. "Shocks, Deadlocks, and Scorched Earth: Reaganomics and the Decline of U.S. Hegemony." *World Policy Journal* 4 (Fall): 555–582.

Ophuls, William. 1977. *Ecology and the Politics of Scarcity*. San Francisco: W. H. Freeman and Company.

Prather, Paul. 1988. "Unions Change with World Economy." *Lexington Herald-Leader*, 9 May, D5, 10, 11.

Reid, Herbert G. 1973. *Up the Mainstream*. New York: David A. MacKay Company.

Reisman, Barbara, and Lance Compa. 1985. "The Case for Adversarial Unions." *Harvard Business Review* 3 (May-June): 1–6.

Rowen, Hobart. 1987. "Japan Builds Better Cars—Here." *Washington Post National Weekly*, 16 February, 5.

Rugeley, Cindy. 1986. "Union Tells Candidates Its Position on Toyota." *Lexington Herald-Leader*, 17 October, C1, 2.

———. 1986. "Hopkins, Hammond Have Failed to Stir Any Excitement." *Lexington Herald-Leader*, 25 October, B1, 12.

Schnaiberg, Allan. 1980. *The Environment: From Surplus to Scarcity*. New York: Oxford University Press.

Settlement and Release Agreement. March 17, 1987. Natural Resources and Environmental Protection.

Snyder, J. Robert. 1987. "The Toyota Package." Paper presented at the Kentucky Political Science Association meeting, Centre College, Danville, Ky. March 6–7.

Sobel, Robert. 1984. *Car Wars: The Untold Story*. New York: E.P. Dutton.

Stephens, John D. 1980. *The Transition from Capitalism to Socialism*. Atlantic Highlands, N.J.: Humanities Press.

Stewart, Fran. 1985. "Toyota Decides on Scott Co." *Kentucky Kernel*, 12 December, 3.

Swasy, Alecia. 1986. "Scott Toyota Plant Called Step 'Backward' Toward Socialism." *Lexington Herald-Leader*, 17 January, B2.

———. 1986. "Shirts, Leaflets New Weapons in Anti-Toyota Campaign." *Lexington Herald-Leader*, 29 August, 1+.

———. 1986. "Union Loyalties Need for Jobs Clash at Toyota Site." *Lexington Herald-Leader*, 5 October, 1, 16.

———. 1986. "AFL-CIO Economists Assail Tax Break for Toyota Plant." *Lexington Herald-Leader*, 31 October, 1, 13.

———. 1986. "Union Rebukes State for Issuing Permit for Scott Waste-Water Plant." *Lexington Herald-Leader*, 7 November, C3.

———. 1986. "Why the Unions Are Fighting Toyota." *Lexington Herald-Leader*, 16 November, 1, 14.

———. 1987. "Toyota Investment Return May Start by '93." *Lexington Herald-Leader*, 29 January, 1, 18.

Swasy, Alecia, and Michael York. 1986. "D.C. Rally to Target Toyota." *Lexington Herald-Leader*, 13 November, 1, 12.

———. 1986. "Unions and Toyota Builder Resolve Hiring Dispute." *Lexington Herald-Leader*, 26 November, 1, 10.

"The Toyota Campaign." N.d. Mimeographed chronology. Frankfort, Ky.: Kentucky Building and Construction Trades Council.

U.S. District Court. January 15, 1987. Motion for Permission to Intervene [Jane Allen Offutt and William N. Offutt IV].

Ward, Joe. 1986. "Labor Groups Feel They're in the Sights of 'Union Busters'." *Louisville Courier-Journal*, 1 September, F1, 2.

———. 1986. "N.Y. Union Workers give Toyota the Cold Shoulder." *Louisville Courier-Journal*, 22 November, 1, 8.

Wiggins, Don. 1985. Letter to the Editor. *Lexington Herald-Leader*, 31 December, A6.

———. February 5, 1986. Testimony. Before the Kentucky House Appropriations and Revenue Committee. Frankfort, Ky.: Legislative Research Commission.

Wilson, Dee. 1985. "Collins Unveils $125 Million Incentive Package for Toyota." *Louisville Courier-Journal*, 18 December, 1, 18.

Wolfe, Alan. 1981. *America's Impasse: The Rise and Fall of the Politics of Growth.* New York: Pantheon Books.

Wrenn, Rob. 1985. "The Decline of Labor." *Socialist Review* 85–86 (July-October): 89–117.

Yanarella, Ernest J. 1985. "Environmental vs. Ecological Perspectives on Acid Raid: The American Environmental Movement and the West German Green Party." In Ernest J. Yanarella and Randal H. Ihara, eds., *The Acid Rain Debate: Scientific, Economic, and Political Dimensions.* Boulder, Colo.: Westview Press, 243–260.

Yanarella, Ernest J., and Herbert G. Reid. 1987. "Class-Based Environmentalism in a Small Town: ERDA's 'Gasifiers in Industry' Program and the Georgetown, Kentucky, Controversy." In Ernest J. Yanarella and William Green, eds., *The Unfulfilled Promise of Synthetic Fuels.* Westport, Conn.: Greenwood Press, 99–125.

York, Michael. 1986. "Hundreds Rally in Washington Against Toyota." *Lexington Herald-Leader,* 18 November, 1, 7.

———. 1986. "Pact to Cover 2,000 Building Toyota Plant." *Lexington Herald-Leader,* 27 November, 1, 14.

Zeigler, Harmon. 1961. *The Politics of Small Business.* Washington, D.C.: Public Affairs Press.

9

Japanese Investment in Tennessee: The Economic Effects of Nissan's Location in Smyrna

William F. Fox

An announcement was made in October 1980 that Nissan would locate its U.S. light truck production facility in Smyrna, Tennessee. The events and decisions leading up to the news generated much attention because numerous states sought to attract the plant and its expected economic and fiscal benefits. After the Tennessee location was announced, there was much speculation regarding the incentives Tennessee had offered to Nissan and many suggestions about whether too much had been spent to "buy" the decision. At the local level, people were concerned that significant population inmigration would cause housing strain and overextend the area's ability to deliver public services such as ambulances, road repair, and education.

This chapter examines the effects of Nissan with the benefit of eight years of retrospect. The first section places the Nissan investment in context by evaluating the overall level of Japanese investment in Tennessee. The next two sections address the magnitude of Nissan's investment and the reasons behind the choice of Smyrna. The public sector's role in attracting Nissan is considered in the fourth section. The economic and fiscal effects are then identified and a brief conclusion closes the chapter.

Table 9.1

Investment by Foreign Affiliates in Tennessee, 1977–1986 (Millions of Dollars)

Year	Gross Book Value of Manufacturing Investment	Gross Book Value of Total Investment	Gross Book Value of Japanese Investment
1977	$1,159	$1,335	$ 24
1978	1,362	1,576	45
1979	1,624	1,897	76
1980	1,798	2,208	87
1981	3,142	3,747	121
1982	3,488	4,514	573
1983	3,523	4,730	724
1984	2,890	4,465	793
1985	2,863	4,609	884
1986	2,854	5,182	1,040

Source: U.S. Department of Commerce, 1985, p. 70.

Table 9.2

Employment by Foreign Affiliates in Tennessee, 1977–1986

Year	Number of Manufacturing Employees	Number of Total Employees	Number of Employees in Japanese Affiliates
1977	26,215	21,542	NA
1978	30,381	25,503	475
1979	37,686	31,114	1,641
1980	44,063	33,178	1,564
1981	57,422	43,972	2,718
1982	58,959	42,730	3,926
1983	59,980	43,598	5,196
1984	63,202	43,151	5,708
1985	69,559	45,641	7,089
1986	78,028	48,415	7,952

NA = not available

Source: U.S. Department of Commerce, 1988, Tables F-7 and F-8.

JAPANESE INVESTMENT IN TENNESSEE

In 1977, Japanese affiliates operating in Tennessee were insignificant contributors to foreign investment and employment in the state (Table 9.1). For
example, total Japanese investment of $24 million (in current dollars) represented
only 1.79 percent of total investment by foreign affiliates in Tennessee. This
share was much smaller than the 4.03 percent of foreign affiliate investment
made by Japanese firms across the entire United States. The same characteristic
could be seen in the employment associated with the investments (Table 9.2).
The 475 employees of Japanese affiliates in 1978 (data were unavailable for
1977) were only 1.56 percent of total foreign affiliate employment in Tennessee.

Again, the Tennessee numbers were very small compared with U.S values which showed that 89,898 employees, or 6.29 percent of the foreign work force employed, were associated with Japanese affiliates.

During the decade between 1977 and 1986, dramatic increases occurred in the economic activity of Japanese affiliates located in Tennessee. Nissan is responsible for a large share of the increase (about 44 percent of Japanese-affiliated employment growth), but national data sources report that in 1986 there were 76 Japanese affiliates with employment and 40 with physical investments in Tennessee (U.S. Department of Commerce, 1988: Tables D-13 and F-7). The value of total investment grew at a compound annual rate of 51.5 percent to reach $1,040 million. This represented 20.07 percent of foreign investment in Tennessee. Total Japanese investment in the United States was also growing at a rapid 26.5 percent annual pace, but that locating in Tennessee grew so fast that by 1986, 7.03 percent of Japanese investment in the United States was in the state. Japanese employment increased 42.2 percent annually in the state and was 10.19 percent of the state's total foreign employment by 1986. Tennessee's share of the nation's Japanese employment also jumped significantly, and at 3.67 percent in 1986 was well above the state's 1.9 percent share of the nation's overall employment. The growth trend appears to have continued, as 12 new operations were announced in 1987 and 9 more in the first 8 months of 1988.

Unfortunately, data are unavailable for identifying the Tennessee industries where the new Japanese investment has occurred. One accounting of a more select group of firms indicates that there are 35 manufacturing and 25 nonmanufacturing Japanese affiliates ("How Japan Is Winning Dixie," 1988: 44). The magnitude of the Nissan project probably means that manufacturing growth has not been a declining share of Japanese affiliate employment in Tennessee. On the other hand, wholesale and retail trade has received a significant share of total new investment and employment for all foreign affiliates in Tennessee (U.S. Department of Commerce, 1988: Tables D-13 and F-11) as manufacturing, though remaining the major industry for both measures, grew slowly relative to the average of other industries. Nonetheless, manufacturing employment for foreign affilitates increased at a dramatic 12.88 percent annually.

Similarly, data are unavailable for measuring the size distribution of Japanese affiliates operating in Tennessee. Overall, Tennessee has a strong tendency to receive relatively small branches of foreign firms, as 44.55 percent of the state's foreign affiliates employ five or fewer workers, and only 2.92 percent employ more than 1000 (U.S. Department of Commerce, 1988: Table F-10). Nationally, only 16.5 percent of foreign affiliate firms employ five or fewer, and 7.91 percent employ more than 1000. Tennessee's tendency for smaller branches has diminished somewhat over the past decade.

NISSAN IN TENNESSEE

In October 1980 Nissan ended its six-year search for a U.S. location with the announcement that it would develop a production facility in Smyrna, Tennessee.

The facility was to be Nissan's third outside Japan, following those in Australia and Mexico, but it was to represent the largest single investment. The plant was initially intended to produce Nissan trucks, to have an investment value of $300 million, and to employ a labor force of 2200. The first truck was completed in June 1983.

The size and expectations for the plant have expanded rapidly. Employment was 3300 and the plant operated two shifts daily in 1987 (Fisher, 1987). Cars were added to the assembly line, with the first Sentra produced in March 1985. Investment to date totals $760 million and includes the capacity to produce 265,000 Sentras and light trucks annually (Japan Center Newsletter, 1988). In 1987, production was 222,000 vehicles of which 117,000 were cars (about one-half of the U.S. Sentra production) and 105,000 were trucks (Fisher, 1987).

Changes have also been made in the Nissan plant's role in the overall production of vehicles. Several examples can be cited. Engineers at the Nissan plant now have some original design responsibility (Nissan Corporation News Release, 1987a). Also, plans have been announced for the plant to begin assembling car engines, truck axles, and bumper parts in 1989 (Schultze, 1988), and an increase in the domestic content has occurred steadily.

NISSAN'S SEARCH FOR A SITE

It has been reported that Nissan considered 34 states in its U.S. siting decision (Horowitz, 1982). After narrowing the potential region to the southeast, the final choice was made between a Georgia site and the Tennessee location. The reasoning for the selection of Smyrna is not known for certain. As is the case with nearly every major business location, the factors entering selection of the final site have not been revealed. Every firm making such a decision has understandable justification for keeping its major factors confidential. One reason is that competitors would be given an advantage if they knew the important determinants in the siting decision of other producers. Also, firms want to avoid making negative statements about another location or state since they want to sell products in the alternative sites' market. Further, firms do not want to reduce their ability to bargain with governments and suppliers in future siting decisions.

Five factors have been hypothesized as being very important in the Smyrna choice.[1] First, it is geographically located in the region where the majority of light trucks are purchased in the United States. Thus, the site is located near much of the market for the final product. Second, the area is convenient to rail service from the West Coast, being one day closer by rail than the alternative Georgia site. Since many parts are shipped from Japan, this means that the location is also easily accessible for inputs.

Next, the perception that the area labor force's work ethic is good was felt to be important. Definitions of the factors which comprise a good work ethic vary widely among analysts. Some potential aspects include low absenteeism, willingness to work, and quality outputs. Evidence of the labor force's quality can be seen in a *Washington Post* report that Nissan trucks built in the United States had 11 percent fewer errors than those built in Japan ("Standing Tall," 1984). Jerry Benefield, president of Nissan's American unit, was quoted in the *New York Times* as saying that the Nissan plant's absentee rate was under 3 percent compared with an industry average of 14 percent, and the plant's turnover rate for employees was below 2.5 percent compared with an average of 10 to 16 percent ("Union Organizers," 1988). Marvin Runyon, former president of the American unit, also reported to the Industrial Trade Commission that the defect rate for U.S. suppliers of Nissan was lower than the rate for Japanese suppliers (7 October 1986).

Another reason for the Smyrna selection may be that wage rates are lower in Tennessee than in many other areas. In 1987, United Auto Worker assembly workers earned between $14.80 and $19.00 per hour plus a cost of living allowance while Nissan employees earned between $12.62 and $16.36 per hour ("Nissan Plant," 1988). In fact, the somewhat lower unionization of employees in Tennessee also may have been a factor in the site selection. UAW efforts to unionize Nissan have been underway for more than five years, though they have been unsuccessful to date (see "Smyrna's Nissan Plant," 1983). An initial effort by union workers to embarrass the plant was staged on groundbreaking day.

Finally, the bedrock surface available at the Smyrna and Georgia sites has been mentioned as an important reason for the regional choice. It was regarded as necessary for the heavy equipment which is used.

THE PUBLIC SECTOR'S ROLE IN NISSAN'S DECISION

Tennessee state and local governments sought to attract the plant by offering incentives and cooperating with Nissan in a wide variety of ways. This section is a discussion of those recruitment activities which necessitated a direct outlay of cash. State government involvement focused on road improvements and training. Tennessee agreed to spend about $7.4 million in state resources and $2.5 million in CETA funds for training of Nissan employees (Burnett, 1981). More than 70 percent of the training funds was for travel and training in Japan. This included sending 380 supervisors (for as long as 40 weeks) and technicians (for an average of six weeks) to Japan for preparation (Nissan Corporation News Release, 1985). State officials made the argument that preparation of the labor force (education) is generally a responsibility of state and local governments and therefore it is acceptable for the state to make such investments in Nissan. They regarded training as an investment in the state's labor resources. Further, the provision of training funds for Nissan was not unique. Tennessee had provided training for employees of 184 new and expanding firms in the preceding two years through its Industrial Training Service.

Whether the training investment is large depends on one's perspective. The cost averaged $4,480 per initial worker at the facility. However, the state of Tennessee funded relatively little of the facility's total training investment. The

total resource expended on training prior to opening of the plant has been estimated at $63 million (Nissan Corporation News Release, 1985). In nine months
of training for Sentra production, Nissan spent another $10.4 million ("Train-
ing," 1984). Further, ongoing training is provided in a special center. Thus,
Tennessee financed less than one-seventh of the training for the plant's opening
and car production, and the overall share provided by the state continues to fall
with Nissan's ongoing investment.

State controlled resources totalling about $15.1 million, including those pro-
vided by state and federal sources, were targeted for road improvements. Most
of the funds went to improve the interchange with U.S. Route 41 and to provide
a connector on Interstate 24 (Cotham, 1981). A little over three-fifths of the
funds were from the state's own sources, and the remainder came from Economic
Development Administration grants (Burnett, 1981). Nissan claims to have contributed about $5.0 million for road improvements. Rutherford County (which
includes Smyrna) also spent about $5.0 million (Martin, 1984) so total highway
improvements were approximately $25 million.

The local governments also provided other types of location inducements.
Rutherford County issued $450 million in revenue bonds to finance construction
of the facility (Rutherford County, 1981). Though revenue bonds offer little
direct financial benefit to Nissan, they do require the setting of an in-lieu property
tax payment since the property is technically owned by the county. Normally a
county would establish an in-lieu payment equal to the property tax bill that
would have been assessed on the property. However, the size of investment by
Nissan was dramatically larger than most business projects and was large relative
to the existing tax base. Thus, a decision was made to set the in-lieu payment
lower than the property tax payment would have been. This is a tax concession
but the in-lieu payment was set such that there was no net fiscal cost to the
county or city.[2]

The annual in-lieu payment from 1981 through 1990 was set equal to the net
new annual operating cost that Nissan would impose on Rutherford County and
Smyrna plus $0.5 million. The $0.5 million was intended to account for nonfiscal
costs imposed on the county's residents, such as congestion and sound pollution.
The net new annual operating costs were defined as new public costs minus new
revenues arising from both the firm and its employees. Primary new costs were
police, fire, and education, and the total annual cost was estimated to be $693,000
in 1980 dollars. The estimate was inflated for subsequent years.[3] New revenues
were anticipated to arise from sales taxes paid on consumption expenditures from
the new incomes, and property taxes would be generated because of 400 new
housing units.

The agreement phased in the in-lieu payments until 1984, the first full year
of operation. In 1984, it was set at $1,268,525 and was to rise annually because
of anticipated inflation to reach $1,829,969 in 1990. Nissan's annual property
tax payment would have been approximately $3.2 million if its property had
been taxed at the effective tax rate that was imposed in 1984. From 1991 through

2010, Nissan's payments are to grow at one-third the combined increase of the city and county effective tax rate. This will likely result in a real (inflation adjusted) reduction in Nissan's in-lieu tax payments during that time interval. Nissan's in-lieu payments were to be increased proportionately for new investments.[4] Nissan will begin making property tax payments in 2011.

The site was annexed into Smyrna at Nissan's request, and the delivery of utility services to the plant required a number of investments totaling about $12.8 million, of which Nissan paid $9.2 million (Martin, 1984). Utility improvements were all deeded to the local area. Expansion of the sewage treatment facility from 2.6 mgd (million gallons per day) to 5.2 mgd entailed about two-thirds of the cost. Doubling the water capacity to 8 mgd, adding water storage, and laying seven miles of gas mains were also important infrastructure investments.

During negotiations for the plant, a letter from state officials to Marvin Runyon (then president of Nissan USA) agreed that Nashville and Rutherford County schools would provide part-time tutors for accelerated mathematics and that Saturday school and adult education in English and American culture would be provided. Interestingly this later led to controversy because there was a question as to who should pay for these services, even though the estimated cost was only $60,000 to $80,000 annually.

Measuring the importance that public sector recruitment and inducement activities played in the actual decision is at least as difficult as measuring the influence of other siting factors. Each firm making a location decision has the incentive to overstate the value of public sector incentives so that governments will want to offer them during other siting decisions. Further, the firms would not want to be quoted as saying that state and local governments had wasted resources in attracting the firm.

The conventional wisdom holds that certain policies, such as the level of taxes and the tax structure, will have a limited effect on the overall amount of manufacturing attracted (Wasylenko, 1985). However, even if the judicious setting of taxes and other state and local government policies is statistically associated with the location of business, the overall effect is so small that the probability of a single location decision being affected by government policies is very low.

The results of research on the effects that taxes and public policies have on business location (as summarized above) are based on research on the entire fiscal structure. Analysts are less in agreement about the influence of the specific incentives which governments offer to attract individual firms, because there has been very little research on the effects of specific incentives. It is tempting to extrapolate the results of broad-based studies to individual incentive agreements, but the reliability of this is questionable. One reason is that the change in the relative cost of producing at one location versus another because of a temporary reduction in the property tax rate cannot be easily assessed from outside the firm and, as noted above, the firm is unlikely to reveal its assessment. Further, if the same incentives, or ones of similar value, are offered by governments at several locations, then no noticeable change is made in a firm's relative costs of producing at each potential site. Also, for many location decisions (though perhaps not in the Nissan case) the value of incentives may be determined after the firm has already made an internal decision about where to locate, and the incentives then become icing on the cake. The minimum that can be said is that Tennessee state and local government efforts served to accommodate the needs of Nissan for information, to cooperate in helping Nissan overcome locational problems, and to lower Nissan's costs at the site. At a maximum, the effect was to help sway the decision for the Smyrna site.

A frequently asked question is whether the public sector's resources should have been allocated in an effort to attract the Nissan location. This question involves consideration of the potential fiscal and economic gains for the area and the importance of treating firms and residents evenly for tax purposes. Unfortunately, there is no simple answer to this question, nor is there a single way to evaluate the issues. One approach to such an analysis would be to determine whether the inducements attracted the firm, and if so, then to measure the public and private sector gains from the location. In the analysis the resources would by definition be wasted if they had absolutely no influence on the decision. If the plant would have located in Smyrna anyway, the inducements were simply an income transfer from the taxpayers of Tennessee and Rutherford County to Nissan, and the taxpayers' well-being would have been improved without the location incentives being offered.

If the incentives offered to Nissan did influence the location decision, a careful economic impact study would be necessary to determine if the public sector on net receives tax revenues above the costs. It would seem likely that the state government did not expend significantly more (if any at all) on incentives than the discounted flow of new revenues minus any increase in services, as the incentives were small relative to the total fiscal flows. At the local level, the in-lieu Rutherford County and Smyrna payments were set to exceed the net public sector costs so the project would have positive public sector benefits unless the projections were in error.[5]

Even if the reverse occurred and the state and local governments had greater expenditures associated with Nissan and its inducements than they received in revenues, there is the subtle question of how much the state should be willing to spend above any expected revenues to attract the private sector jobs and incomes that located in the state. The incentives could conceivably be justified by the state or local government if the firm's location would raise per capita incomes or reduce unemployment. Improvements in such nonquantifiables as quality of life could also justify incentives. Little consideration has been given to this issue by the economics literature.

However such an analysis resulted, the distributional effects of benefits may be more important than the magnitude of the overall gains. Even if both the public and private sectors gain on net from Nissan's location, it is still likely that some taxpayers, such as new employees or nearby retailers, are better off if the public sector's Nissan-related investments attracted the firm, and others are worse off because they do not receive any new income from Nissan, but some of their taxes must pay for public sector investments.

NISSAN'S EFFECTS ON RUTHERFORD COUNTY

Nissan's location may have led to economic stimulus in the immediate area and across much of the state; to changes in the fiscal climate in Rutherford County, other counties, and the state; and to other influences. This section addresses the extent to which this stimulus caused significant changes in Rutherford County.

First, consider the economic effects, which are described here but not fully quantified. The plant had the obvious benefit of providing employment during the construction phase and continuing employment during the operations phase. Because of the expansion, the economic benefits exceed those expected during negotiations for the plant, though some anticipated during the negotiation phase that the plant would be expanded. Nissan's payroll is currently $95 million annually. More than 85 percent of the jobs at the plant have gone to Tennesseans, so the employment benefits were substantially directed inside the state (Runyon, 1987). The jobs, which pay more than the state's average manufacturing earnings ($25,161 in 1986), are also regarded as highly desirable. One evidence of the high regard can be seen by the fact that the Tennessee Department of Employment Security interviewed 52,000 people for the 700 jobs which were added with the second shift ("Nissan in Tennessee," 1987).

Income and employment have also been generated by the network which supplies Nissan. Japanese automobile companies are much less vertically integrated than U.S. companies and this offers greater flexibility in the choice of suppliers. Nissan is 20 to 25 percent vertically integrated while General Motors is about 70 percent (Runyon, 1987). The economic benefit to Tennessee from the supplier network depends on the number of parts which are purchased and the location where they are purchased. Approximately 37 percent of the parts used in Nissan vehicles are manufactured in the United States (Runyon, 1987), and the overall U.S. content is 61 percent ("Nissan Expanding," 1988).[6] At the same time, Nissan's just-in-time system makes it desirable for many suppliers to be near the plant. Nissan is reported to use 136 domestic suppliers and to purchase $546 million annually in inputs; 46 of the suppliers are in Tennessee ("Nissan Supply," 1987). Fourteen of the 46 in-state suppliers are said to have moved to Tennesse to supply Nissan. In 1985, when there were only 29 Tennessee suppliers, the value of the annual intermediate product purchases was $101.7 million (Nissan Corporation News Release, 1985). Though the supplier purchases cannot be directly translated into income, the employment and income benefits of suppliers are substantial.

Income and employment arising through the multiplier process, which occurs as direct incomes attributable to Nissan expenditures are spent in the state on other products, must be added to both the supplier and direct incomes created by Nissan to measure the total value that the plant contributes to the state's economy. Also, new income and employment could be generated in the area if firms which are not suppliers of Nissan choose to locate in the surrounding area because of visibility created by Nissan's presence, the desirability of hiring from the same labor pool, or other reasons.

Quantifying the specific influence which Nissan has had on the state and immediate surrounding area cannot be achieved by examining available statistics such as growth in income, because many other changes have occurred simultaneously. A fully specified econometric model would be necessary for this purpose. Thus, general analysis of the area is at best indicative of Nissan's economic effects. The number of nonagricultural jobs in Rutherford County grew at a compound annual rate of 5.7 percent between 1979 and 1986, much faster than Tennessee's 1.4 percent, and this was the second highest growth rate among Nashville's 8 MSA counties (below Williamson County which is immediately to the west). Manufacturing jobs grew 9.3 percent annually in Rutherford County during this time, with Nissan providing 46.9 percent of these jobs. On the surface this would seem to be evidence that Nissan was an important source of rapid growth in the county.

Personal income in Rutherford County has grown at a compound annual rate of 11.1 percent since 1979, also much faster than the state's 8.1 percent rate, and again the growth rate is second only to Williamson County's in the MSA. Similarly, Rutherford County's 3.4 percent population increase is second fastest in the MSA and much faster than the state's 0.8 percent rise. However, the population increase offset much of the income growth so that per capital income in Rutherford County has grown at a compound annual rate of 7.4 percent, which is only slightly faster than the state's 7.2 percent growth rate. Rutherford County's per capital income growth rate is fourth among the eight MSA counties.

Examination of the historical context prior to 1979 would seem to indicate that Rutherford County's growth rates have not accelerated as a result of Nissan. Personal income, population, and per capital personal income all had lower annual growth rates between 1979 and 1986 than between 1970 and 1979, though this is also true for the state. However, the county's per capita income grew only 3.9 percent faster than the state's in the 1979 to 1986 time period, compared with 17.6 percent faster between 1970 and 1979. Thus, Rutherford County's growth rates have been good relative to other counties, but have not been spectacular and do not appear to have accelerated in the intervening years since Nissan's location. This may indicate that economic activity that otherwise would have come to Rutherford County located elsewhere after Nissan's decisions. Concerns about wage rates being too high or workers not being available may be some reasons for this. Similar statistics for the state fail to reveal a significant shift in overall economic activity.

Also, the location of Nissan does not appear to have led to undue fiscal stress on Rutherford County or its cities. Per capita non-debt operating expenditures for the aggregate of Rutherford County local governments were much lower in 1986 than for the average of Tennessee counties ($652.08 versus $751.96, as

Table 9.3
Per Capita Local Government Expenditures and Revenues

	Nondebt Operating Expenditures	Debt	Total Operating Expenditures	Own Source Revenues
		1986		
Rutherford County	409.50	70.32	479.82	368.45
Local Governments[a]	402.67	44.33	447.00	448.42
		1980		
Rutherford County	285.62	39.43	325.05	216.37
Local Governments[a]	280.46	11.09	291.55	131.44

a. Includes Smyrna, Murfreesboro, Eagleville and Lavergne

Source: State of Tennessee, Comptroller of the Treasury, Division of Local Finance, County and Municipal Finances for Fiscal Year Ended June 30, 1980 and June 30, 1986.

indicated in Table 9.3). Rutherford County's growth in expenditures since 1980 has been somewhat faster than the average counties' growth (7.4 percent versus 7.1 percent), but this small difference is consistent with Rutherford County's faster employment and income growth. Debt service payments for the county are also lower than average ($97.03 versus $166.26).

The equalized property tax rate[7] for both Rutherford County and Smyrna was moderately volatile between 1979 and 1986 but was lower in 1985 than in 1970. The equalized property tax rate in Rutherford County rose slightly from $1.93 per $100 of assessed value in 1979 to $1.97 in 1986. Smyrna's rate rose slightly from $2.42 to $2.59 in the same time period. Rutherford County increased its local option sales tax rate from 1.5 percent to 2.25 percent in October 1983, following the 1982 recession.

CONCLUSION

Nissan's investment in truck and automobile assembly capacity in Tennessee was an early and important part of the rapid growth of Japanese investment in Tennessee during the past decade. The magnitude of Nissan's investment made it important, but it represents less than one-half of the total new activity by Japanese affiliates in the state. Though the Japanese investments have been made by numerous firms and across many different industries, the Nissan decision was also important because it has proved to be a positive influence on the decision by some other firms to consider Tennessee. Further, the economic benefits from Nissan probably exceed those anticipated when the location decision was made because of subsequent decisions to expand the facility to its current size of approximately 3,330 employees. Thus, the chances are even higher that inducement activities were a sound investment. Despite expansions in Nissan's plant, however, the immediate area appears to have accepted Nissan in stride without suffering a sudden shift in its economic or fiscal climate. Further, no significant negative noneconomic influences appear to have resulted because of the facility.

NOTES

1. Some of these are cited in "Tennessee Has a Lot Going for Japanese Business," 1981.

2. See Fox and Neel, 1987, for a discussion of issues related to setting an in-lieu payment which is below the potential tax liability for large projects.

3. The inflation forecast available in 1980 ranged between 6.95 and 9.21 percent for subsequent years and represented rates which were higher than have occurred. Thus, a greater payment in real terms has resulted than was anticipated.

4. One-third of the assessed value of investments above $450 million would be taxed at the current tax rate. The $450 million is the part of Nissan's initial investment which was regarded as potentially part of the tax base. Assessed value would be equal to 40 percent of land and improvements plus 30 percent of machinery and equipment less 30 percent front-end depreciation. Capitalized interest, financing costs, and architectural and engineering fees were not to be included in calculation of new value.

5. Local governments surrounding Rutherford County could have experienced some diminution in their fiscal position because they likely became the residence site for some Nissan employees who moved to the area, but these counties received none of the firm's in-lieu payments. This assumes that residents' taxes would not be sufficient to cover all services that they received. The problem of surrounding counties experiencing some costs from a large plant locating nearby is the result of the state's tax structure and is independent of any location inducements.

6. Nissan started with 38 percent U.S. content (Runyon, 1987) and is aiming for 75 percent according to Benefield ("Nissan Expanding," 1988). Proportions of content depend on the prevailing currency exchange rate.

7. The equalized property tax rate is calculated by adjusting the nominal tax rate for the appraisal ratio.

REFERENCES

Burnett, Wilton. 1981. "Nissan Budget." Unpublished Tennessee Department of Economic and Community Development working paper, 23 January.

Cotham, James. 1981. "Fact Sheet: State Commitments, Nissan Project." Unpublished working paper, 17 February.

Fisher, Gene. 1987. "Nissan's Smyrna Plant Earns High Marks." *Nashville Tennessean*, 23 June.

Fox, William F., and C. Warren Neel. 1987. "Saturn: The Tennessee Lessons." *Forum for Applied Research and Public Policy* 2 (Spring): 7–16.

Horowitz, Bruce. 1982. "Japan Inc.'s Beachhead in Tennessee." *Industry Week*, 17 May, 45–47.

"How Japan Is Winning Dixie: The Tennessee Story." 1988. *U.S. News and World Report*, 9 May, 43–47.

Japan Center Newsletter. Spring 1988. Middle Tennessee State University.

Martin, Don. 1984. "A Look at Smyrna—The Nissan Impact." *Local Planning News*. Tennessee Department of Economic and Community Development. 16 (September): 1–8.

Nissan Corporation News Release. 1 August 1985.

"Nissan Expanding Smyrna Operations." 1988. *Nashville Banner*, 7 April.

"Nissan in Tennessee Celebrates Production of 500,000th Vehicle and Achieves Capacity Increase." 1987. Nissan Corporation News Release, 30 March.

"Nissan Motor Manufacturing Corporation USA Engineers to Assume New Design Responsibility." 1987. Nissan Corporation News Release, 2 December.

"Nissan Plant in Tennessee is UAW Target." *New York Times*, 26 January.

"Nissan Supply Firms Move to Midstate." 1987. *Nashville Tennessean*, 22 September.

Runyon, Marvin T. 1986. Speech text, 7 October.

———. 1987. "Remarks to the Congressional Automotive Caucus." 5 May.

Rutherford County, Tennessee. 1981. "Nissan Project." Unpublished working paper.

Shultze, Cathy. 1988. "Nissan Expanding Smyrna Operations." *Nashville Banner*, 7 April.

"Smyrna's Nissan Plant Has Non-Union Utopia." 1983. *Nashville Tennessean*, 28 September.

"Standing Tall: We Make the World's Best Japanese Trucks." 1984. *Washington Post*, 19 August.

Tennessee Department of Economic and Community Development. 1981. "Cost-Benefit Ratios of Nissan Project, Smyrna, Tennessee." Unpublished working paper, 10 February.

———. 1985. "Training at Nissan." Unpublished working paper.

"Tennesse Has a Lot Going for Japanese Businessman." 1981. *Asian Wall Street Journal*, 11 February.

"Training." 1984. Nissan Corporation Information Packet.

"Union Organizers Task is Uphill at Nissan Plant." 1988. *New York Times*, 3 April.

U.S. Department of Commerce, Bureau of Economic Analysis, 1985. *Foreign Direct Investment in the United States, Operations of U.S. Affiliates, 1977–1988.* Table D-14: 70.

———. 1988. *Foreign Direct Investment in the United States, Operations of U.S. Affiliates Preliminary 1986 Estimates.* June. Tables D–13 through F–11.

Wasylenko, Michael. 1985. "Business Climate, Industry and Employment Growth: A Review of the Evidence." Occasional paper no. 98. Syracuse, N.Y.: Metropolitan Studies Program, October.

PART III

SEARCH FOR AN AMERICAN INDUSTRIAL POLICY

10

The National Level Roots of the Failure of State Industrial Policy

David Lowery

PROBLEMS IN THE STUDY OF STATE INDUSTRIAL POLICY

While often denied by those opposed to the use of governmental power and authority in economic affairs, it is a truism to suggest that every nation has an industrial policy. That policy is defined by the total set of governmental actions that influence private economic development, including both a wide array of microeconomic policies and strategies of macroeconomic intervention. Even when such policies are designed for other purposes, their impacts may be more far reaching than the kinds of interventions usually suggested in discussions of systematic industrial policy. Thus, the real questions about industrial policy in the United States have less to do with whether the federal government should adopt an industrial policy than with the degree to which that policy should be conscious and its component strategies subject to the discipline of intentional coordination.

To date, we have decided not to pursue a strategy of conscious and coordinated industrial policy at the national level. But by the mid-1980s, a number of analysts began to focus on the states as the locus of American industrial policy, arguing that others had failed to find evidence of systematic industrial policy in the United States simply because they looked in the wrong place (Wilmoth, 1984; Grady, 1987; Clark, 1986; Peters, 1986: 64). Under the pressure of declining industries, new attention to economic development, and a rapid series of recessions during the previous decade, it was argued, the states were, by the early 1980s, adopting a set of new policies and practices under the rubric of "industrial policy" (Hudson, Hyde, and Carroll, 1987; Grady, 1987; Goldstein and Bergman, 1986; Peters, 198: 64).

There are any number of examples of such state policies to be found in the case literature. The most often noted examples include the $752 million Greenhouse Compact proposal in Rhode Island, Pennsylvania's Ben Franklin Partnership, and Minnesota's expedited passage of a tough antitakover law to protect the Dayton-Hudson Corporation. In each of these cases, proponents of industrial policy at the state level note that joint and concerted efforts on the part of business, labor, and government were an essential foundation of policy success. Most of these case analyses of state industrial policy are optimistic in tone, and usually cite the traditional argument that states can be more successful in developing such policies because of the diversity of approaches inherent in their role as "policy laboratories."

While these cases are suggestive, many analysts remain suspicious of such optimistic conclusions. One of the central issues underlying this skepticism concerns the epistemological foundation of claims made about the success or failure of state industrial policy. To date, studies of state industrial policy have generally been of one of two types. On one hand, and as illustrated by the examples cited above, we have intensive analyses of the policies of single states. But while rich in detail, the key cases underlying the optimistic assessment of state industrial policy were largely noncomparable, usually analyzing policies that are dramatically different in scale and focus. And, in one way or another, these policies examined seemed almost unique products of their own state's political and economic conditions. While such "policy uniqueness" might be expected from a strict "states as policy laboratories" perspective, and even interpreted as supportive of that view, the limitations on generalization inherent in such empirical evidence are obvious. Just as it is impossible to conclude that a forest is healthy by intensively studying one elm tree, we cannot conclude that state industrial policy "works" by finding that Pennsylvania's Ben Franklin Partnership has been effective in achieving its specific goals.

On the other hand, the few genuinely comparative state analyses of state industrial policy have largely failed to find much supportive evidence for such optimistic conclusions (Hansen, 1984; Ambrosius, 1986; Gray and Lowery, 1988, 1989). The problem with such studies, however, is that they are poorly designed to assess the impact of policies that are very different in scale and focus and that are uniquely configured for their own political and economic environments. Conducting such analyses requires that we compress the diversity inherent in state approaches to industrial policy into a few, very general categories that may miss the essential details that ultimately are responsible for policy success or failure. In terms of our metaphor, it is hard to accurately assess the health of a forest when one has to employ a common definition of health for elms, spruces, birches, oaks, and pines. In sum, we have two very different kinds of studies that have provided strikingly different conclusions about the success of state industrial policy, with both types of studies suffering from profound inferential limits.

These mutual limitations highlight the essential epistemological contribution of the case analyses presented in this volume. In contrast to either the single case or the fifty state comparative approaches dominating most of the literature on state industrial policy, we find here a set of analyses that address state industrial policy efforts that are more truly comparable. All are addressing state actions vis-à-vis a common type of industry—the auto industry. All of the states are in the same general region, auto alley, running from Michigan to Tennessee, thereby facilitating some control over important political and economic variables that might influence industrial policy. All are concerned with initial siting decisions about very large industrial complexes rather than such varied efforts as preventing plant closings or spurring the development of small, innovative firms. In short, these studies provide a much firmer empirical base from which to assess the success or failure of state industrial policy efforts than either of the two dominant approaches to analyzing such policies.

Given this inferential foundation, what do these case analyses tell us about state industrial policy? Two conclusions seem warranted. First, they strongly suggest that the efforts by states to develop independent industrial policies have been less than entirely successful, or at least not as successful as they might have been. And second, they strongly imply that the roots of this at least partial failure are to be found at the national level of government. As so baldly stated, both of these conclusions may be surprising. Several of the individual case analyses in this volume end on a somewhat optimistic note. Even more problematically, not one of the cases even mentions the federal government. Thus, neither conclusion seems obvious on its face given an uncritical reading of the several case studies.

A more critical assessment, however, supports both conclusions. This argument is developed in three steps. First, the consistent similarities in the conclusions of the case studies are noted. In the following section, I then discuss the one major contextual variable that the case studies fail to address: the role of federal macroeconomic policy during the 1980s. We will see that federal macroeconomic policies account for the observed similarities in the findings of the case reports. And finally, I will offer an alternative history of federal policy during the 1980s to suggest how national policy could have created a more benign environment for the effective operation of state industrial policy.

THE SIMILARITIES OF THE CASE FINDINGS

The case analyses of Japanese automobile investment included in this volume do not present a single, uniform evaluation of the processes and impacts associated with the experience. Still, three general themes are evident that are relevant to our overall assessment of the success or failure of the states' efforts to lure a Japanese auto plant.

First, all allude to an almost wrenching *political desperation* on the part of the politicians overseeing the negotiation for the privilege of being selected as the site of the next Japanese auto plant. There is, of course, some variation in this description. The Blair, Endres, and Fichtenbaum chapter on West Central Ohio presents a picture of that state's officials as being a bit more future oriented and controlled in their dealings with Honda. But from there on, one receives a picture of truly desperate officials pullling out all the stops to have a plant sited in their states, with perhaps the most frightening portrait provided by Green's analysis of Kentucky's bid for a Toyota plant. The source of that desperation is evident in each of the cases. All of these states suffered high unemployment levels during the period under consideration, and in each, unemployment became one of the central political issues governing the political lives of its officials.

There is, moreover, something of a temporal aspect to this picture of political desperation. That is, the level of desperation hinted at by the case analyses of the earliest siting decisions seems less than that of the latter sites. This pattern would be consistent with the hypothesis that the earlier successes of some states in attracting a Japanese auto plant served to harden the expectation on the part of officials whose state had so far failed that their political future depended on landing a plant. When only one state had been successful, it might be dismissed as good fortune. But when all one's neighbors have landed a new factory, a voter might begin to question whether his or her own government was less than competent. Some perception of Japanese auto plants as a scarce good may also have contributed to this escalation in expectations. There are only so many Japanese auto producers. As the last of the major companies were making their siting decisions, officials must have begun to ask if they were gambling on their last opportunity to get into the Japanese auto plant game.

A second aspect of this descriptive theme concerns the asymmetrical bargaining relation between the state and local governments and the Japanese auto firms, or rather, the pattern of asymmetrical information inherent in the negotiation. The actions of the state and local officials as well as the size and character of the incentive packages being offered were, by the very nature of being official acts of government, exceedingly public. In contrast, the firms' decision processes and criteria were unknown. Fox's analysis of Nissan's decision to locate in Tennessee, in particular, notes both the reasons for this confidentiality and the disadvantages it created for the state and its localities. In the present context, this inherent asymmetry could only have heightened the sense of political desperation governing the bargaining relationship over plant siting.

The second general theme, one that will be a major part of our ultimate evaluation of the success or failure of the Japanese auto plant experience, concerns the *descriptions of the incentive packages* offered by the states. To put it simply, the separate case descriptions are remarkably repetitive in their listing of the incentives offered the several Japanese auto firms. This is by no means a criticism of the authors of the case studies; the packages were objectively similar, at least in terms of the kinds of benefits offered by the respective state and local governments. In virtually all of the cases, we find property tax abatements, enhanced funding for infrastructure, and state absorption of some portion of training costs. But while similar in terms of what kinds of incentives were offered, the states offered varying amounts of incentives, amounts that, according to Milward and Newman's analysis, escalated sharply over time.

Two aspects of this second descriptive theme deserve further attention. The first and most easily understandable concerns the escalation of the value of the incentive packages offered by the states. If the earlier observation that the political desperation of state officials grew over time is accepted, then we have an obvious explanation of the forces underlying the escalation process. But a second and less obvious aspect of our second theme concerns the underlying similarity of the contents of the incentive packages. The common basket of incentives is remarkable in the face of the prevailing wisdom about the states as "policy laboratories," which might be interpreted as implying that the states would experiment with widely different incentives for, approaches to, and strategies of economic development. Thus, both the underlying uniformity of the contents of the incentives packages, as well the escalation of specific bids, must be accounted for if we are to understand Japanese auto siting experience.

The third general theme concerns the "cooperative" character of the negotiations over the siting decisions. The "cooperative" spirit among management, government, and, in some cases, labor, are often referred to in Bachelor's chapter on Mazda's Michigan plant, in Blair, Endres, and Fichtenbaum's chapter on the Honda plant in Ohio, in Lind's analysis of Diamond-Star Motors in Illinois, and, to a much lesser extent, in Fox's analysis of Nissan in Tennessee. In only the Toyota cases, examined by Yanarella and Reid as well as Green, is the theme of cooperation missing. Such broad references to cooperation imply that these new plants and the processes that led to their siting embody an evolving American form of corporatism along the lines of European interest group systems. Virginia Gray and David Lowery, balancing among many competing definitions of corporatism and meso-corporatism, have defined its American form as "tripartite agreements between business, labor, and government sanctioned by political parties that resolve traditionally conflicting issues in the interest of the public good" (Gray and Lowery, 1989).

Do the present cases meet this definition of mesocorporatism? On its face, the answer would seem doubtful. Fox's interpretation of cooperation in the Nissan case is extremely tentative. And while Lind's chapter stresses cooperation as its major theme, labor is virtually never mentioned. For the Ohio and Michigan cases, the respective authors assert that substantial cooperation between labor (in one case unionized and the other nonunionized), management, and government characterized the siting decision. But even in these cases of apparent cooperation, the relative bargaining power that the three parties brought to the table is hardly discussed, and, thus, the authors fail to demarcate submission from true mutual resolution of conflicting interests. So while corporatist-like cooperation is a theme of several of the chapters, they largely fail to explore its underlying base. When that base is explored critically, as in the Yanarella and Reid chapter on the Georgetown Toyota plant, conflict, rather than cooperation, is the dominant theme.

Beyond articulation of these three themes, we are most interested in how these cases ultimately evaluated the success or failure of their respective states' experiences in securing a Japanese auto plant. How did the costs of the incentive packages offered to the Japanese auto firms balance against the employment and economic opportunities that the politicians were desperate to secure for their states? In developing a summary answer to this question based on the separate case reports, I will restrict the analysis to consideration of only the direct economic tradeoffs made by the state governments. Importantly, this is the criterion used by most of the individual papers. As Perrucci and Patel note, whether appropriate or not, it is on this issue that the debates over the new plants hinged.

This is not the only basis on which to consider the auto siting experience, however. Two of the chapters are generally negative in overall assessment, though they address political rather than economic criteria. Perrucci and Patel conclude that newspaper coverage of Toyota in Kentucky and Subaru-Isuzu in Indiania generally served to suppress discussion of the distributive and environmental consequences associated with the siting of a major new auto plant. Green's review of the constitutional crisis created by Toyota's incentive package was resolved in a way that undermined the legitimacy of Kentucky's political-legal system. And Yanarella and Reid's discussion of the weaknesses of the anti-Toyota coalition in Kentucky highlights the political liabilities confronting those opposed to a state's efforts to land a major auto plant. And while none of the chapters attempts to deal with the issue in any direct manner, several raise the question of distributive consequences in a manner that suggests that the plants might have had less than uniformly positive economic impacts. These are clearly important issues that must be considered in any final assessment of policy success or failure. But not all of the cases address these issues. Thus, our evaluation will be restricted to the economic criteria that would, presumably, be most likely to lead to a favorable assessment of the impacts of the new auto plants.

Starting with the most optimistic evaluation, we find that Blair, Endres, and Fichtenbaum's analysis of Honda's plant in Ohio presents that experience as an unambiguous success. Bachelor's assessment of Michigan's experience with Mazda and Lind's analysis of Diamond-Star Motors in Illinois also appear optimistic, but they are much more constrained in their enthusiasm than are Blair, Endres, and Fichtenbaum. In contrast to the Honda case, Bachelor and Lind are both concerned that their respective states "might have paid too high a price," and recognize that a complete answer to this question is not yet in. Still, apparently more on faith than evidence, they remain hopeful about the ultimate payoffs for Illinois and Michigan. The remaining cases in which judgments about impacts are made offer a far more pessimistic view of their respective state's experiences. Fox's analysis of Nissan's plant in Tennessee is by and large negative in its consideration of specific employment consequences, though he too ends up modestly hopeful in the conclusion of the paper. Even more negatively, Hansen's review of Pennyslvania's Volkswagen plant episode, the only case for which enough time has passed to allow for accurate assessment of economic consequences, concludes with the hard fact that the plant eventually closed.

On balance, I would argue that these varous conclusions add up to a generally pessimistic view of the auto siting experience. With the exception of the Ohio case, any optimism in the results seems to be based more on hope than factual evidence. And this slim reed of optimism must be discounted given a single question that is asked in several different forms in nearly all of the essays. With the exception of the Ohio case, each of the case analysts report that all observers were left with the nagging question of whether too much was given away or too high a price was paid. With the exception of the study of the Pennsylvania Volkswagen plant which has closed, none of the authors asking this question are able to provide a firm answer to this fundamental issue. And in terms of a strict economic balance sheet, no specific answers can be offered until enough time has passed to see if the new plants grow into a thriving industrial complex, as Honda in Ohio appears poised to do, or fail, as did Volkswagen in Pennsylvania. Still, the fact that this question is asked in nearly every case analysis, when combined with the bargaining characteristics of the situation, almost certainly means that the states paid more than they should have for the auto plants. While the question of the economic success or failure of these siting decisions remains open, I will argue that they represented a clear policy failure by failing to secure as much benefit as possible from the new plants. To fully understand this conclusion, however, we must go beyond what the several authors of the case studies have written to consider issues that they have collectively failed to address.

THE CONTRADICTORY AND TRAGIC ROLE OF THE NATIONAL GOVERNMENT

It was earlier noted that all nations have an industrial policy, though in the United States, overt industrial policy at the national level has been largely a strategy of default. Industrial policy, of the type we have seen in these cases, has been left to the states. While even this lack of action on the part of the national government *is* industrial policy of a sort, it is also obvious that many of the explicit economic policy actions of that government have profound implications for economic development. In terms of the present cases, two such overt policy concerns of the national government—international trade policy and macroeconomic policy—have had a major impact on the effectiveness of state industrial policy.

Before we consider the impacts of these policies, it should be noted that, with the partial exception of the Yanarella and Reid chapter, the case analyses in this volume say little about national level policy concerns in evaluating the effectiveness of state industrial policy. In part, this is understandable; the authors were considering the impacts of specific actions of states within states. External forces influencing the actions of state officials, when considered from such an analytic focus, are often, and sometimes appropriately, dismissed as simple environmental constraints that can be treated as constants. In our present cases, however, federal actions in the fields of international trade and macroeconomic policy both helped to create the initial opportunity for states to attract Japanese firms and, at the same time, undermined their bargaining position vis-à-vis those firms. Thus, we cannot understand the success or failure of the state incentive policies, nor answer the ultimate question of whether or not the states paid too high a price for their new Japanese auto plants, unless we understand the backstage roles the federal government played in state industrial policy.

The federal government played at least two different and ultimately contradictory roles in the Japanese auto plant story. Actions taken by the federal government in the name of international trade policy clearly exerted some pressure on the Japanese auto firms to locate plants in the United States. Informal and formal trade actions, and the threat of quotas on imported automobiles, almost certainly made sites in the United States more attractive to Japanese auto firms than they might otherwise have been. This alone, of course, may not have led to decisions to establish plants in the United States. Milward and Newman note, for example, that the rise in the value of the yen and proximity to markets were major contributing reasons to the decision to invest in U.S. production facilities. But they also cite the threat of protectionist legislation as the most "immediate" concern of the Japanese companies. Thus, through its international trade policy, the federal government, in so far as federal actions or threats of trade sanctions encouraged Japanese auto investment in the United States, acted in a manner that created significant opportunities for state policy makers.

If national industrial policy consisted solely of the federal government adopting trade policies designed to encourage direct investment in the United States on one hand, and leaving the states to compete for the siting of the new plants on the other, the policy might have been more successful. Unfortunately, other policies of the federal government—especially the macroeconomic policies of the Reagan administration during the early 1980s—served to minimize the states' abilities to bargain effectively for the new plants. Simply put, the Reagan administration, in conjunction with the Federal Reserve Board, adopted a series of policies designed to purge the economy of inflation via recession. Thus, the early 1980s saw the most severe recession since the depression, with unemployment levels skyrocketing to over 10 percent. The economic desperation resulting from such policies, of course, is the source of the political desperation governing the politics of Japanese auto plant siting noted earlier.

The macroeconomic policies of the Reagan administration can be criticized on any number of grounds. Some, for example, have questioned whether such policies were needed, arguing that the social consequences of even high levels of inflation are less troublesome than high levels of unemployment (Hibbs, 1987;

Page, 1983), or that the engine driving inflation was a series of unique price shocks that would have run their course irrespective of national macroeconomic policy (Thurow, 1983). Others have argued that selective wage and price controls could have wrung out underlying inflation without the social consequences of high unemployment (Galbraith, 1987). For our immediate purposes, however, these debates are less important than the secondary impacts of restrictive macroeconomic policy on states' efforts to attract new plants. To put the issue simply, federal macroeconomic policy precluded effective state industrial policy.

The roots of this contradiction in national level policy are found in the bargaining situation confronting state officials. As we have seen, they were pursuing a commodity—new Japanese auto plants—that was perceived to be in finite supply. Indeed, the sequential manner in which the Japanese auto companies came to the United States may have created the perception at any given time that the next plant was the last plant that would be available. Moreover, the states were in direct competition with each other with a finite set of policies and incentives that they might adopt to make themselves more attractive. And finally, the bargaining situation was one characterized by asymmetrical information; the states had to be entirely open with each other in terms of what they were offering, but the Japanese firms did not have to disclose the criteria they were employing in selecting among the states. All of these factors created a bargaining situation that was firmly imbalanced against the states and in favor of the Japanese auto companies.

The final, crucial element that the federal government added to this unfortunate situation, thereby transforming it into a policy disaster of foregone opportunity, was its restrictive macroeconomic policy. By driving unemployment to double digit levels, the federal government essentially made the states' demand for new plants inelastic. State politicians simply could not afford to bid less than everything they had to secure a Japanese auto plant. At the same time, as pointed out by Yanarella and Reid in the Kentucky case, high levels of unemployment undermined any opportunity for developing an effective antigrowth coalition. Federal macroeconomic policy, thereafter, transformed a bad bargaining situation into something more like an open auction for the last piece of bread before 50 starving individuals. In such situations, cooperative bargaining as mutual resolution of competing interests is unlikely.

The evidence for this interpretation is found in the earlier noted similarities in the states' incentive packages and industrial policies. In the early 1980s, the states were adopting several different strategies of economic development. Hansen (1984), in a factor analysis of a number of policies described in the *Directory of Incentives for Business Investment and Development in the United States* (1983), found evidence of four distinct strategies of economic development in four typical sets of incentive packages. When this analysis was replicated using 1988 data from the *Directory* (Gray and Lowery, 1989), 15 distinct factors with an eigenvalue of greater than one were found, but they together accounted for less variance in the use of incentives than Hansen's simple four factor solution had found only a few years earlier. These results suggest that, with the possible exception of a few new policies (such as venture capital programs), the states were rapidly imitating each other by adopting all possible types of incentives. From the perspective of this interpretation, the new factor scores represent evidence of only leads and lags in a system that was quickly becoming saturated with nearly identical incentive packages.

Such policy homogenization is understandable in light of the situation created by federal macroeconomic policy. That policy created desperate economic conditions. And the resulting desperate political situation state officials found themselves in deprived them of any realistic opportunity to experiment with different strategies of economic development; they were compelled to try all possible strategies. Thus, instead of the states acting as laboratories of industrial policy, developing and testing competitive strategies of economic development, they acted in blind imitation of one another, each offering whatever incentive any other state was willing to bid.

When each of the states are offering essentially similar incentive packages in terms of the types of benefits being provided, their next recourse is to offer more of each. And again, this is just what we observe in the case analyses presented here. In particular, Figure 2.2 in the Milward and Newsman chapter strongly suggests a rapid and substantial escalation in the per worker cost of the incentive packages offered by the states as the supply of Japanese auto plants was depleted. Nor does the desperate bargaining game stop even when the states have escalated their bids to their legally constrained limits. Once the states had exhausted all of the resources that they legitimately could offer the Japanese auto companies, their last recourse was to pursue less legitimate incentives. In this regard, Green's analysis of Kentucky's mutilation of its own constitution is perhaps the first example of the next round of state industrial policy, should we again experience severely restrictive macroeconomic policy on the part of the national government.

Such an outcome in the future is a distinct possibility because of the likely long-term consequences of this episode of policy homogenization. Once policies of the type discussed here have been adopted, it is very difficult to step away from them. It is likely, therefore, that the unfortunate consequences of the economic policies of the Reagan administration will reach far beyond the specific bargains struck for a few Japanese auto plants during the early 1980s, necessarily restricting the range of options the states have in confronting future economic crises.

The impacts of federal macroeconomic policy, moreover, go beyond minimizing the interstate bargaining power of officials to also distort the intrastate bargaining that precedes a siting decision. It was earlier noted that several of the chapters stress "cooperation" as a major theme in their assessment of their respective state's experience with the new Japanese auto plants. And it was pointed out that the authors largely failed to distinguish between cooperation as submission and cooperation as mutual satisfaction of conflicting interests, with only the latter being truly consistent with our understanding of an evolving American form of mesocorporatism. But given Reagan administration macroeconomic policies, as well as its union busting efforts symbolized by the crushing of PATCO, it is almost certain that any apparent cooperation between unions and management during the plant siting processes was of the cooperation-as-submission form. When unions have a substantial portion of their members out of work in an economy characterized by weak demand, they have little bargaining power. So while there may have been "cooperation," even within a union context as in the Michigan case, federal macroeconomic policy guaranteed that it was weighted for the benefit of the auto producers. This is highlighted by the fact that the tangible benefits derived from "cooperation" in Bachelor's Michigan case do not appear, on their face, to be all that different from the fruits of "confrontation" outlined in Yanarella and Reid's Kentucky case.

In sum, the policies of the federal government both created an opportunity for states and undermined their ability to maximally benefit from it. Restrictive macroeconomic policy transformed state policy laboratories into a desperate auction. *And it is in this light that we must interpret the central question of whether or not the states gave away too much to secure the Japanese auto plants.*

We still cannot say that the bargains made by the states will not ultimately prove to be economically beneficial; over time, the growth in jobs and income associated with the new plants may balance the prices paid through the incentive packages. As we have seen, however, such interpretations of ultimate economic success or failure are still largely matters of hope in the cases considered in this volume.

Clearly, however, and irrespective of their ultimate economic success or failure, we can describe the states efforts to attract new auto plants as a policy failure. *Even if the states receive a net return on their incentive packages at some unspecified time in the future, they paid far more for the new plants than they would have if the economic environment had been more benign.* With a more elastic political demand for new jobs, the states would have been better prepared to strike bargains more beneficial to themselves. And the roots of this policy failure lies not in the states, but with the macroeconomic policy of the federal government. By choosing not to adopt overt industrial policy itself, and by adopting macroeconomic policies which guaranteed high levels of unemployment, the federal government insured that the states could not engage in effective industrial policy.

ALTERNATIVE PASTS AND ALTERNATIVE FUTURES

The case analyses on the siting of Japanese auto plants offer, at best, a very mixed picture of our efforts to develop successful industrial policy at the state level. The most optimistic interpretations of the individual cases base their optimism on largely unsubstantiated hopes, hopes that what Hansen's review of Pennsylvania's earlier experience with Volkswagen suggests may be unwarranted. More fundamentally, we have seen that in the absence of coordinated national *and* state policies, state efforts to develop successful industrial policy are inherently vulnerable to the competitive pressures built into federal systems. Given such uncoordinated national and state policies, the individual efforts of the states to lure the private good of a Japanese auto plant must almost inevitably degenerate into a seller's market where the Japanese auto companies have most of the bargaining advantages.

This is a pessimistic conclusion, especially so given the deliberate use of such phrases as "inherently vulnerable" and "almost inevitable." Is such pessimism really warranted? When the conditions outlined here—restrictive macroeconomic policy, competition among the states for a private good, and asymmetrical bargaining—apply, the outcomes we have observed do have an inherent or inevitable character. But these conditions do not apply to all of the actions of state officials that fall under the heading of state industrial policy, nor were they necessarily the conditions that must have governed the process of siting Japanese auto plants in the United States. We can explore the implications of this observation by answering two final questions.

First, does the analysis presented here imply that all state industrial policies will inevitably fail? The answer to this question is clearly no. Earlier, it was suggested that these cases provided a solid inferential foundation for analyzing the processes and impacts of state industrial policy. The cases provide essential details about the policies of states that would be lost in 50 state aggregate analyses, which can lead to comparisons between apples and oranges for so diverse a set of policies as state industrial policy. Just as importantly, the cases share a number of important similarities, including their focus on a common type of plant and location choice, that make comparisons of the type presented here meaningful.

But while the inferential base of these analyses is solid, it is also narrow. The interpretations presented here apply most directly to cases in which several states are competing for a single, large, foreign manufacturing plant. They do not apply to the many other governmental actions falling under the heading of state industrial policy. Many of these actions, such as setting up investment programs for small, innovative firms or state support of technical training, probably do not suffer from the competitive pressures and asymmetrical bargaining found in our present cases. Accordingly, the interpretations of the success and/or failure of state industrial policies of the type considered here need not apply more generally.

Second, were the conditions of a lack of overt national industrial policy, state competition, restrictive macroeconomic policy, and asymmetrical bargaining that undermined the states' abilities to bargain effectively with the Japanese auto firms historically inevitable? In a practical sense, it seems reasonable to suggest that at least some of these conditions were historically fixed. For instance, it is possible to image a scenario in which the United States substantially weakened or abandoned its federal system of government, but such a course is so unlikely as to be implausible. Only slightly more plausible is Lind's proposal for a federally enforced cartel, however attractive the proposal might be. Similarly, the asymmetrical bargaining of the states and the Japanese auto firms might conceivably be altered by very stringent, national disclosure laws governing foreign investments. But given the status of private corporations in this country, the foreign base of the Japanese auto companies, and the economic power of Japan, we should have little expectation that such laws might be adopted any time soon. Thus, several of the conditions that governed the siting decisions examined in this volume must be viewed as essentially fixed.

Still, at least two other conditions outlined here could have developed in a very different manner. On the one hand, instead of leaving industrial policy to the states, the United States could have adopted a national industrial policy in the early part of the 1980s. Such a policy would have balanced monopoly bargaining power on the part of the Japanese firms with monopsonistic bargaining on the part of the United States, thereby dramatically altering the respective power positions of the two parties. The reasons for our failure to adopt a national industrial policy have been examined in some detail (Salisbury, 1979; Wilson, 1982; Peters, 1986), generating an impressive array of plausible reasons for the failure of systematic industrial policy in the United States, including Americans' antipathy toward interest groups and governmental intervention in economic affairs, as well as the nation's social diversity and decentralized political and interest group systems. These conditions have not changed. But what must be at least somewhat shaken by the case studies presented here is our faith that the states can easily fill the gap in policy left by the lack of explicit national action. Thus, one implication of the chapters presented in this volume must be that it is essential to reconsider our decision to eschew national industrial policy.

On the other hand, and accepting for the moment that likelihood that overt national industrial policy was and still is untenable, the cases presented here could have had very different outcomes if the national government had pursued an alternative macroeconomic policy. If, instead of relying on restrictive monetary policy and the resulting high levels of unemployment to purge the economy of inflation in the early 1980s, the federal government had adopted some form of selective wage and price controls, as have West Germany, Austria, Switzerland, Holland, and, perhaps most notably, Japan, the political desperation that so severely constrained the bargaining power of state officials would have been dramatically reduced. Such a policy would not have been a substitute for national industrial policy. But while some degree of competition and asymmetrical bargaining would have remained even with selective wage and price controls, the states would have been in a much better condition to simply walk away from any prospective siting deal if the price became too high. As it was, the states simply could not afford to walk away, which would seem to be a good definition of the origins of many bad deals.

REFERENCES

Ambrosius, Margery M. 1986. "Effects of State Development Policies on the Health of State Economies: A Time Series Analysis." Paper delivered at the Annual Meeting of the Midwest Political Science Association, Chicago, Illinois, April.

Clark, Susan. 1986. "Urban American Inc.: Corporatist Convergence of Power in American Cities?" In Edward M. Bergman, ed., *Local Economies in Transition*. Durham, N.C.: Duke University Press.

Galbraith, John Kenneth. 1987. *Economics in Perspective*. Boston: Houghton Mifflin Company.

Goldstein, Harvey A., and Edward M. Bergman. 1986. "Institutional Arrangements for State and Local Industrial Policy." *Journal of the American Planning Association*. 52 (Summer): 265–276.

Grady, Robert C. 1987. "The Appeal of Corporatism in American Politics." Paper delivered at the Annual Meeting of the Southern Political Science Association, Charlotte, North Carolina, November.

Gray, Virginia, and David Lowery. 1988. "State Industrial Policy: The American Form of Corporatism?" Paper presented at the Annual Meeting of the American Political Science Association, Washington, D.C., September.

————. 1989. "The Corporatist Foundations of State Industrial Policy." Paper presented at the Annual Meeting of the Midwest Political Science Association, Chicago, Illinois, April.

Hansen, Susan B. 1984. "The Effects of State Industrial Policies on Economic Growth." Paper delivered at the Annual Meeting of the American Political Science Association, Washington, D.C., August.

Hibbs, Douglas A. Jr. 1987. *The American Political Economy: Macroeconomics and Electoral Politics in the United States*. Cambridge: Harvard University Press.

Hudson, William E., Mark S. Hyde, and John J. Carroll. 1987. "Corporatist Policy Making and State Economic Development." *Polity* 19 (3): 402–418.

National Association of State Development Agencies and the Urban Institute. 1983. *Directory of Incentives for Business Investment and Development in the United States*. Washington, D.C.: Urban Institute Press.

Page, Benjamin I. 1983. *Who Gets What from Government*. Berkeley: University of California Press.

Peters, Guy B. 1986. "The Politics of Industrial Policy in the United States." In Steven A. Shull and Jeffrey E. Cohen, eds., *Economics and Politics of Industrial Policy*. Boulder, Colo.: Westview Press, 47–68.

Salisbury, Robert H. 1979. "Why No Corporatism in America?" In Philippe C. Schmitter and Gerhard Lehmbruch, eds., *Trends in Corporatist Intermediation*. London: Sage Publications.

Thurow, Lester, 1983. *Dangerous Currents: The State of Economics*. New York: Random House.

Wilmoth, David. 1984. "Regional Economic Policy and the New Corporatism." In Larry Sawers and William K. Tabb, eds., *Sunbelt/Frostbelt*. New York: Oxford University Press, 259–270.

Wilson, Graham. 1982. "Why is There No Corporatism in the United States?" In Gerhard Lehmbruch and Philippe Schmitter, eds., *Patterns of Corporatist Policy-Making*, London: Sage Publications, 259–280.

Select Bibliography

Alperovitz, Gar, and Jeff Faux. 1984. *Rebuilding America*. New York: Pantheon.

Barfield, Claude E., and William A. Schambra, eds. 1986. *The Politics of Industrial Policy*. Washington, D.C.: American Enterprise Institute.

Bartik, Timothy. 1984. "Business Location Decisions in the United States: Estimates of the Effects of Unionization, Taxes, and Other Characteristics of States." *Journal of Business and Economic Statistics* 3: 14–22.

Bell, Michael, and Paul Lande, eds. 1982. *Regional Dimensions of Industrial Policy*. Lexington, Mass.: Lexington Books.

Blair, John C., and Robert Premus. 1987. "Major Factors in Industrial Location: A Review." *Economic Development Quarterly* 1: 72–85.

Bowman, Ann O'M., and Richard C. Kearney. 1986. *The Resurgence of the States*. Englewood Cliffs, N.J.: Prentice-Hall.

Carlton, Dennis W. 1983. "The Location and Employment Choices of New Firms." *Review of Economics and Statistics* 65: 440–449.

Carroll, John C., Mark Hyde, and William E. Hudson. 1987. "State-Level Perspectives on Industrial Policy. The Views of Legislators and Bureaucrats." *Economic Development Quarterly* 1: 333–342.

Chernow, Ron. 1979. "The Rabbit That Ate Pennsylvania: Governor Shapp Builds Volkswagen a $70 Million Hutch," *Mother Jones* 2 (October): 19–24.

Clarke, Marianne K. 1986. *Revitalizing State Economies: A Review of State Economic Development Policies and Programs*. Washington, D.C.: National Governors' Association.

Cole, Robert E., ed. 1981. *The Japanese Automobile Industry*. Ann Arbor: Center for Japanese Studies, University of Michigan.

Cole, Robert E., and Donald R. Deskins, 1988. "Racial Factors in Site Location and Employment Patterns of Japanese Auto Plants in America." *California Management Review* 31: 9–22.

Cole, Robert E., and Taizo Yakushiji, eds. 1984. *The American and Japanese Auto Industries in Transition: The Report of the Joint U.S.-Japan Automotive Study*. Ann Arbor: Center for Japanese Studies, University of Michigan.

Council on Competitiveness. 1988. "Reclaiming the American Dream: Fiscal Policies for a Competitive Nation." *Challenge* 2 (December): 5–8.

Cumberland, John H. 1971. *Regional Development Experiences and Prospects in the United States of America*. The Hague: Mouton.

Dohse, Knuth, Ulrich Jurgens, and Thomas Malsh. 1985. "From 'Fordism' to 'Toyotism'?" *Politics & Society* 74: 141–178.

Dolbeare, Kenneth. 1986. *Democracy at Risk: The Politics of Economic Renewal*, rev. ed., Chatham: Chatham House.

Dubnick, Mel. 1984. "American States and the Industrial Policy Debate." *Policy Studies Journal* 4: 22–27.

Due, John F. 1961. "Studies of State-Local Tax Inferences on the Location of Industry." *National Tax Journal* 14: 163–173.

Dunphy, Dexter. 1987. "Convergence/Divergence: A Temporal Review of the Japanese Enterprise and Its Management." *Academy of Management Review* 12: 445–459.

Eisenger, Peter K. 1989. *The Rise of the Entrepreneurial State: State and Local Government Economic Development Policy in the United States*. Madison: University of Wisconsin.

Elder, Ann H., and Nancy Lind. 1987. "The Implications of Uncertainty in Economic Development: The Case of Diamond Star Motors." *Economic Development Quarterly* 1: 30–40.

Epping, G. Michael. 1982. "Important Factors in Plant Location in 1980." *Growth and Change* 13 (April): 47–51.

Falk, William W. 1988. *High Tech, Low Tech, No Tech: Recent Industrial and Occupational Change in the South*. Albany, N.Y.: SUNY Press.

Fino, Susan P. 1987. *The Role of State Supreme Courts in the New Judicial Federalism*. Westport, Conn.: Greenwood.

Fosler, R. Scott. 1986. *Leadership for Dynamic State Economies*. Washington, D.C.: Committee for Economic Development.

———. ed. 1988. *The New Economic Role of the American States: Strategies and Institutions for a Competitive World Economy*. New York: Oxford.

Fox, William F. 1978. "Local Taxes and Industrial Location." *Public Finance Quarterly* 6: 93–114.

———. 1981. "Fiscal Differences and Industrial Location: Some Empirical Evidence." *Urban Studies* 18: 105–111.

Fox, William F., and C. Warren Neel. 1987. "Saturn: The Tennessee Lessons." *Forum for Applied Research and Public Policy* 2: 7–16.

Fulton, William. 1988. "VW in Pennsylvania: The Tale of the Rabbit That Got Away." *Governing* 2 (November): 32–37.

Gardner, Mona J., Kang Han Bin, and Dixie L. Mills. 1987. "Japan, USA: The Impact of the Diamond-Star Plant on the Bloomington-Normal Economy and Housing Market." *Illinois Business Review* 44: 7–9.

Gelfand, M. David, and Peter W. Salsich. 1985. *State and Local Taxation and Finance in a Nutshell*. St. Paul, Minn.: West.

Gilmore, Donald R. 1960. *Developing Little Economies*. New York: Committee for Economic Development.

Gold, David M. 1985. "Public Aid to Private Enterprises Under the Ohio Constitution: Sections 4, 6, and 13 of Article VII in Historical Perspective." *Toledo Law Review* 16: 405–464.

Goodman, Robert. 1979. *The Last Entrepreneurs: America's Regional Wars for Jobs and Dollars*. Boston: South End Press.

Grady, Dennis O. 1987. "State Economic Development Incentives: Why Do the States Compete?" *State and Local Government Review* 19: 86–94.

Gray, John, and Dean Spina. 1980. "State and Local Industrial Location Incentives: A Well-Stocked Candy Store." *Journal of Corporation Law* 5: 517–587.

Gray, Virginia, and David Lowery. 1988. "Interest Group Politics and Economic Growth in the American States." *American Political Science Review* 82: 109–132.

Grossman, Ilene. 1985. *Initiatives in State Economic Development*. Lombard, Ill.: Midwest Conference, Council of State Governments.

Hamilton, William W., Larry C. Ledebur, and Deborah Matz. 1986. *Innovations in Economic Development: Lessons from the States*. McLean, Va.: Aslan Associates.

Hamilton, William W., Larry C. Ledebur, and Stephen Rabinowitz. 1986. *State Constitutional Barriers to Economic Development*. McLean, Va.: Aslan Associates.

Hansen, Susan B. 1987. "State Governments and Industrial Policy in the United States." In Joachim J. Hesse, ed., *Regions, Structural Change and Industrial Policies in International Perspective*. Frankfurt: Nomos Verlag.

———. 1989. *The Political Economy of State Industrial Policy*. Pittsburgh: University of Pittsburgh.

Heckman, John S. 1982. "Survey of Location Decisions in the South." *Economic Review* 19: 6–19.

Hellman, Daryl, Gregory H. Wassall, and Laurence H. Falk. 1976. *State Financial Incentives to Industry*. Lexington, Mass.: Lexington Books.

Helms, L. Jay. 1985. "The Effect of State and Local Taxes on Economic Growth: A Time Series-Cross Section Approach." *Review of Economics and Statistics* 67: 574–582.

Hunker, Henry. 1974. *Industrial Development: Concepts and Principals*. Lexington, Mass.: Lexington Books.

Jacobs, Jerry. 1979. *Bidding for Business: Corporate Auctions and the Fifty Disunited States*. Washington, D.C.: Public Interest Research Group.

John, Dewitt. 1987. *Shifting Responsibilities: Federalism in Economic Development*. Washington, D.C.: National Governors' Association.

Junkerman, John. 1987. "Nissan, Tennessee: It Ain't What It's Cracked Up to Be." *The Progressive* 51 (June): 16–20.

Kerson, Roger. 1988. "Flint's Fight to the Finish." *Washington Monthly* 20 (September): 19–24.

Keys, J. Bernard, and Thomas R. Miller. 1984. "The Japanese Theory of Management Jungle." *Academy of Management Review* 9: 342–353.

Kincaid, John. 1984. "The American Governor in International Affairs." *Publius: The Journal of Federalism.* 14: 95–114.

———. 1988. "State Constitutions in the Federal System." *Annals of the American Academy of Political and Social Science* 496: 12–22.

Kline, John. 1985. "The Expanding International Agenda of State Government." *State Government* 55: 57–64.

Krause, Kitry. 1986. "Americans Can Build Good Cars: They're Doing It in Marysville, Ohio." *Washington Monthly* 18 (July-August): 41–46.

Kujawa, Duane. 1986. *Japanese Multinationals in the United States.* New York: Praeger.

Lawrence, Paul R., and Davis Dyer. 1983. *Renewing American Industry: Organizing for Efficiency and Innovation.* New York: Free Press.

Ledebur, Larry C., William W. Hamilton, and Deborah Matz, eds. *Industrial Incentives: Public Promotion of Private Enterprise.* McLean, Va.: Aslan Associates.

Lind, Nancy S., and Ann H. Elder. 1986. "Who Pays? Who Benefits? The Case of the Incentive Package Offered to the Diamond-Star Automobile Plant." *Government Finance Review* 2: 19–23.

Magaziner, Ira C. 1981. "Japanese Industrial Policy: Source of Strength for the Automobile Industry." In Robert E. Cole, ed., *The Japanese Automobile Industry: Model and Challenge for the Future.* Ann Arbor: Center for Japanese Studies, University of Michigan.

Magaziner, Ira C., and Robert C. Reich. 1982. *Minding America's Business.* New York: Harcourt, Brace, Jovanovich.

Markusen, Ann. 1987. *Regions: The Economics and Politics of Territory.* Totawa, N.J.: Rowman and Littlefield.

Marlin, Martin R. 1957. "Industrial Revenue Bonds at 50: A Golden Anniversary Review." *Economic Development Review* 1: 153–179.

Matz, Deborah. 1985. *An Analysis of Innovative State Economic Development Financing Programs.* Washington, D.C.: National Association of State Development Agencies.

Milward, H. Brinton,. 1986. "Can a Governor Determine the Location of Private Industry?" *Kentucky Economy* 10: 3–4.

Milward, H. Brinton, and Heidi H. Newman. 1988. "The Escalation of State Incentive Packages and Japanese Automobile Alley." *Review and Perspective* 12: 2–5.

Nathan, Richard P., Fred C. Doolittle, and Associates. 1987. *Reagan and the States.* Princeton, N.J.: Princeton University Press.

National Association of State Development Agencies (NASDA). *Directory of Incentives for Business Investment and Development in the United States: A State by State Guide,* 2nd ed. Washington, D.C.: The Urban Institute Press.

National Governors' Association. 1987. *Making Americans Work Again: Productive People, Productive Policies.* Washington, D.C.: National Governors' Association, Center for Policy Research.

Newman, Robert J. 1983. "Industry Migration and Growth in the South." *Review of Economics and Statistics* 65: 76–86.

Newman, Robert J., and Dennis H. Sullivan. 1988. "Econometric Analysis of Business Tax Impacts on Industrial Location: What Do We Know and How Do We Know It?" *Journal of Urban Economics* 23: 215–234.

Osborne, David. 1987. *Economic Competitiveness: The States Take the Lead*. New York: Praeger.

―――. 1988. *Laboratories of Democracy: A New Breed of Governor Creates Models for Economic Growth*. Cambridge, Mass.: Harvard Business School Press.

Pinsky, David E. 1963. "State Constitutional Limitations on Public Industrial Financing: An Historical and Economic Approach." *University of Pennsylvania Law Review* 111: 265–325.

Plaut, Thomas R., and Joseph E. Pluta. 1983. "Business Climate, Taxes and Expenditures, and State Industrial Growth in the U.S." *Southern Economic Journal* 50: 99–119.

Rasmussen, David W., Marc Bendick, and Larry C. Ledebur. 1984. "A Methodology for Selecting Economic Development Incentives." *Growth and Change* 15: 18–25.

Reich, Robert B. 1983. *The Next American Frontier*. New York: Penguin Books.

Schmenner, Roger W. 1982. *Making Business Location Decisions*. Englewood Cliffs, N.J.: Prentice-Hall.

Schmenner, Roger W., Joel Huber, and Randall Cook. 1987. "Geographic Differences and the Location of New Manufacturing Facilities." *Journal of Urban Economics* 21: 83–104.

Schultze, Charles L. 1983. "Industrial Policy: A Dissent." *Brooking Review* 2: 3–12.

Sobel, Robert. 1984. *Car Wars: The Untold Story*. New York: Dutton.

Springs, Ricardo C. 1981. *Pilot Study: The Decision by Nissan Motor Manufacturing Corporation U.S.A. to Build a Light Truck Assembly Plant in Smyrna, Tennessee*. Washington, D.C.: Government Printing Office.

Stein, Herbert. 1983. "Don't Fall for Industrial Policy." *Fortune* 108 (November 14): 64–78.

Sullivan, Jeremiah, and Richard B. Peterson. 1982. "Factors Associated with Trust in Japanese-American Joint Ventures." *Management International Review* 22: 30–40.

Tarr, G. Alan, and Mary Cornelia Aldis Porter. 1988. *State Supreme Courts in State and Nation*. New Haven, Conn: Yale University.

Tolchin, Martin, and Susan Tolchin. 1988. *Buying into America*. New York: Time Books.

U.S. Congress. House Committee on Government Operations. December 2, 4, and 5, 1986. *Federal and State Roles in Economic Development: Hearings Before the Intergovernmental and Human Relations Subcommittee of the Committee on Government Operations*. Washington, D.C.: Government Printing Office.

Vaughan, Roger J. 1983. *Rebuilding America*. Washington, D.C.: Council of State Planning Agencies.

Vaughan, Roger J., Robert Pollard, and Barbara Dyer. 1986. *The Wealth of States: Policies for a Dynamic Economy*. Washington, D.C.: Council of State Planning Agencies.

Walker, Jack L. 1969. "The Diffusion of Innovation among the American States." *American Political Science Review* 63: 880–889.

Wasylenko, Michael. 1981. "The Role of Taxes and Fiscal Incentives in the Location of Firms." In Roy Bahl, ed., *Urban Finance: Emerging Issues*. Beverly Hills, Calif: Sage.

Wasylenko, Michael, and Theresa McGuire. 1985. "Jobs and Taxes: The Effect of

Business Climate on States' Employment Growth Rates." *National Tax Journal* 38: 497–510.

Weidenbaum, Murray L. 1987. "International Trade and Economic Development." *Economic Development Quarterly* 1: 4–12.

Williams, Bruce A. 1990. "Regulation and Economic Development." In Virigina Gray, Herbert Jacob, and Robert Albritton, eds., *Politics in the American States*, 5th ed., Chicago: Scott-Foresman.

Yoshida, Mamoru. 1987. *Japanese Direct Manufacturing Investment in the United States*. New York: Praeger.

Zysman, John. 1983. *Governments, Markets, and Growth*. Ithaca: Cornell University Press.

Index

Contributors

LYNN W. BACHELOR, an Assistant Professor of Political Science at the University of Toledo, has written on economic development and policy and is the coauthor with Bryan Jones of *The Sustaining Hand*. She has a continuing research interest in urban policy issues and the problems of the homeless.

JOHN P. BLAIR is a Professor of Economics at Wright State University. Formerly a policy analyst with the U.S. Department of Housing and Urban Development, he has written extensively on urban economics, real estate, and public policy. He is at work on a study entitled *Urban and Regional Economics*.

CAROLE ENDRES is a Compensation and Benefits Manager for the City of Dayton and an Adjunct Professor of Economics at Wright State University. She was chosen 1988 Urban Fellow by the University of Dayton.

RUDY FICHTENBAUM is an Associate Professor of Economics at Wright State University. His research interests are labor economics and regional development. His articles have appeared in *Journal of Business and Economic Statistics, Eastern Economic Journal, Growth and Change*, and *Urban Affairs Quarterly*.

WILLIAM F. FOX is an Associate Professor of Economics and the Associated Director of the Center for Business and Economic Research at the University of Tennessee. His many research studies and articles on state economic development and industrial location have appeared in the *Forum for Applied Research and Public Policy*, *Urban Studies*, and *Public Finance Quarterly*.

WILLIAM C. GREEN is an Associate Professor of Government at Morehead State University and Research Associate with the Institute for Mining and Minerals Research at the University of Kentucky. His articles on civil liberties issues, labor grievance arbitration, and pharmaceutical policy have appeared in *Valparaiso University Law Review*, *Labor Law Review*, *Food Drug Cosmetic Law Journal*, and *Policy Studies Journal*. He is also coeditor with Ernest J. Yanarella of *The Unfulfilled Promise of Synthetic Fuels* (Greenwood Press, 1987).

SUSAN B. HANSEN is an Associate Professor of Political Science at the University of Pittsburgh. Her research interests include state politics, economic policy, and women's issues. Her numerous articles have appeared in the *American Political Science Review*, *American Politics Quarterly*, and the *Journal of Politics*. She has also written three books, the most recent of which is *The Political Economy of State Economic Policy*.

NANCY S. LIND is an Assistant Professor of Political Science at Illinois State University whose areas of specialization include public administration, organization theory and behavior, and government budgeting. She has served as Director of the National Conference on Small City and Regional Community. Her publications have appeared in *Economic Development Quarterly* and *Government Finance Review*.

DAVID LOWERY is a Professor of Political Science at the University of North Carolina at Chapel Hill. His research interests include political economy, the politics of state and local public finance, and local political behavior. His publications on these topics have appeared in the *American Political Science Review* and the *American Journal of Political Science*. He is also coauthor with William D. Berry of *Understanding United States Government Growth: An Empirical Analysis of the Post-War Era* (Praeger, 1987).

H. BRINTON MILWARD is the Director of the School of Public Administration and Policy at the University of Arizona and Associate Dean of the College of Business and Public Administration. He has published widely in the areas of public administration and business management. His articles have appeared in *Administration and Society*, *Public Administration Review*, *Social Science Quarterly*, and the *Academy of Business Management*.

HEIDI HOSBACH NEWMAN is the project manager and a research associate with the Center for Business and Economic Research at the University of Kentucky.

MADHAVI PATEL is a graduate student in sociology at Purdue University who is interested in the study of industrial organizations and multinational corporations.

ROBERT PERRUCCI is a Professor of Sociology at Purdue University. He has published numerous articles and ten books on the interplay of technology and society, work and occupations, and complex organizations. He is currently studying the impact of foreign transplants on local communities.

HERBERT G. REID is a Professor of Political Science at the University of Kentucky who teaches and does research on contemporary political philosophy, American political thought and culture, Appalachian politics, and the problems of ideology in advanced industrial societies. His articles have appeared in leading journals of political and social theory.

ERNEST J. YANARELLA is a Professor of Political Science at the University of Kentucky. He teaches political theory and public policy, including energy and environmental policy, arms control and defense policy, and agricultural policy. His work in critical studies is reflected in two dozen scholarly articles and five previous books. He is currently completing a book on contemporary science fiction and the ecological imagination.